The Military Transition

Civilian control of the armed forces is crucial for any country hoping to achieve a successful democratic transition. In this remarkable book, Narcís Serra, Spanish Minister of Defence between 1982 and 1991, explains the steps necessary to reduce the powers of armed forces during the process of a democratic transition. Spain's military reform proved a fundamental and necessary element for the consolidation of Spanish democracy and is often viewed as a paradigm case for the transition to democracy. Drawing on this example, Serra outlines a simple model of the process and conditions necessary to any democratic military reform. He argues that progress in military transition must include legal and institutional reforms, changes to the military career structure and doctrine, and control of conflict levels.

NARCÍS SERRA has a BA in Economics from the University of Barcelona and a PhD in Economics from the Autonomous University of Barcelona (UAB). In 1976 he was appointed to the post of Professor in Economic Theory, first at the University of Seville and then at the UAB.

Following this academic experience, in 1977 he was appointed Catalan Minister of Town and Country Planning and Public Works in the Regional Government (Generalitat de Catalunya), and in April 1979 he became the first elected Mayor of Barcelona since the Spanish Civil War. In December of 1982 he was appointed Spanish Minister of Defence in the Government of Felipe González, and left the post in 1991 to become Vice-president of the Spanish Government. From 1986 until 2004, Narcís Serra was member of the Spanish Parliament representing the province of Barcelona.

Since 2000 Narcís Serra has been the President of the CIDOB Foundation. During this time, he has promoted the creation of the Barcelona Institute for International Studies (IBEI) and has acted as expert consultant for a number of Ministries of Defence of Latin American and Eastern European countries.

The Military Transition

Democratic Reform of the Armed Forces

NARCÍS SERRA

Translated by
PETER BUSH

CAMBRIDGE
UNIVERSITY PRESS

CAMBRIDGE UNIVERSITY PRESS
Cambridge, New York, Melbourne, Madrid, Cape Town, Singapore,
São Paulo, Delhi, Dubai, Tokyo

Cambridge University Press
The Edinburgh Building, Cambridge CB2 8RU, UK

Published in the United States of America by Cambridge University Press, New York

www.cambridge.org
Information on this title: www.cambridge.org/9780521133449

Originally published in Spanish as *La Transición Militar: Reflexiones en torno a la
reforma democrática de las fuerzas armadas* by Random House Mondadori 2008 and
© Random House Mondadori 2008

First published in English by Cambridge University Press 2010 as *The Military Transition:
Democratic Reform of the Armed Forces* © Narcís Serra 2010

English translation © Peter Bush 2010

Esta obra ha sido publicada con una subvención de la Dirección General del Libro,
Archivos y Bibliotecas del Ministerio de Cultura de España.

This publication is in copyright. Subject to statutory exception
and to the provisions of relevant collective licensing agreements,
no reproduction of any part may take place without
the written permission of Cambridge University Press.

Printed in the United Kingdom at the University Press, Cambridge

A catalogue record for this publication is available from the British Library

ISBN 978-0-521-11667-1 Hardback
ISBN 978-0-521-13344-9 Paperback

Cambridge University Press has no responsibility for the persistence or
accuracy of URLs for external or third-party internet websites referred to in
this book, and does not guarantee that any content on such websites is,
or will remain, accurate or appropriate.

Contents

Figures and tables

Figures

Tables

Introduction

This book has its origins in a lecture I gave in 1999 at the London School of Economics at the invitation of Professor Paul Preston. The initial idea was to examine military policy during Spain's transition to democracy. Soon afterwards I left my post as general-secretary of the Catalan Socialist Party, and although I continued as a member of parliament until March 2004, I had more time available to act as a consultant to programmes of military reform for a number of governments in Latin America and one or two in Europe.

My growing awareness of the political realities in different countries revealed both the complexity and similarities of the problems to be resolved, starting with the lack of knowledge of military issues displayed by civilians responsible for reform in almost all of these countries. A lecture I gave in the Latin American Faculty of Social Sciences in Santiago de Chile in 2002 and another in Belgrade in 2003 forced me to start to articulate my personal experiences in government in Spain and the wealth of experience I was now acquiring through my consultancies. I began to think of a model that would allow me to demonstrate the complexity of the process and, at the same time, help develop policies to reform the armed forces.

Obviously, the key factor was my previous stint as Minister of Defence. I held this post from the end of 1982, when Felipe González entrusted me with that portfolio after the Socialist Party had won a decisive victory under his leadership in the October elections. I remained in post for eight years, until I was appointed vice-president in the government. As a result, I was responsible for a large part of the process of reforming the Spanish military during the period I describe in this book as one of democratic consolidation. Before my appointment I had had no opportunity to find out the issues involved, even though I had to take decisions almost immediately. In my previous post as mayor of Barcelona, I had learned that it was not necessary to have extensive technical competence in an area in order to have the political and moral authority to take sensible decisions. Clearly one must read reports and study many issues in depth, particularly in the first few months in post. Longevity in post increases competence, even in the more technical areas. When I left my post, I was the minister of a European democracy who had held the defence portfolio for the longest period of time. This time factor is crucial in tasks like military reform that demand that authority be backed by knowledge and continuity in order to be able to put flesh on guidelines and move from the pages of the Official Bulletin of State to everyday practice. It has always been my belief that the short period in post of Latin American ministers of defence has been their greatest undoing when it comes to solving the problems they have with their armed forces.

Not that I had time to reflect on questions of military policy in the years immediately after my period as Minister of Defence. It was several years before I could read the existing literature on civilian–military relations and think about aspects of Spanish policy that might be of use in other latitudes. Two developments fuelled a renewed interest in the analysis of civilian–military relations at that time: on the one hand, transitions to democracy in Eastern Europe and Latin America and, on the other, the frictions and conflicts between the Clinton administration and the military in the 1990s. I doubt that Samuel Huntington would write now, as he did in his preface to his seminal work, *The Soldier and the State*: 'the study of civilian–military relations had suffered from too little theorizing'.[1] In the 1990s, numerous monographs were published on the state of civilian–military relations in several Latin American countries. In the mid-90s, the academic world in the United States began a serious debate on government control of the armed forces that was truncated at a stroke by the terrorist attack on New York in September 2001. All this literature has been of enormous help in the preparation of this book. Nonetheless, there are few books that discuss what happened in Spain, although I was able to draw on Felipe Agüero's pioneering book, which I hope to complement.[2]

By reading the existing literature and analysing different case studies, I began to give shape to a book that does not set out to be a chronicle of the process of military reform in Spain. Instead, the approach I have

---

[1] See Huntington 1957: VII.
[2] I am referring to Agüero 1995a, a book that will be quoted extensively in the following pages.

tried to adopt is normative, rather than descriptive or historical: a narrative account of Spain's lengthy process of military reform has yet to be written. I have attempted to reflect on the military policy that should be developed as part of a process of military reform in a transition to democracy. In the academic field, even within the political sciences, it is usually claimed that theories should help anticipate outcomes on the basis of their cogent explanation of the facts. This is a somewhat limited approach. Steve Smith's view seems much more fruitful when he argues that: 'theories do not simply explain or predict, they tell us what possibilities exist for human action and intervention; they define not merely our explanatory possibilities, but also our ethical and practical horizons'.[3] This admittedly hybrid approach is the one I have tried to adopt in my study.

I have already indicated that one feature which impressed me as I studied situations in countries as different as Chile and Serbia was the similarity of the issues to be confronted. Many scholars of civilian–military relations share this perspective. In a recent work, Thomas Bruneau and Scott Tollefson state 'in all democracies, new or old, issues of civil–military relations are fundamentally the same'.[4] In fact, Juvenal already posed the basic issue at stake between civil governments and the armed forces, almost twenty centuries ago when he asked *Quis custodiet ipsos custodes?* That is, who will guard the guards? The control by society and its representatives over the group to which it has granted the use of force, precisely to free it from those who pose a threat, is, has been and will always be the key issue in civilian–military relations.

Edmund Burke was very pessimistic on the matter of control of the armed forces. He believed that 'an armed, disciplined body is, in its essence, dangerous to liberty; undisciplined, it is ruinous to society'.[5] Much more recently, S. E. Finer, a pioneer of the study of relations between governments and the armed forces, concluded that the only single stable solution is for the military to accept that its subordination to civil power is an entirely necessary prerequisite for a country to function in a democratic way. I agree with Finer and would add that this subordination is also necessary if the military as a group is to serve the state effectively. If we add to the criterion of control the need for efficiency that must be pursued in any sector of state administration, we

---

[3] Quoted in Burchill 2001: 2.   [4] Bruneau and Tollefson 2006: 3f.
[5] See the introduction in Howard 1959.

have the two essential goals of military policy. This position informs the suggestions in chapters 5 and 6, which focus on the analysis of the different measures that should comprise military policy.

An issue that follows directly from this, and which must be addressed in a transition, is whether the government decides that the military must share the same values as society: in other words, how much does it want the military to differ from the society in which it is located? There are two, almost contradictory, responses given by the two most influential studies published in the last fifty years. Huntington argues that to be effective, the military has to be different, and Janowitz states that it must move closer to civilian values and procedures in order to improve its efficiency in the new context. This debate, like the previous one, is almost as old as the existence of the armed forces. Machiavelli in his *Art of War* had already stated: 'there is nothing which has less in common with another, and that is so dissimilar, as civilian life is from the military'.[6]

Those were other times. On the brink of the First World War, Max Weber expressed an opposite point of view: 'a person holding rank in the military domain, in other words, an official, is no different to a bourgeois civil servant. In effect, the modern mass army is also a bureaucratic army, and an official is a special kind of civil servant, in contrast to the noble, condottiere, bandit-leaders or heroes of Homer'.[7] It goes without saying that in this book I criticize the position defended by Huntington as wrong and dangerous. I believe that the passage of time, the end of the Cold War and the growing awareness that there have to be legitimate reasons for the use of force on the international stage, make Janowitz's criteria valid for the twenty-first century. The United States' enormous military power has blinded them to this necessary development to the extent that in the case of Iraq, the US administration believed military victory was sufficient to win the war.

The path opened by Max Weber leads us to another problem linked to relations between the military and the government. It is an issue that arises frequently and in quite dissimilar countries: the transition from an army that considers itself, and is considered to be, an institution in dialogue with the other institutions of the state, to an army that is integrated into the state as a special area within it. This question has been much discussed, even in Spain where it was at the centre of

---

[6] Machiavelli 2003 [1520]: 7.   [7] Weber 1968: Chapter IX, Section 3.

parliamentary debate in the process of drawing up the Constitution of 1978. I analyse this issue in chapter 5 from the perspective of someone convinced that the necessary route to the adaptation of the armed forces to democracy passes through its integration into the state administration.

The following pages attempt to follow the suggestions of two American academics well known for their work in this field. The first, Samuel Fitch, concludes in one of the most lucid studies on this question in relation to Latin America that 'there are no simple recipes or proven strategies for civilian governments seeking to redefine relationships with the military'.[8] In this book I have tried to simplify those recipes, following the criterion I have always found useful in my professional life, namely that clarity of thought is the best instrument with which to confront complex situations.

The second, Eliot A. Cohen, writes in his study of the relations between political leaders and armies in the great warring conflicts of the past century: 'There is nothing obvious or inevitable about the subordination of the armed forces to the wishes and purposes of the political leadership'.[9] In effect, the satisfactory evolution of military reform is not predetermined by the conditions in which it takes place and the beginning of a process of democratization, however promising, does not guarantee that it will reach a satisfactory conclusion. In other words, if I am clear about one thing after my experiences in the field, it is that policy is important and that the way a process of military reform is planned and carried out is central to its eventual success. This conviction permeates the whole book.

This study is structured over eight chapters. In the first, I review part of the literature on the transition to democracy in order to draw some conclusions on the way it is connected to policy for military reform. In the second, I analyse studies that concentrate more directly on the relationship between the transition to democracy and military policy in order to demarcate the different phases in the process. In the third, I attempt to define the concepts that are necessary to show what in my view constitutes proper military reform and to articulate a model that can act as a guide to the design and implementation of military policy. What I consider to be the first part of the book concludes in chapter 4 with an analysis of various reform measures structured according to the axes of the model suggested in the previous chapter.

---

[8] Fitch 1998: 169.   [9] Cohen 2002: 226.

Chapters 5 and 6 analyse the Spanish process as divided into periods of transition and consolidation, respectively. They represent the application of my model to the situation I know best, which is obviously Spain. This allows me to evaluate possible measures, their advantages and risks, as well as their inclusion in a global policy of military reform. I include the reflections in chapter 7 concerning the US debate on the control of the armed forces, because I want to show that an active policy on the part of the government in order to retain control of the armed forces and their effectiveness is a necessity in all circumstances, even in a consolidated democracy. Finally, in line with the book's normative approach, I conclude with a series of reflections and suggestions on military reform policy in processes of transition and on the control of the army in various situations, in the hope that these may be of use to civilians who from ministerial or other similar positions of responsibility must propose or implement decisions in the area of military policy.

Many people have helped me in writing this book. I should mention, from within the academy, Professors José María Maravall and Felipe Agüero. Among my colleagues in my time as minister I must mention Gustavo Suárez Pertierra, José Enrique Serrano and Generals Ramón Fernández Sequeiros and Jesús del Olmo. Pol Morillas and Laia Mestres helped me with the notes, bibliography and final editing. The following pages were written over numerous weekends and holidays. Without the help or interest of Conxa, my wife, I would never have finished.

It behoves me to say that all the errors are exclusively my responsibility, but I think a fitting conclusion to this introduction might be the last paragraph to Hugo Grotius's preliminary discourse to his *The Rights of War and Peace*:

Whatever Liberty I have taken in judging of the Opinions and Writings of others, I desire and beseech all those, into whose Hands this Treatise shall come, to take the same with me. They shall no sooner admonish me of my Mistakes, than I shall follow their Admonitions. And moreover, if I have said any thing contrary either to Piety, or to good Manners, or to Holy Scripture, or to the Consent of the Christian Church, or to any Kind of Truth, let it be unsaid again.[10]

---

[10] Grotius 2005 [1625]: 132.

1 | *The study of the transition to democracy*

I will begin by considering some of the studies of transitions from authoritarian regimes and the subsequent interactions between civilian and military spheres developed over the last twenty years, in order to scrutinize approaches to, and definitions of, democratic transition and consolidation. This is the first step to be taken before applying these terms to a case study of Spain and the experiences accumulated there. It is not my intention to track down the theory that best explains the process of political transformation generated in Spain after the death of General Francisco Franco. My aim is rather to consider critically the policies needed to encourage a democratic transition in the area of the control of the military. If a normative focus is to be of use, the process one wishes to nurture or control must be understood. It is not sufficient to reflect on the adequacy of policies and measures taken in the field of defence during the process of the transition. In this first chapter I will try to review some of the many advances that have been made in a field which some have dubbed 'transitology'. This will enable us to set the procedures belonging to military control within a more general view of the process that brought democracy to Spain. I would also like to establish the groundwork in order to determine whether the Spanish experience, together with an analysis of processes of reform in other countries, might suggest a line of political action that could be applied to current processes of transition, even though none are strictly comparable.

A brief glance at the large number of countries that have been able to overcome authoritarian regimes in the last twenty-five years is enough to explain why the field of political science has been so fascinated by these processes. If we take 1974, the year of the Revolution of the Carnations, as our point of departure for the third wave of democratizations, we have moved from a situation in which out of 145 existing countries, 39 were democracies, that is 26.9 per cent, to a very different balance sheet: in 1997, 191 countries existed in the world of which 117, or 61.3 per cent, were democracies.[1] In fact, between 1974 and 1999, 85 authoritarian regimes fell, of which 30 are now stable democracies, 34, new authoritarian regimes and the remaining 21, pseudo-democracies or countries that have fallen into the hands of war lords.[2] We are thus faced by a new, wide-ranging phenomenon that has inevitably, and most fortunately, attracted the interest of scholars from different social sciences.

Given the intense concern for these issues shared by academics, it should come as no surprise that the studies carried out have created new, widely used terms despite the lack of real consensus as to their content. The two most used terms are transition and democratic consolidation. Different authors endow these terms with different meanings, but that is far from unusual, as we can see from other concepts, such as development and globalization, widely used in the political sciences. Nonetheless, we should note that the expression 'transition to democracy' is ambiguous because it implies that the final outcome of the process is a democratic regime. A summary scrutiny of the situations in most countries in Latin America and Eastern Europe, however, reveals that consolidated democracy is not the only possible outcome for transitions sparked by the collapse of a dictatorship: that result is in fact the least likely and the most difficult to achieve.[3]

It is possible that the success of the changes in three southern European countries (Portugal, Spain and Greece) has led researchers to wax optimistically about the results of processes of transition and drawn them towards a determinism that had hitherto been the domain of structuralists, and towards a so-called 'teleology'.[4] Clearly, the Spanish process of transition has constantly belied any determinist vision of history, from the designation of Adolfo Suárez as president of the government to the resolution of the 1981 attempted coup d'état via the Moncloa Pacts or the re-establishing of the regional government of Catalonia (Generalitat de Catalunya). Suárez himself wrote:

One comforting lesson that I, at least, have drawn from the Spanish transition, in which I played a central role, is that there is no such thing as historical

[1] Diamond 1999: 25.   [2] Geddes 1999: 115.   [3] Przeworski 1991: 51.

[4] A term proposed by Guillermo O'Donnell that he later rectified. In his May 1997 Postscript to 'Transiciones, continuidades y algunas paradojas', O'Donnell admits that the idea of democratic consolidation the article puts forward is wrong (O'Donnell 1997b: 253). In a later article, 'Otra Institucionalización', O'Donnell, considers that the previous article is an example of the very teleology he himself criticizes (1997c: 305ff.).

determinism. By living and making history in this phase, I experienced a most important justification of an essential idea: that the future, far from being decided in advance, is always an open, unstable realm of freedom, even though one can foresee possible outcomes from the analyses we make of structural conditions and the forces at work in the society in which we live, which include, as a vital impulse, the free will of men, who are the protagonists of history.[5]

I use this quotation to emphasize the fact that there is a broad field for a study of the behaviour of leading political players, and of the scope for compromise and the impact of these on the subsequent process of transition. As we shall see later, the analysis of political action in these contexts is much more relevant and enlightening when related to underlying structural and cultural factors.

In any case, the way different realities developed dealt a final blow both to 'teleology' and historical determinism. Situations with similar departure points, for example, as those in which the military ceded power in Latin American countries, have evolved quite distinctly. Even worse, very few of the thirty countries that have become stable democracies (perhaps only Portugal, Greece and Spain) have carried the process of transition to democracy, in the real meaning of that term, to its conclusion. There are many countries that have not reinstated dictatorial regimes, but neither have they progressed to a situation that could be called democratic. As a consequence, expressions such as formal democracy, pseudo-democracy, weak democracy, partial democracy, *delegative democracy* and *low-intensity democracy*[6] have arisen, which try to encompass recognition of the sad fact that the fall of a dictatorship does not inexorably lead to democracy. In this respect, a study of transition and military reform in Spain is clearly of interest as it focuses on a process that can be called a true and proper transition to democracy, since it led to the consolidation of a state of law.

The analysis of transition processes

The pioneering work of Dankwart A. Rustow stands out in the field of transition studies. It is quite astonishing, with the hindsight of what

---

[5] Adolfo Suárez, 'La Transición Política' in 'Historia de la Transición', Madrid, *Diario 16*, 1983. Quoted by Colomer 1998: 9.
[6] O'Donnell 1994. For the concept of low-intensity democracy and its relationship to social and civil rights, see O'Donnell 2001: 601 and following.

happened in Spain, Greece or Portugal, that in his article of 1970, written five years before these processes of transition had begun, he was able to describe so precisely their most salient features. Rustow starts from a view that 'the factors that keep a democracy stable may not be the ones that brought it into existence: explanations of democracy must distinguish between function and genesis'.[7] In this way, he opened the door to the specific study of transitions to democracy. From this departure point, Rustow considers such transitions as a process that could be divided into three phases, with a single prerequisite in order to be operative: national unity. Rustow thus denies that a minimal level of economic development is a necessary prerequisite for democracy.

The first phase, which he describes as preparatory, is one of struggle and conflict over power between different social forces. The initial aim of the latter is not necessarily to establish democracy. The second phase, decision making, can be viewed as an act of explicit consensus in which 'political leaders accept the existence of diversity in unity and, to that end, agree to institutionalise some crucial aspects of democratic procedures'. In the third phase, habituation, politicians and citizens alike apply the new rules to other issues and adjust to the new democratic structure.

Rustow based his article on his knowledge of the situations in England, Sweden and Turkey, and was of course unable at that stage to analyse the numerous cases of transition that occurred in the 1970s and 1980s. Nonetheless, I can point to many elements in his description that anticipated what was to happen, at least in Spain. One could mention his affirmation that small groups of leaders play a disproportionate role in the decision-making phase. There are also his references to the fear of civil war as an incentive for gradualism; to the importance of political consensus in what he describes as the decision-making phase; or his statement that education for the masses and the welfare state are the consequences of democracy rather than a precondition for democracy itself.

The notion of process and division into phases is a starting point in the contributions by O'Donnell and the group of academics he and Philippe Schmitter brought together to research *Transitions from Authoritarian Rule* at the Woodrow Wilson Centre in Washington. From his assessment of what had happened in several countries in

---

[7] Rustow 1970: 346.

South America, O'Donnell suggested it would be useful to divide the process into two phases: 'The first goes from the previous authoritarian regime to the establishing of a democratic government. The second goes from that government to the consolidation of democracy or, in other words, to the effective existence of a *democratic regime*.'[8] These definitions frame the paths for two lines of study: the one distinguishing between the two transitions, that is, between what would be later called transition and consolidation; and the other defining the features of a democratic regime that the process should embody in order to be judged a success.

We should not be surprised if the attention of scholars has been drawn to the concept of consolidation rather than to that of transition. In terms of time-span, the transition is usually a shorter period, as well as being simpler: the replacing of authoritarian rules and structures by democratic ones.[9] It is understandable that the very nature of a concept susceptible to many interpretations should give rise to other definitions of transition and, above all, of democratic consolidation. These are

---

[8] O'Donnell 1997b: 221.

[9] In the same study written in 1997, O'Donnell himself advanced his definition of consolidated democracy on the basis of the meeting of five requirements linked above all to the behaviour and attitudes of the main political actors and groups. It is an insightful but not very practical proposal, whether in terms of analytical or normative outcomes, since these are complex factors that are difficult to calibrate and relate as much to formal issues as they do to the behaviour and attitudes of society and the main political actors. See: O'Donnell 1997b: 251–2: 'a consolidated democracy is a regime 1) where political democracy rules (or polyarchy, to recall Robert Dahl's definition) and none of the democratic players is principally concerned about preventing the (slow or sudden) return of authoritarianism and consequently nobody subordinates their decisions (or omissions) to that concern; 2) where the social and political players who control the most important resources of power (even when they are not strictly democratic) customarily submit their interrelations to the specific institutions of political democracy through practices that are compatible with the reproduction of those institutions, institutions that, whether they like it or not, they believe will continue to exist indefinitely; 3) where the routine character of these practices, the strengthening of those institutions (that have consequently managed to assert themselves as important, if not exclusive, spaces of power in the nation) maintain the "procedural consensus" that Schmitter and I mention in the work quoted and promote the uncertain nature of results from clean, competitive elections; 4) where this set of political relations is increasingly consistent with the extension of similarly democratic (or at least not despotic or archaic) relations to other spheres of social life; 5) where those in government assume the distinction between the public and the private and reasonably effective mechanisms exist to sanction their anti-republican actions.'

based on formal aspects rather than a description of the process. In a study devoted to Spain, Mario Caciagli therefore states that consolidation takes place when election results decide changes in who holds power.[10] Some years later, Huntington caricatured this criterion.[11] In the concrete case of Spain, Huntington's proposal takes us back to 1996, when the Socialists gave way to the Partido Popular in the general elections. It is a focus that is far too limited, based solely on election results, and although it is a conclusion in line with Schumpeter's well-known definition of democracy,[12] it belongs to what Linz and Stepan have called 'the electoral fallacy', that is, the idea that free elections, although a necessary condition for democracy, become the single sufficient requirement.[13]

Other writers have based their criteria on the acceptance of the rules of the game of democracy. Di Palma believes consolidation to be 'the establishing of rules of competition able to prevent the key players from boycotting the game'.[14] Even Linz, who together with Alfred Stepan would later put forward a complex definition of consolidation, proposed a definition of a similar kind when he believed the situation was one in which

> none of the most important political actors, parties or organised interest groups, forces or institutions, considers that an alternative to the democratic process exists in order to hold the reins of power. And ... no group or political institution has the prerogative to veto the actions of democratically elected governments ... To say it in the simplest terms possible, democracy must be considered 'the only game in town'.[15]

Guillermo O'Donnell has quite rightly criticized this view, given that numerous Latin American democracies fulfil the formal rules of polyarchies but cannot be thought of as consolidated democracies because they have unacceptably low levels of protection for rights, insufficient accountability of governments, or a proliferation of the plague that O'Donnell dubs favouritism or nepotism. To express it in

---

[10] Caciagli 1986: 3–14.

[11] Huntington 1991: 267. I say it is somewhat of a caricature because he states that a democracy is consolidated after two peaceful changes of government.

[12] Schumpeter defined democracy as 'The democratic method is that institutional arrangement for arriving at political decisions in which individuals acquire the power to decide by means of a competitive struggle for the people's vote' (Schumpeter 1950: 269).

[13] Linz and Stepan 1996: 4.   [14] Di Palma 1988: 78.   [15] Linz 1990: 156.

his words: 'Individuals are citizens in relation to the only institution that functions in a way that is prescribed by formal rules: elections. In every other sphere, only members of a privileged minority are full citizens.'[16]

We can conclude that the more an analysis of these transformations is tied into formal elements and definitions of formal democracy, the less it will clarify the real problems of transition understood as a process and provide criteria to enable us to distinguish the various phases within a transition.[17]

However, these attempts to define consolidation do not provide useful starting points if we wish to include the armed forces as a key player in our analysis. In fact, and I shall return to this in greater detail later on, the process of democratic consolidation does not finish, but starts, in relation to the military, when, to borrow Juan Linz's expression, they lose their prerogative to 'veto the actions of democratically elected governments'.

Adam Przeworski in his work *Democracy and the Market* outlines a very similar position although he expresses it in terms that are more akin to the rational decision-making approach:

Democracy is consolidated when under given political and economic conditions a particular system of institutions becomes the only game in town, when no one can imagine acting outside the democratic institutions, when all the losers want to do is to try again within the same institutions under which they have just lost. Democracy is consolidated when it becomes self-enforcing, that is, when all the relevant political forces find it best to continue to submit their interests and values to the uncertain interplay of the institutions.[18]

Przeworski's focus could be the object of the same criticisms as the previous approaches, including the fact that his position rests on a degree of tautology: a democracy is consolidated when everybody accepts it, that is, when everyone is a democrat.

Nonetheless his definition is relevant because Przeworski includes the military as a sector it is essential to control. He argues as follows: in

---

[16] O'Donnell 1997c: 320.

[17] A clear case of this nature is Giuseppe Di Palma, who centres his analysis on the existence of a democratic accord as the basis for the process of transition. From this perspective, as Di Palma states, in the ideal situation, the process must be very short lived. The recommendation that the processes of consolidation are short is in Di Palma 1988: 74. For his most detailed explanation, see Di Palma 1990.

[18] Przeworski 1991: 26.

terms of rational decision-making analysis, when a player in a demo-cratic system tries to overthrow the regime, both the likelihood that this subversion will be successful and the cost associated with its failure depend on the will expressed by the other political forces to defend the institutions. However, Przeworski continues, 'yet the actors in the democratic game are not identical; democracy is not just a matter of numbers. Obviously, the institutional framework of civilian control over the military constitutes the neuralgic point of democratic consoli-dation.'[19] This is clear recognition of the importance of the role of the armed forces and an insight to spur us on in our reflections. But it remains an insight Przeworski never develops.

Another approach views consolidation as a long process that can extend over a decade to a generation. In this sense, democratic consolidation would be the process that diminishes any possibility that democratization could slip backwards and 'may be said to have been completed when there is evidence that the political culture is being made in a system-supportive direction, thus removing the last of the uncertainties remaining in the aftermath of transition'.[20] This process can be divided into two, negative and positive consolida-tions. The first implies the effective or final removal of any hope being placed in non-democratic alternatives. In positive consolida-tion, the democratic system settles down operationally and gains in credibility. Apart from warning about the time span necessary for the process – which did not last anything like a generation in Spain – this approach does not help us in our attempts to find elements that can link the theory of democratic transition to the attitude of the armed forces and the process of imposing control on them. And one must also bear in mind that negative consolidation may not be followed by positive consolidation, if the process of evolution stagnates.

To return to the non-formalist current within 'transitology', stem-ming from the work of O'Donnell and Schmitter, the more rounded, mature definitions of the terms we are using come from the joint think-ing of Juan Linz and Alfred Stepan.[21] For them

---

[19] Przeworski 1991: 29.   [20] Pridham 1995: 171.
[21] See Linz and Stepan 1995, an article that defines the approach in their important 1996 study.

[a] democratic transition is complete when sufficient agreement has been reached about political procedures to produce an elected government, when a government comes to power that is the direct result of a free and popular vote, when this government *de facto* has the authority to generate new policies, and when the executive, legislative and judicial power generated by the new democracy does not *de jure* have to share power with other bodies.[22]

Their definition of democratic consolidation emphasizes that democracy is consolidated when democracy really has become 'the only game in town'. But to that end one must consider three aspects that refer respectively to the way the political actors behave, public opinion develops and the domain of legal structures and procedures is established.

In spite of Linz and Stepan's noteworthy attempts to clarify approaches, they do not fully succeed in providing a useful demarcation between definitions of transition and consolidation nor, although they mention it as an important factor, do they offer a clear framework for integrating the evolution of relations between civilian society and the military within the analysis. Consequently, we must conclude that neither the development of the various perspectives on political transition nor the diverse definitions of transition or consolidation have succeeded in incorporating a study of the attitudes of the military and the relations between military and civilian spheres into their more general analyses or combined approaches.

The inclusion of the armed forces in the analysis

Among the many contributions to understanding the concept of democratic consolidation, J. Samuel Valenzuela's contains new elements that help articulate military reform theoretically within the overall process. Firstly, Valenzuela points out the frequent need in the period of consolidation to abandon agreements or rules that were useful during the process of transition: 'The process of democratic consolidation would require redefinitions, sometimes at considerable risk, of the regime's institutions and/or of the relations between political

---

[22] Linz and Stepan 1996: 3.

actors'.[23] Secondly, Valenzuela uses a new tool to facilitate bringing the analysis of the behaviour of the military within the vision of the entire process.

It involves creating a space in the analysis for what Valenzuela calls *perverse elements* in the process of institutionalizing democracy. Democratic consolidation takes place through a continued functioning of the democratic institutions that have been created, but rather than studying the characteristics of this benign process, scholars should attend to the perversions of the system that could undermine it. Democratic consolidation consists in reducing these *perverse elements* until they have been eliminated. Although a list of such elements could be very long, he suggests identifying four main *perverse elements*: the existence of tutelary powers not generated by democratic means; the existence of important 'reserve domains' of policy making; significant exclusions from the electoral process; and, finally, a situation in which elections are not the only way to create a government.

We will focus on the first two of these elements independently of the fact that it is arguable whether the last two fit the category of possible *perversions* of the process or relate to situations that undoubtedly make it impossible to meet a definition of democracy, however minimalist that may be. In effect, experiences in Spain, and many other countries, show that the element most likely to undermine the process of consolidation is the military when it asserts itself as a tutelary power or creates its own autonomous space and takes areas of political decision making away from the government. The armed forces assert themselves as tutelary powers when they consider themselves guarantors of the nation's essence and permanent interests and from this position impact on an elected government.

As examples of tutelary power one can mention the Revolutionary Council included by the military in the 1974 Portuguese Constitution, or in Latin America, the case of Bolivia, where the Organic Law of the Armed Forces includes among other doctrinal principles 'To exemplify the heroism, courage, power and strength of the Bolivian people; they symbolise the history of Independence and strengthening of the

---

[23] Valenzuela 1992: 59.

Republic, being thereby custodians of its freedom, progress and territorial and spiritual integrity.'[24]

The 'reserve domains' may be a product of impositions by diverse political actors, from the judiciary to the economic powers-that-be, but the analysis of third-wave processes of transition demonstrates that they are usually constituted by the armed forces. The most obvious example is perhaps Chile, but it is a constant that can be traced in almost all recent processes of democratic transition in Latin America. It leads Valenzuela to make the following definition of democratic consolidation:

Once the first transition has been accomplished, the process of reaching democratic consolidation consists in eliminating the institutions, procedures, and expectations that are incompatible with the minimal workings of a democratic regime, thereby permitting the beneficent ones that are created or re-created in the transition to a democratic government to develop further. It reaches closure, following the basic conception presented above, when the authority of a fairly elected government and legislative officials is properly established (i.e., not limited as noted) and when major political actors as the public at large expect the democratic regime to last well into the foreseeable future.[25]

---

[24] This is the first article in the Organic Law of the Armed Forces of Bolivia, that states as follows:

'The Armed Forces of the Nation are the fundamental and permanent armed Institution of the Bolivian state and they sustain the legal principles:

a) To preserve the Mandate of the Constitution, peace, National Unity and the democratic institutions of the State.
b) To defend the nation, to be a faithful expression of civic values, the honour and greatness of the Fatherland, its traditions and its glories.
c) To exemplify the heroism, courage, power and strength of the Bolivian people; they symbolize the history of Independence and the strengthening of the Republic, being thereby custodians of its freedom, progress and spiritual and territorial integrity.
d) They constitute the bastion of National Security and the sovereign Defence of the Fatherland, contribute to the general well-being of the Bolivian people, are the mainstay of the vigour of the Political Constitution of the State, democracy and the rights and guarantees of the citizenry.
e) They are the indispensable factor for the achievement of National Objectives, the overall development of the country and the irrevocable resolution of maritime demands.
f) To sustain itself through the coherence of its structures, its mission and vertical organization, based on the fundamental principles of discipline, hierarchy, order and respect for the Political Constitution of the State, its laws and regulations.'

[25] Valenzuela 1992: 70.

Starting from this definition, it is possible to locate military reform within the process of transition and consolidation to the extent that a programme of reform for the armed forces will begin their adaptation to the new regime's democratic procedures. That is, to the extent that their tendency to intervene politically and shape the process of democratization is reduced, as well as their propensity to create a 'reserve domain' on issues affecting their own sphere, thus contributing to the completion of the process of consolidation.

When analysing the distinction made by O'Donnell between what he calls the two transitions, I noted that his article introduced the idea of two lines of study, the demarcation of different phases and the analysis of the characteristics of the democratic regime towards which the process should be moving. We have pinpointed the shortcomings in the definitions under scrutiny, with the partial exception of J. Samuel Valenzuela, at least from the perspective of an analysis that allows detailed study of the interrelationship between the transition and the process of establishing democratic control of the armed forces. To that end, it is helpful to explore a potential definition of the period of democratic consolidation by focusing on the analysis of the process of moving towards or fulfilling the attributes of a regime that may be described as democratic.

However turbulent, the present international context favours such an approach. Przeworski has stated that 'the final destination (that is, the establishing of a democracy) is as important as the point of departure', against those who cultivate the path-dependent approach maintaining that the circumstances of the transition or the so-called route to transition determine or seriously condition the characteristics of the new regime. He does not deny that the nature of the previous regimes influences the context and trajectory of the transition, but considers that recent transitions to democracy have come about as part of a tide of change and have taken place influenced by similar ideological and political conditions throughout the world.[26] The thinking of Linz and Stepan shifted in the same direction when they used the expression *zeitgeist* (spirit of the times) to analyse international influence on processes of transition: 'by the late 1970s the *zeitgeist* in southern Europe ... was such [that] there were no major ideological contestants to democracy as a political system'.[27]

---

[26] Przeworski 1991: 190.   [27] Linz and Stepan 1996: 74–6.

On the other hand, stagnation in the progress to acceptable levels of democracy in so many countries on the American continent and in Eastern Europe means we must separate out the notion of democratic consolidation from the idea of a successful culmination of an irreversible process once the transition is underway or from the idea of its stability. Many weak democracies are in situations that can be described as irreversible. And there are multiple examples of semi-democracies stagnating in a possible evolution to a consolidated democracy.

The need for a non-aggregate approach

The crucial drawback for our study stems from a problem shared by all the approaches we have examined up to now. A general or combined perspective creates enormous difficulties when it comes to investigating the nature of democratic consolidation. The complexity of the process does not allow such general approaches, and the variety of situations resists the formulation of a paradigm that can be applied to each and every one. Pure common sense almost leads us to conclude that if we want to explain the process as a process and not as the final outcome, then we must break it up and study it in its parts in order to analyse the behaviour of the political actors in a given field and their contribution to the overall process.

Leonardo Morlino pinpointed this issue when he declared that a process of consolidation cannot start simultaneously for the different components of a democratic regime. Hence his definition of consolidation as 'the multifaceted process through which the structures, norms and relations between the regime and civil society are firmly established and entirely democratic'.[28] Years earlier, David Stark also stated that 'within any given country, we find not one transition, but many, occurring in different domains – political, economic, and social. These processes are often asynchronous and their articulation seldom harmonious'.[29]

I believe that similar considerations led Philippe Schmitter to formulate the concept of *partial regimes*. Schmitter states that 'it is not democracy as such that is consolidated in the aftermath of the demise of an authoritarian regime. Rather, it is a bundle of diverse institutions or 'partial regimes' that link citizens to public authorities, thereby

[28] Morlino 1998: 14.   [29] Stark 1992: 301.

rendering these authorities accountable'.[30] Schmitter sums up the case for a non-aggregate approach in four points:

1. Democratic consolidation is a process implying the structuring of several partial regimes, linking each one of them to different institutions with its respective publics, clients, members or voters.
2. Despite the shared *appellation non-contrôlée* of democracy, it is probable that these partial regimes are organised around different principles or decision–making rules in relation to their domains and resources.
3. It is also probable that the rhythm of these partial structural changes will vary from one case to another; moreover, it is probable that those institutions that are first consolidated in their domains and resources in the evolution of a transition of a regime, will have significant impact on those that appear afterwards.
4. The resulting overall kind of democracy will be defined by the permutation (and hence by the sequence) of the partial regimes that are formed during the consolidation.[31]

Schmitter refers to some of the partial regimes that make up an overall process of democratic consolidation: the electoral process, representation, or collective bargaining in terms of relations between government, employers' federation and unions. The corollary of such a conception of the processes of regime change is that if they comprise the consolidation of a set of partial regimes, it is necessary to analyse these regimes in an individual way in order to understand how they work.[32] Thus, from this perspective, we can consider the relations between the civilian and the military as a partial regime, and, likewise, a partial regime of collective bargaining, and we can study separately, though not in isolation, their process of evolution from an authoritarian regime to a consolidated democracy. In the Spanish case, to give another example, one would no doubt have to consider the partial regime of territorial division as one of the essential elements in that set of transitions.

In a study centred on the partial regime of civil–military relations, we can draw on the approach developed by Valenzuela, namely, one that

---

[30] Schmitter 1995: 285.   [31] Schmitter 1995: 287.
[32] For an analysis of several recent studies of processes of transition from the perspective of an aggregate or non-aggregate focus, see Encarnación, 2000.

eliminates the perverse elements in the process of democratic institutionalization that may pertain to the armed forces.

Initial conclusions on political transition and military reform

The previous reflections enable us to focus the analysis I will develop in the following chapters which, I emphasize, have as their main aim the study of military policy, that is, policy referring to the field of relations between democratic institutions and the armed forces. For the moment, we can establish a series of premises.

There is no single paradigm accepted by all scholars as a way of explaining processes of regime change from authoritarian situations, and if one ever existed, it is now in deep crisis, since the majority of countries that began these processes are not in transition to democracy, but are currently stagnating in semi-democratic situations.[33]

In keeping with the normative aim of these reflections, I share the point of view expressed by Rustow in his seminal article that 'the political scientist, moreover, is entitled to his rights within the general division of labour and may wish to concentrate on some of the political factors without denying the significance of the social and economic ones'.[34]

There are two schools into which 'transitology' can be divided, namely, a more formal one, concerned with such aspects as free elections or the alternating of power, and one more centred on content, concerned, for example, with citizens' rights or the real exercise of power by those elected. Only the second encompasses military reform in its analysis.

It is necessary to study the process of transition as such: a process that implies improvements and which cannot be mistaken for the permanence of democracy. To that end, we must be concerned less with preconditions and the goal to be attained than with the actual development and thrust within a process of transition, that from the angle of military policy is fundamentally one of reforms.

The differentiation of stages is useful for normative purposes. If we focus on the area of military control, then the distinction between transition and consolidation is very helpful. The stage of democratic 'persistence' must be added and that will be the focus of chapter 7.

---

[33] On this issue see Carothers 2002.   [34] Rustow 1970: 344.

We must adopt a non-aggregate approach if we want to analyse in detail the process of military reform within the transition in general, and use the notion of 'partial regime' coined by Schmitter.

Within such an approach, that is, from within the 'partial regime' of the relations between the armed forces and society, we must decide whether we can consider the process of consolidation to be a period when the 'reserve domains' retained by the armed forces are gradually reduced.

2 | Democratic transition and the armed forces: military autonomy

After examining in the previous chapter some of the main lines of thought in studies of processes of transition and their potential for encompassing the issue of control of the military, in this chapter we shall examine in greater detail the existing analyses in this field before embarking on a definition of phases that I think fits the case of Spain.

The fact that most of the transitions belonging to the so-called third wave have taken place following totalitarian military regimes (every single one if we refer to Latin America), has led to the study of civilian–military relations in the broader context of political transformation. Robert Dahl includes the issue of the control of the military, albeit briefly, in *Democracy and its Critics*:

> In order for a state to be governed democratically, evidently two conditions are required: 1) If military and police organizations exist, as they surely will, then they must be subject to civilian control. But civilian control, while necessary, is not sufficient, for many nondemocratic regimes also maintain civilian control. Therefore, 2) the civilians who control the military and police must themselves be subject to the democratic process.[1]

Dahl does not develop this insight in the rest of his book, apart from some historical reflections on the relationship between the evolution of military organization and the potential for democracy in ancient Greece and Rome. He does, however, develop ideas about civil control and military professionalism that are of interest since he defends a position that is opposed to Huntington's concept of objective control. But it is a reflection on consolidated democracies and not on processes of transition.[2]

We can mention many 'transitologists' who consider the role of the armed forces as one of the key factors when studying changes in authoritarian regimes if we are to determine whether democracy has been consolidated. Adam Przeworski, already quoted, states 'the

---

[1] Dahl 1989: 245.   [2] I discuss this issue in chapter 7.

institutional framework of civilian control over the military constitutes the neuralgic point of democratic consolidation'.[3] But he fails to develop his analysis with this statement in mind. Przeworski's book includes an interesting discussion of the initial situation in a transition: the risk of a coup and the probable acceptance of military tutelage, which, as the author notes at the moment of writing (1991), only Spain and Greece have avoided. Consequently he considers that 'transitions through a process of gradual emancipation leave institutional features intact, a significant one being the autonomy of the armed forces'. And later he adds: 'wherever the armed forces have remained free of civilian control, the "military question" is a permanent source of instability for the democratic institutions'.[4] In my view, the tendency of the armed forces to defend their area of autonomy in the process of transition is a constant in every single instance, whether it is gradual, has been produced by the collapse of an authoritarian regime or, to use terms coined in the case of Spain, there is *reforma* or *ruptura*. What I want to emphasize, however, is that neither Przeworski nor other scholars who have recognized the importance of the role of the armed forces in the process have then located it at the centre of their analyses or made it a priority in their research.

Valenzuela did not do so either, although he articulated many valuable insights pertaining in particular to the stage of consolidation. As for the role of the armed forces, he writes:

Placing the military under the authority of the elected government is a key condition facilitating democratic consolidation. Insofar as elected government officials are unsuccessful in their attempts to subordinate the military, the subsequent autonomy of the military is contrary to the consolidation of democracy since, following the idea indicated above, it becomes a reserve domain containing a fundamental ingredient of state power: force of arms. In this case the reduction of military autonomy is an indispensable step towards consolidation.[5]

In Valenzuela's writing, we find a suggestion to which we shall return later: the struggle against military autonomy is indispensable for democratic consolidation He goes on to state: 'a fully democratic regime should contain in its constitutional and other basic laws the formal bases of military subordination to elected government officials,

---

[3] Przeworski 1991: 29.   [4] Przeworski 1991: 188–9.   [5] Valenzuela 1992: 87.

exclusive of any provisions suggesting military tutelage'. It is obvious nonetheless that it is not enough for democracy to be prescribed in law, but that it must determine procedures and actions in practice. Thus, Valenzuela maintains: 'Consequently, the key question for democratic consolidation is whether or not the second transition succeeds in removing or preventing the spectre of coup politics from emerging.'[6] There is a flaw in Valenzuela's line of argument because the absence of the threat of a coup d'état does not resolve all the problems relating to interventions by the military, and even less so the issue of military tutelage or their attempts to retain autonomy as a body. In any case, we confront two tasks for the second transition or consolidation: the resolution of the problems of possible coups d'états and military autonomy. This situation should be seen as part of an overview that locates the military question within the analysis of the process.

However, we still lack studies that tackle this approach as one of their main goals. Alfred Stepan has complained of this void in the scholarship on transitions, and, as one of the scholars who has most helped to fill it, he is well placed to do so: 'Unfortunately ... the military has probably been the least studied of the factors involved in new democratic movements'.[7] We must go to the literature generated in relation to Latin America to find any serious studies of the role of the armed forces in processes of regime change. In the case of Spain, there is scant scholarship in this field,[8] and what exists is always by specialists working on civilian–military relations, and never 'generalists' who integrate the issue within their analyses.

Stepan himself opened a promising line of analysis when he explained how he thought it was possible to break the cycle often repeated in Latin America of military intervention followed by a period of democracy that is ended by another military intervention. 'To prevent the return of the cycle described above, the democratic leadership of the state must implement a well conceived, *politically led* strategy towards the military (a *política militar*).'[9]

In my view, Felipe Agüero has made an unparalleled contribution to the study of periods of transition in the area of the military and to the articulation of the process of reforming the armed forces as part of a general process of transition. At this point I should single out the

---

[6] Valenzuela 1992: 88.   [7] Stepan 1988: xi.   [8] Agüero 1995a: 28.
[9] Stepan 1988: 138.

application of Pridham's definitions to the military field. Adopting his
terminology, Agüero considers that civilian elites need to know how to
find a way to progress from negative to positive consolidation.
'"Negative consolidation" would be elite satisfaction with the creation
of conditions that prevent military rebellion against the process of
democratization. "Positive consolidation" would refer, instead, to conscious, long-term efforts by civilian elites to devise policies and strategies for the incorporation of the military into the goals and institutions
of the new democratic regime.' Agüero here locates the task of preventing coups d'états in a different phase in the elaboration of a military
policy or strategy aimed at integrating the military within the democratic state. However, the definition he proposes of this task is not
entirely satisfactory:

A positive reincorporation is one which, while securing indisputable civilian
supremacy, grants the military enough institutional autonomy for the efficient
pursuit of its mission. Using civilian leadership to develop the framework for
such a positive incorporation, in which the military feels its institutional
interests are guaranteed, may ultimately facilitate the expansion of attitudinal
change among members of the armed forces in support of a democratic
regime. This kind of civilian leadership, then, emerges as a key factor differ-
entiating the Southern European from the South American cases.[10]

For Agüero, a degree of autonomy is the sweetener to ensure the
military support the new democratic institutions, and it is also a precondition for their professional behaviour, and the pursuit of their
mission. But this is surely dangerous terrain to tread, since an increase
in autonomy for the military is not at all compatible with steps to
encourage the necessary change in values and professional self-
definition on the part of the military. As I shall explain in the following
chapter, military autonomy entrenches itself in the final stages of consolidation via control of its training, its definition as a profession and its
corporate features. The process of democratization cannot be considered finished if it does not produce a change in the principles and beliefs
of the military and make them loyal to the democratic regime.

It is clear that this requires more time than we would normally expect
for a process of institutional transition. Consequently, Agüero states
'more often than not, the "military problem" has not been resolved by

[10] Agüero 1995b: 165.

the time the transition ends'.[11] However, can we consider a process of transition to be finished that has not managed to resolve the issue of the military? A response can only come from a correct definition of the process and of its stages.

The stages in the transition of the military to democracy

For Agüero, two different tasks make up the process of the transition to democracy: the exclusion of the military from political affairs and the elimination of protests from the military, along with the affirmation of the prerogatives of civil government in military and defence matters. These goals were probably not reached in Spain until the transition was completed, and that is why it is necessary to extend the analysis to the specific process of *post-transition*.[12] The two tasks have to go in tandem, since I know of no case of a process of transition in which civil authority has been asserted without first returning the military to their barracks and preventing them from intervening in politics. But other scholars do not use the word 'post-transition' and it may create confusion. It is unclear if Agüero is referring to the stage commonly described as one of consolidation, or to what Gunther, Diamandouros and Puhle have dubbed 'democratic persistence'.[13] For Agüero, democratic consolidation 'was not achieved in Spain until approximately seven years after the death of Franco'.[14] That means that Agüero considers, along with many other authors, as we shall see, that the consolidation was settled by the 1982 elections. In my opinion, one cannot say that at that moment 'the prerogatives of civilian rulers were affirmed over military matters', without broaching the fact that we need a simpler, more verifiable formula to encapsulate this situation. In that sense, it is worth making the effort to focus on the military when clarifying the various stages in a transition and their content.

A democracy cannot be considered as consolidated, at least from the perspective of the 'partial regime' of civil–military relations, until civilian supremacy has been consolidated. In relation to this concept, Agüero offers a definition that reproduces some terms from a key law

---

[11] Agüero 1995b: 148. [12] Agüero 1995a: 33.
[13] Gunther, Diamandouros and Puhle 1995: 412. [14] Agüero 1995b: 138.

for the reform of the Spanish military, namely the reform carried through in 1984 of the 1980 Organic Law of Basic Criteria for National Defence: 'We shall define civilian supremacy as the ability of a democratically elected civilian government to carry through general policies without interference from the military, to define the goals and general organization for national defence and oversee the application of military policy.'[15] The two sides of the question emerge again in this definition. The first is more in evidence and is underlined: there is no democracy if the military are in charge. The second is proposed by Alfred Stepan in his seminal work on Brazil: the need for civilians to follow a policy-led strategy in relation to the military. However, it is obvious that a situation of civilian supremacy requires investment of time and effort, and cannot be reached overnight in the wake of an authoritarian regime.

When it comes to analysing necessary changes to the military in a process of transition or, to formulate it in other terms, from the 'partial regime' of civil–military relations, the two-phase division most authors apply to the general process of transition and consolidation should be used. This makes sense because they correspond to different transformations and policies.

The phase of *transition* occurs when democratically elected civilians manage to end military interference in the policy-making process, either because the military stops participating in the tasks of government or because any leverage it had to veto or pressurize the activities of the elected authorities is eliminated. On the other hand, the phase of *consolidation* occurs when the elected civilian government is able to establish military and defence policies, ensures they are implemented and directs the activities of the armed forces.

These definitions are applicable, in particular, from the perspective of the partial regime of civilian–military relations. Nevertheless, they can decide the phases in the general process if the interplay of changes in this specific field is decisive for the whole. They have the virtue of simplicity and of being consistent with a vision of transition as a process and not as a situation that can or cannot be established. Finally, they are definitions that are quite free of any danger of tautology: we are not using expressions such as reinforce, habituate, affirm or prop up which would

---

[15] Agüero 1995a: 47. In relation to the Organic Law consult Suárez Pertierra 1994: 51.

move us in that direction.[16] Although it is comparison with reality that validates any categorization, I want to emphasize the advantages of these definitions, at least in terms of simplicity, before examining what they imply for the demarcation of stages in Spain's transition to democracy. In effect, each stage represents a different process that is easy to define and understand. According to the approach I am suggesting, the key factor in the transition, and enough to define the stage by itself, is the phenomenon the Anglo-Saxons call 'extrication': the relinquishing of positions of power and political intervention by the military. As I understand it, the existence of a military and defence policy developed and applied by representative government is enough to guarantee that a particular country has entered the stage of consolidation.

It is worth emphasizing that I have not mentioned the reduction in privileges for the military as a feature that defines either of the two stages. The experience in Spain and other countries in Southern Europe and Latin America shows that the elimination of military privileges is a task that belongs to both stages and not just one. The same can be said of the legal reforms that encourage the armed forces to depend on civil authority and adjust to democratic procedures. In this case, I believe legal reforms, sometimes of a constitutional nature, have to be enacted at both stages, and it is more than likely that in the period of consolidation legal reforms will have to be introduced to improve on those implemented in the previous phase. Sometimes this involves correcting what some authors have called defects in the birth of democracy. On other occasions, it means enacting the legal reforms that are possible at a particular moment. The mere fact legal reforms exist, does not distinguish one stage from another. Their content must be the defining issue. As I have indicated previously, legal reforms in the transition, the pact that leads to the creation of democratic institutions, must encompass provisions to prevent political intervention by

---

[16] Others ways of dividing the process of reform into phases exist. Cottey, Edmunds and Forster have suggested distinguishing between first- and second-generation challenges to reform. First-generation issues are those that centre on structural reform, while the second relate to the consolidation of the new framework and subsequent injection into that framework of what they call democratic substance. This stage is marked by the 'ability of democratic state structures to provide for effective management of the armed forces and defence policy' (2002: 40). This represents a distinction that is not opposed to the one we are suggesting, but in my view the one defined in this chapter is clearer and less of a tautology.

the military and eliminate any ambiguity in this area if we are to consider the transition complete.

It is inadequate to try to differentiate the two stages as a function of the existence or not, or simply the threat, of military coups d'état. Coups are a symptom of a sick democracy. And, in politics, as in medicine, one must fight the illness and not just the symptoms. This means that the aim of military policy must be the inclusion of the military within the structure of the new democratic state. It implies establishing the armed forces' relationship of dependency in respect of the government that is 'normal' in any consolidated democracy. Coups d'état will cease to be a threat to the extent that these policies are reinforced.

Finally, the previous definitions do not tackle the issue of the loyalty of the military to democracy nor the end of uncertainty as features of a particular stage. Uncertainty is a problematic term if not used carefully, since, in very different ways, the transition and consolidated democracy are characterized by uncertainty, not in terms of institutional framework, in the case of the latter, but in the way it turns out, especially in electoral terms. Democracy has been defined as the institutionalizing of a normal, limited political uncertainty. Thus, it is wrong to try to define democratic consolidation as that situation in which uncertainty has been eliminated, even though we are referring to uncertainty in relation to possible coups. On the other hand, without discounting threats of coups in the slightest, I believe they do not constitute a sufficient criterion to define the stages or tasks the elected government must undertake in each phase of the process.

It goes without saying that the loyalty of the military to democratic government is a basic feature of a stable democracy. This implies that military policy in the period of consolidation must successfully implement enough changes in the values and professional profile of the military to guarantee this loyalty. I must emphasize again, nonetheless, that it is not a feature that can define a stage in the process. It suffices for the elected government to begin to implement suitable military policy for these features to become reality.

The academic world has recently experienced a debate on the control of the Latin American military that touches on the issues we have been examining, in particular the stages in asserting control and their content in a process of democratization.[17] In the first article, Pion-Berlin starts

---

[17] David Pion-Berlin 2005 and Thomas Bruneau 2006 led this debate.

from the fact that although the processes of democratization in Latin America began long ago, there are still very few civilian experts in areas related to the military, security and defence. He finds several reasons for this, among which he cites the non-existence of threats of invasion by foreign armed forces, the lack of job-generating military industries and the fact that the electorate does not bring either executive or legislative politicians to task for not formulating a security or defence policy. Hence he states: 'The balance of power has unquestionably tilted in favour of civilians over the course of 15 to 20 years, but *the balance of competence has not.*'[18] The problem arises, according to Pion-Berlin, from the fact that definitions of civilian control presume that control of the military is inseparable from managing defence and, while civilians in Latin America have every incentive to control the military, they have no incentive to develop expertise on defence issues. From these premises, he proposes separating the issue of relations with the military from the issue of defence policy management by making a distinction between 'civilian control'– the classic concept – and 'civilian-political control' defined as 'a low-cost means of achieving a relative calm in civil–military affairs, without investing in extensive institution building, expertise, legislative oversight, and large budgets'.[19] Pion-Berlin justifies his proposal with the fact that the classic definition imposes unfair, unachievable standards on Latin America.

Thomas Bruneau reacted with an article in which he used the well-known metaphor of the fox and the hedgehog, images that correspond to the military and the civilians, respectively. Here, Bruneau disagrees with Pion-Berlin and states that the civilians responsible for controlling the military 'must know enough to be sure that the armed forces are doing what is required of them, not only in terms of their subordination to civilian control [which is the central issue for Pion-Berlin] but also fulfilling the broad spectrum of tasks and missions assigned to the diverse security forces in Latin America'.[20] Apart from reminding us that in a consolidated democracy there are no areas of administration outside the control of the elected leaders, which, as we examined in the previous chapter, is tantamount to rejecting any possibility of reserved domains, Bruneau suggests three concepts that can give content to civilian–military relations: *democratic civilian control*; *effectiveness*,

---

[18] Pion-Berlin 2005: 21. [19] Pion-Berlin 2005: 28 and 29.
[20] Bruneau 2005: 113.

or the ability to carry through tasks determined by elected civilians; and *efficiency* as the requirement to do so as cheaply as possible. All this clearly requires the government to formulate proper policies for security and control of the military. Pion-Berlin responded by accepting Bruneau's positions from a normative perspective while affirming that it is essentially an empirical question and that effectiveness and efficiency are not priorities in a world with diminishing resources for defence.

Pion-Berlin's position can be described as an acceptance, or recognition, that the process of democratization can come to a halt in the period we have called the transition without the period of consolidation taking place, and that this situation can be stable and long-lasting. He drives this point home in his use of the expression 'live and let live'. The period of transition we have looked at and will look at in more detail in the next chapter can stabilize and be extended in a situation where the military does not intervene in politics or attempt coups d'état, but where civilians do not decide issues in the domain of the armed forces. This will no doubt be the case in situations of weak democracy that have not managed to build the institutional strength that is the mark of consolidated democracies. But the fact that the situation is stable does not mean the armed forces have been correctly articulated within the state administration in the terms of a functioning democracy.

For his part, Bruneau proposes a 'trinity' that is compatible with the definition of consolidation I have suggested, since it is impossible to control effectiveness and efficiency if the government does not implement military policy. When Bruneau says there is no control without the control of the effectiveness and efficiency of the armed forces, he is saying it cannot exist if the government does not implement military policy. And the fact is that in present circumstances, issues of military effectiveness and efficiency are linked to the question of military autonomy. It is practically impossible in the present context for an army that has organizational and budgetary autonomy to be efficient. Colombia, the only country in the hemisphere where the armed forces have to conduct large-scale fighting against an internal enemy, is a good case in point. The control of the armed forces is not independent of the missions the latter must undertake. Pion-Berlin himself accepts this when he says: 'Politicians seek military help in development assistance in Ecuador, counter-narcotic programmes in Brazil, and disaster relief in Honduras and Guatemala. In each case, political pragmatism dictated that civilian leaders made the decisions to deploy their militaries for the unorthodox assignments cited.'[21] Pion-Berlin clearly does not criticize the use of the military on such missions, but the fact that he calls them 'unorthodox' shows that he is not taking into account the profound transformation that has taken place in the role of the armed forces in recent years, in particular after the end of the Cold War. In this context, on the one hand, the autonomy of the armed forces is even less imaginable and, on the other, the civil authorities are better prepared to control the efficacy and efficiency of their armed forces.

Pion-Berlin is, however, mistaken when he centres his analysis on the problem of the expertise of civilians in matters of security and defence. The most important problem in Latin America is not the lack of knowledge or expertise of the executive or the legislature. One has to look to the institutional weakness of many South American democracies; the lack of prestige of the political class in relation to the armed forces; the lack of political will to carry through a process of democratization on all fronts; instability in public posts, in particular that of defence minister, if we wish to find real explanations for the stagnation of democratizing reforms and the modernization of the armed forces. Consequently, we cannot go along with Pion-Berlin's conclusion when he indicates that 'Our definitions and analyses should be less normative and more analytical. Civilian control definitions which impose unfair standards on a region not able to meet them should be stripped of their most exacting requirements.'[22]

Nonetheless, it is necessary to point to the set of prerequisites that allow one to consider a particular configuration of relations with the armed forces to be one of democratic control in order to establish how far a particular country must go to achieve this goal. The fact that the criteria are beyond reach at a given time does not mean they are unfair and that they must be redefined so that some day they can be achieved. That is why I believe it is essential to undertake a description of the whole process and its division into periods of transition and consolidation as I have in this chapter.

The stages of the process in Spain

In terms of deciding on the stages in the Spanish process, it is worthwhile reviewing conclusions from those who have studied its evolution.

[21] Pion-Berlin 2006: 55.   [22] Pion-Berlin 2005: 31.

One of the first studies was by Maravall and Santamaría, who state that the period between December 1975 and July 1976, the date when King Juan Carlos I appointed Adolfo Suárez as president of the government, must be seen as the 'preparatory phase'. This was the beginning of the transition as such, and they divide it into two phases. The first comprises political reform and finishes with the related referendum and the first general elections, in June 1977. The second phase comprises the Moncloa Pacts, the constitutional accord and the agreement of territorial organization that created the State of the Autonomies and ended with the general and municipal elections in the spring of 1979.[23] The period of consolidation then began, which they consider an extended process that in some cases can last for a whole generation. At the time they did not signal an end date for this period. They suggest that the 1982 elections belonged to the category of critical elections that greatly influenced the new party structure and consolidated the regime for three reasons. The first two were the renewal of the system's legitimacy that was brought by the high electoral participation and the alternation in power. The third comprised the widening of the government's scope for initiatives, particularly in its policy towards the armed forces.[24]

A few years later, Linz and Stepan gave us a precise formulation:

[W]e maintain that the Spanish transition began with the death of Franco on November 20, 1975, and was completed at the latest on October 25, 1979, when the Basque and Catalan referendums on regional autonomy were held. A case could of course be made that the transition was completed when the principle of government accountability to the parliament was established formally in November 1977 or when the new democratic constitution was approved in the referendum on December 6, 1978. However, we believe that only after the formula for Basque and Catalan regional autonomy had been negotiated and voted upon did Spain meet our three requirements for a *completed transition*: a government was in office that was the result of a free and popular vote, the government had sovereign authority to generate policies, and the government did not *de iure* have to share power with other bodies.[25]

This is an approach that focuses particularly on aspects of territorial organization, and especially on the establishing (or rather re-establishing) of the autonomous governments in Catalonia and the Basque country.

[23] Maravall and Santamaría 1986: 80–9, following Rustow's terminology.
[24] Maravall and Santamaría 1986: 100–2.   [25] Linz and Stepan 1996: 106–7.

However, this perspective needs to encompass a longer time-span, since the State of the Autonomies was far from being established in 1979.

In terms of democratic consolidation, Linz and Stepan coincide with the majority opinion and consider that Spanish democracy was consolidated no later than with the transfer of power to the Socialist Party in the elections of October 1982. They even believe that an earlier date could be posited: that of the imprisoning of General Milans del Bosch and Colonel Tejero, after the attempted coup, when 'there was no politically significant movement in the military or in civil society to grant them clemency'.[26] The reasons they give to justify the choice of this date relate above all to the armed forces, since from the moment there was a clear parliamentary majority decided in the ballot-boxes, 'military contestation shifted from politics to more strictly corporate concerns, and from resistance to accommodation'.[27] The military become the key factor because they constituted the only doubtful element in relation to their definition of consolidated democracy that we have duly examined. In effect, in terms of the three dimensions of a consolidated democracy – attitudes, constitution and behaviour – the authors recognize that the first two were fully met in so far as they considered Spanish public opinion and the constitutional legislative bloc to be fully democratic. The behavioural dimension was still outstanding, and that is met when no significant actor attempts to achieve his aims by violent means or from outside the democratic framework. The assessment of change in the behaviour of the armed forces is the decisive factor for Linz and Stepan to be able to decide whether their conditions for consolidation have been met.

However, the situation did not change overnight, and that is why I continually defend the notion of a process while at the same time stating that it is dangerous to look for dates of crucial events in order to define periods, rather than thinking of dates, whether they coincide or not with crucial events, that might be viewed as moments when processes of transformation were completed. Following this same logic, I think that the 1982 elections opened rather than closed the period of consolidation in terms of the military. The increased legitimacy these elections granted the Spanish democratic system and the authority that they lent the government, allowed the latter to develop its defence and military policy and accelerate the process of adaptation or, as I prefer

---

[26] Linz and Stepan 1996: 108.   [27] Linz and Stepan 1996: 110.

to call it, of normalization, of the armed forces in relation to the newly created state of law.

This suggestion differs not only from those I have reviewed, but also from those of Mario Caciagli[28] and Guillermo O'Donnell[29] and even Felipe Agüero,[30] which coincide in the main with Maravall and Santamaría, and Linz and Stepan. However, I would like to emphasize that from the perspective of the military's position, and from that of other partial regimes, such as, for example, the territorial organization of the new democracy, I do not think it is accurate to see the 1982 elections as closing the phase of consolidation. At that moment, for example, there were still unapproved statutes of autonomy, parliaments to be created and autonomous governments to be constituted.

Víctor Pérez-Díaz, more inclined to analyse social processes than the behaviour of political protagonists, must have understood that the 1982 elections made the consolidation possible rather than bringing it to its denouement, when he wrote that 'in Spain, this point [consolidation] was reached during the first socialist government, between 1982 and 1986'.[31] The fact is that the amount of time given to the stages of political change also depends on the perspective from which one scrutinizes the different aspects of reality. The more we focus on the political actors, dwell on aspects such as elections, interactions between elites or political groupings, the alternating between different options, the shorter the time span for the processes of transition will be. If institutional aspects, that is the assimilation of new realities and analysis of determinants of the process, are privileged then the processes get longer because they require more time.

In any case, in the area of the partial regime of civilian–military relations and in line with the descriptions of the periods that I have suggested, I believe that the transition to democracy began in Spain with the appointment of Adolfo Suárez as president of the government,

---

[28] Caciagli 1986: 7–13, considers that the political transition begins with the appointment of Adolfo Suárez as President of the Government in July 1976 and finishes with the verdict in the ballot boxes in October 1982.

[29] O'Donnell 1997b: 232, is forthright: 'Spanish democracy was on its way to consolidation, which happened in 1982 when the PSOE defeated the UCD and Felipe González formed his government as established in the Constitution'.

[30] Agüero 1995b: 138, is of the opinion that consolidation took place in Spain 'approximately seven years after the death of Franco', that is, in 1982.

[31] Pérez-Díaz 1993: 3–4.

although, if we wanted to be more exact, it would begin with the appointment, months later, of General Gutiérrez Mellado as Vice-President to replace General de Santiago. This period ended with the change in government as a result of the 1982 elections. Although the distinctions between stages are not so clear-cut and all contain elements from previous and subsequent phases, the axis of politics in this period was marked by the armed forces distancing themselves from positions of political power and by the safeguarding of the process of democratization in respect of a group that considered itself guarantor of the principles and institutions of the previous regime.

The 1982 elections and the end of the trial of those accused of instigating the February 1981 coup opened a new period: that of democratic consolidation, in which the government could tackle the tasks proper of consolidation, that is, the development of military and defence policy and the implementation of the reforms necessary to guarantee and guide their application. As I see it, this period had a similar length to the transition as it extended to 1989, the year that finalized the integration of Spanish security policy into the Western system with entry into the Western European Union (WEU), the approval of the system of cooperation with NATO and the signing of new accords with the United States. This was also the year when the Law Regulating the Conditions for Military Personnel was passed, structuring the armed forces like a branch of the state administration. On the other hand, with the fall of the Berlin Wall, a period of new changes opened up for the Spanish armed forces: these changes were no longer the result of the process of adaptation to the democratic system, but were prompted by the end of the Cold War and developments on the international scene. Spain had already, even from the perspective of democratic military change, entered the period some authors have described as 'democratic persistence'.[32]

From this point of view, the complete process of transition to democracy, in terms of what we have called the partial regime of civilian–military relations in Spain, required thirteen years; a longer period than that usually set by transitologists for the overall process. There are several reasons why the process in this partial regime is so prolonged, or rather delayed, in relation to the general process. In the first place, unlike the period of transition, the passage of time is crucial for the

---

[32] Gunther, Diamandouros and Puhle 1995: 412.

period of consolidation.[33] The military develops attitudes of loyalty to the democratic system when they can see that there is a light at the end of the tunnel of loss of privileges and changes in their professional profile: new missions accepted by the system and a professional profile that guarantees their corporate future. All that requires time. For their part, it is not easy for the civilians who occupy posts of responsibility in this field to become competent and acquire the ability to lead and control. I am referring to the different posts in the structure of the Ministry of Defence and to the need for the Ministry of Foreign Affairs to have experts in these fields, for intelligence services to recruit civilians and for the committees for defence in both chambers to consist of elected individuals with knowledge of the issues concerned. And once again, all that needs time. Those reasons aside, it needs more time because the new political system must appear gradually as consolidated, or legitimated, for the military to accept the idea of the loss of their privileges, first, and of their autonomy, later. The third set of reasons is linked to the longer nature of processes when the psychological adjustment of particular groups is necessary. A change in the value system of the military, or even in their professional profile, requires more time than establishing elections, to mention another example of adjustment in the process of transition.

We should not be surprised, then, if the reform of the partial regime of civilian–military relations proceeds at a slower rate than that of other partial regimes or the main thrust of the overall process of transition. We must, nevertheless, ask ourselves if it is possible to describe the stages in an overall process very differently to the process in relation to its partial regimes. The answer must be that it will depend on the transcendence of each partial regime in the overall process. In the Spanish case, as in so many others, the adjustment of the armed forces to the new democratic situation was so crucial for the general process that I am afraid it is impossible. In other words, if one agrees that the process of democratic consolidation in relation to the armed forces began substantially in Spain after the 1982 elections, it is very difficult, if not impossible, to argue that it came to an end at that date.

---

[33] Diamond 1999: 115.

3 | *What is military reform?*

In the previous chapters, we saw that there is no theory of transitions that can be applied across the board. Authoritarian regimes fall in different ways according to whether they are military, presidential or single party. Several authors have emphasized that in the case of military regimes, internal divisions usually kick-start the process, and the military usually negotiates an orderly transition to a greater extent than the other two authoritarian systems mentioned.[1] But from there on, the differences are so great that no theoretical model exists which can explain these kinds of processes and anticipate outcomes. Even less so if we want to encompass transitions from other types of authoritarianism. If the process of democratization advances successfully, that is, if it manages to enter a process of consolidation, then different countries begin to show more similarity since, although several kinds of democracy exist, they move towards processes and behaviour that have more in common.

If we focus on the partial regime of civilian–military relations, points in common are more plentiful even though we are looking at contexts as distinct as one country in the Andes and another in the Balkans. Here there is no general theory either, but it may be useful to describe a process based on one concrete situation, in this case, Spain, and to try to sketch out the numerous elements (legal changes, transformations in organization, guidelines and new orientations) that comprise a reform of the military in a process of transition that has been successfully brought to conclusion.

This chapter will review policy for military reform in the framework of the partial regime of civilian–military relations, starting from the definitions of transition and consolidation formulated in the previous chapter. Following the path marked out by J. Samuel Valenzuela of a reduction in reserve domains, I will outline the successive stages of the

---

[1] See, for example, Whitehead 1986: 18, Fitch 1998: 24–29, Geddes 1999: 120.

reform and try to pinpoint the relationship between different reforming measures and the evolution of a social and political framework: in a process of democratic consolidation it is more important to be aware of the restraints on possible actions at each moment in time than the final goal. I must underline the fact that I am not attempting to develop *the* model for military reform, but rather to set out a series of stages in the process, to describe the different measures that make up policy and show the way all elements interrelate in order to propose suggestions, but not norms, for other cases, although their context is different.

Preliminary considerations

Before tackling the division of the process into stages, it will be helpful to analyse three more general issues that shape the process itself.

First, we must understand that military reform cannot be isolated from the process of transition or general democratic reform in which it is embedded. If the general process moves forward, it is possible to advance military reform, but if the democratic transition slows down or is curtailed altogether, is almost impossible for it to progress in the area of the armed forces as if it were an isolated sector. In the case of Spain, legal reforms, agreements between social agencies and the transformation of institutions were carried through at a brisk pace, especially in the first four years of transition. Even so, when the government weakened, particularly due to problems of internal cohesion in the party that was its mainstay, the UCD (Unión de Centro Democrático), opposition and military insubordination grew. In Latin America, the stagnation of most processes of transition and the weakness of presidential systems[2] have backtracked the process through which the armed forces lose their prerogatives and privileges. Colombia is a clear case of the legislature's resistance to reforming initiatives and the democratic strengthening of the system led by recent presidents of the Republic. Until 2005, the lack of agreement between the two most powerful democratic options in Chile put a brake on the necessary constitutional reform that would subordinate the armed forces to the elected civil authority. In such conditions, or when corruption and favouritism are growing rather than being tackled, it

---

[2] O'Donnell 1994: 66, describes these presidential systems in South America as 'a curious mixture of omnipotence and impotence'.

is equally impossible to execute a process of democratic military reform, since the military, like any other corporate body, will resist a reform they believe only impacts on them: 'delegative democracy', as O'Donnell called it, is a good breeding ground for military autonomy. The need to reform the judiciary, to refashion the police system, to combat mafias and paramilitary groups in parallel with the military reform, shows that this is also the case in Eastern Europe.

Secondly, it must be understood that military reform is not a process that takes place on two fronts – the government and the democratic institutions on one side, the armed forces on the other – but on three: we must also take society into account. In this process, relations between institutions are a very important factor. In the case of Spain, think of the vital role of the consensus between the political protagonists regarding the basic steps in the transition, as set out, partly, in the Moncloa Pacts. The absence of such pacts in this period of fundamental transformations would have hugely reinforced the potential of the military (and the so-called *búnker*) to influence the pace and the outcomes of the process. The consensus between the political parties on military policy – and foreign policy – is also a key factor moderating military political and corporate demands in the course of these changes.

To continue with relations between institutions, it is important to mention the support of the legislature, which can be decisive if it is sustained, inasmuch as executive control carried out from parliament can be a powerful factor supporting the government and minister of defence in their endeavours to assert gradual control over the armed forces. In other cases, the actions of parliament can become an element holding back the minister of defence. This happens in many Latin American countries given the frequent weakness of the presidents in their respective parliaments and the lack of party discipline among the elected representatives. As I have already mentioned, the military must see that politicians are united in their wish to achieve the aims of democratic transition and military reform.

In this sense, tacit or explicit agreement on the part of political parties and leaders to refrain from using the armed forces to support their personal or party positions is vital. This was not a problem in the Spanish transition. Although some of the interventions by Alianza Popular in the debates on the Constitution and the Organic Law of National Defence might give the opposite impression, their position was more the consequence of their ideology than a wish to curry favour with the military. In contrast, manipulation of the armed forces for party ends is unfortunately frequent in Latin America. Alfred Stepan has dubbed such attitudes 'Brumairean moments', as Karl Marx described them as characteristic of Bonapartist regimes in his pamphlet on the Eighteenth Brumaire of Louis Bonaparte. Stepan quotes examples from the recent history of Brazil that we could find in almost all countries in the Southern Cone.[3] It was also a frequent phenomenon in Restoration Spain when the Spanish – and Catalan – bourgeoisie handed power to the military in exchange for their decisive help in the repression of anarchist movements. This issue is also present in several countries in Eastern Europe, and strikingly so in those that comprised the former Yugoslavia.

The relations between society and the democratic institutions are factors that are often decisive. A solid electoral majority is usually a necessary element to ensure each step is carried through successfully, and in particular the first steps in the reform of the military. Otherwise resistance from the military only increases. Spain is a good case in point: the large overall majority in October 1982 was necessary to enact the reforms that put an end to attempted coups and culminated in the process, already underway, of integrating the armed forces into the structure of the democratic state. One way to analyse this issue is through the concept of legitimacy, something 'transitologists' consider essential for the process of democratic consolidation. Juan Linz has given us the clearest definition of democratic legitimacy: a regime becomes legitimate when it is considered the best or the least bad of all possible systems.[4] It is evident that as the military perceive the legitimacy of the newly formed institutions, they become more ready to accept the changes that democracy implies in their own relations with government and civil society, changes that include such key questions for them as their own mission, organization and many principles they have considered as immutable. The overriding importance of legitimacy in democratic consolidation and the experiences in so many countries where the collapse of authoritarian regimes has not led to democratic situations, in the strict sense of the term, means we must progress from

---

[3] Stepan 1988: 10–11.
[4] The exact words of Linz 1978: 18, are: 'ultimately, democratic legitimacy is based on the belief that, for a particular country at a particular moment of time, no other regime could better ensure success in the pursuit of collective goals'.

the simple linear government–military relationship studied in the 1980s to the triangle of institutions–civil society–military.[5] Larry Diamond has stated this in the clearest possible terms: 'Thus, the single most important requirement for keeping the military at bay is to make democracy work, to develop its institutional frameworks and problem-solving capacities so that it accrues a broad and unquestioned legitimacy.'[6]

Thirdly, we must analyse the fact that withdrawal from power usually leads the armed forces to entrench themselves in military autonomy. The military increase their control over their own organizations and fight off attempts at control from outside, reinforcing, in some cases, the elements that set them apart from the rest of society. Though an area of autonomy will always survive, even in democracies that have been functioning in a consolidated fashion for a long time, the issue is that these levels of autonomy should be decided by the political authorities and not by the military themselves.

Levels of intervention and military autonomy

As a transition takes its initial steps, the military will try to ensure that the institutions and features of the previous regime are maintained, regardless of whether they were the protagonists and guarantors or were identified with the party that held power. If the process advances, they will attempt to shape its evolution. But in any case, as the organization of the military is a corporate body, it strives to keep control of its profession from inside and to protect itself from external political control.[7] As we will see in chapter 7, tensions between the executive and the armed forces over the latter's scope for autonomy have existed and will continue to exist, even in the United States.

Consequently, I believe one can study the adjustment of the armed forces to the process of transition to democracy in terms of the reduction of its reserve domains to areas of autonomy compatible with the state of law and that the reduction in their levels of autonomy can help gauge the advances being made in this process. To pursue this line of thought, military reform is no more than a process driving and guiding the

---

[5] See the interesting reflections on democratic legitimacy in Diamond 1998: 5f. and in Morlino 1988: 25f.
[6] Diamond 1996: 87.   [7] Perlmutter 1982: 4.

military to shift gradually to positions of greater democratic normalcy and to fit coherently into the new democratic state.

If we start with the experiences in Spain and the two other southern European countries that underwent the process at similar times, we can distinguish various kinds of intervention by the military in the areas of political power and autonomy in respect of the elected government, that can also be detected in most countries in Central and Southern America. Ordered in a sequence from greater to lesser intervention and autonomy, they can be listed as follows:

1. *The control of political power.* In this scenario, a member of the military is usually president or head of state. Military decision-making bodies exist, many political posts are occupied by military representatives and the internal security apparatuses, including the information and intelligence services, are usually filled and controlled by military personnel.

2. *The military as guardians of national essences.* The armed forces consider themselves to be above politics and parties, and not a branch of the state administration. They maintain their threat, which they consider a right, to act when they consider collectively that their mission demands it, rather than doing so as an arm of government. Something similar happened in Spain in the debate over the Constitution of 1978. Even the United States has experience of this attitude, since it was the position taken by General MacArthur when he denounced the 'new and as yet unknown and dangerous concept that the members of our armed forces owe primary allegiance and loyalty to those who temporarily exercise the authority of the executive branch of government rather than to the country and its Constitution which they are sworn to defend'.[8]

3. *The military as constraints on government policy,* limiting reforms or vetoing particular actions. In such cases the military usually maintain full autonomy and levels of direct intervention in political questions and the management of the state. An example of this situation is the attempt by the Spanish military to prevent the legalization of the Communist Party at the beginning of the process of reform.

4. *Defenders of their organizational and operational autonomy.* This is the situation that usually obtains when the military have lost or are

---

[8] The quotation comes from Huntington 1957: 353.

losing the possibility of intervening in politics and state administration. They react by preventing the intervention of the civil authorities in those fields they consider to be the preserve of the military general staff. This situation has arisen in Latin America through unwritten agreements that have subsequently been respected during transitions from military regimes, Colombia being a good example.[9] Currently this marks the boundary limit for potential control in many South American countries.

5. *Formal but partial acceptance of civil supremacy.* Although the military do not issue manifestos or act against the laws consecrating civil supremacy, they disobey certain orders and act on their own initiative in a way the civil authorities neither order nor desire. One example could be the way the military command acted at the beginning of the Spanish transition when they gave out minimal sentences to those who committed acts of insubordination towards the democratic government or the attempt, by the Supreme Council for Military Justice, to pardon those responsible for the attempted coup of 23 February 1981.

6. *The retaining of ideological controls over the military.* In general, the military yield control over their organization and operations but retain control over their professional profile and the values they should uphold, in particular through the control of military training and access to the officer class.

7. *Democratic civil control over the armed forces.* In this situation the executive defines military policy: the Minister gives the lead in its implementation and exercises control and leadership over the armed forces, the legislature controls the executive and the military, and military justice is integrated into a judiciary system that in a democracy is one and unitary. The arrival of this situation does not mean an end to tensions and conflict. The problem of how to delimit the area for military autonomy persists in a democratic situation, as do attempts by the armed forces to influence government policies and

---

[9] The speech by President Lleras Camargo to the military general staff in the Teatro Patria, 9 May 1958, clearly defines this attitude: 'When the Armed Forces enter into politics the first thing that is damaged is its unity because it opens up controversy in its ranks … I do not want the Armed Forces to deliberate about how to govern the nation … But I do not want, by any means, that politicians decide on how to manage the Armed Forces, in their technical functions, in their discipline, in their regulations, and in their personnel.' See Bruneau 2005: 115.

defend the corporate interests of the military. As we shall see in
chapter 7, controlling the military is a recurrent problem and a
government needs an active military policy even in consolidated
democracies such as the United States.

It must be emphasized that in real situations there is no clear line of
demarcation between stages of transition and consolidation, which
means that several of the situations described above may run into
each other in practice. Although we described the third position as
that where the military condition government policy, it is evident that
this can also happen at the seventh level, which we have characterized as
one of democratic civil control, although here the armed forces do not
have the ability to veto and do not enjoy organizational autonomy.

Nor can one assert that once the process has begun, sooner or later
the final level will be reached or that progress from one level to another
guarantees the passage to the next. We saw in the previous chapter how
David Pion-Berlin, in his reflections on the present state of play in
civilian–military relations in the majority of Latin American countries,
considers it very difficult for them to reach the level when the government defines defence policy. On the other hand, in almost every case the
successful management of relations with the armed forces has prevented
coups and military interference in government policy. Consequently he
proposes a less demanding definition of civil control, one that is more
realistic and which he dubs 'political civilian control'. Civilian ministers
are generally sufficiently skilful to keep the military off the front pages,
to 'put out fires' and promise help without that help implying acceptance of military priorities, but rather the desire to channel them
through the chain of command. According to Pion-Berlin, political
civilian control 'adheres to the maxim "live and let live". Civilian
leaders do not meddle in core military interests if the military observes
similar rules about the government's core interests.'[10] As I signalled in
chapter 2, we must accept that the process does not move inexorably
from the first to the seventh level, and that the movement from the stage
of transition to that of consolidation is extremely difficult to achieve in
most countries in South America. They have found it relatively easy to
progress from the first situation of military dictatorship to the fourth,
which we could redefine as the one in which the military have

---

[10] See Pion-Berlin 2005: 28–30.

organizational autonomy but do not interfere in government policy. However, the process seizes up there and Pion-Berlin describes this situation as one of political civilian control, in order to distinguish it from the final stage, which I have termed democratic civilian control. According to Pion-Berlin, the reasons for this rest with the executive and legislature's lack of knowledge of military and defence matters which prevents them both from formulating military and defence policy and from taking the initiative until they have reached the level of democratic civilian control. I will repeat that in my view Pion-Berlin is right when he describes the obvious situation of stagnation in Latin America, but is not right about the causes, which are more complex, or in his acceptance of this situation as obvious or inevitable, to use Cohen's adjectives. As we shall see, the gradual creation of a genuine ministry of defence is probably the most practical remedy.

As I have already pointed out, to be in control of the process it is more important to define the possible progress one can make at each moment and the caution necessary in terms of pacing pressure on the military than to be clear about one's final goal (for that it suffices to study a consolidated democracy). Figure 3.1 sums up what might be a complex process of transition and consolidation from this perspective, although one must emphasize that the boundaries between one stage and another will never be clear cut and that experience shows that in every case, it has been necessary to resolve 'frayed edges' from previous stages or tackle issues together which here are presented as being separate.

Alfred Stepan has studied the process from the perspective of the reduction of the institutional prerogatives enjoyed by the military.[11] This approach can fit perfectly well with a focus on a gradual reduction in levels of autonomy, although I prefer the latter because it enables the time factor to be introduced in the planning of policies to be implemented, in order to know if one is advancing the process and, consequently, best ordering priorities and possibilities at each moment in time. Besides, as I have indicated, the need to control military autonomy remains an issue even if the process of transition has concluded and we are in a situation of consolidated democracy. Felipe Agüero also tackles this problem when he distinguishes between notions of 'expansive entrenchment' in which the armed forces control or influence political decision making, and 'protective entrenchment', when the

---

[11] Stepan 1988.

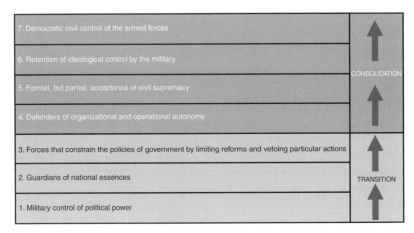

Figure 3.1. Stages in the reduction of autonomy and gradual civil control over the military

armed forces make it difficult or impossible for the government to assert control.[12] I believe the sequence I have included in Figure 3.1 embodies Agüero's idea, without making it explicit.

Stepan defines 'institutional prerogatives' as 'those areas where, whether challenged or not, the military as an institution assumes it has an acquired right or privilege, formal or informal, to exercise effective control over its internal governance, to play a role within extra-military areas within the state apparatus, or even to structure relationships between the state and political or civil society'.[13] From this definition Stepan goes on to list eleven fields in which de facto or *de jure* prerogatives on the part of the armed forces can be detected: 1) the constitution, which can actually sanction an independent role for the military in the political system, 2) the relationship of the military to the head of the executive, 3) the coordination of the defence sector within the executive, 4) the presence of the military in the cabinet, 5) the role of the legislature, 6) the holding of senior posts in the civil service in the defence sector, 7) the role of the military in the intelligence services, 8) their relationship with the police, 9) the system for promoting the military, 10) the role of the military in state enterprises, and 11) the role of the military in the judiciary. I will analyse all these contexts later, though I

---

[12] Agüero 1992: 164–6.   [13] Stepan 1988: 93.

will give them an order that facilitates advances in the process of democratizing civil–military relations.

A first approach to military reform

We have seen how democratic reform can be described in the first instance as the process that drives and guides the military in a movement towards positions of democratic normalcy (in which the prerogatives defined by Stepan do not exist) and a coherent location within the new democratic state. The latter requires well-nurtured relations of institutional loyalty, respect for the laws of the land and subordination to the elected authorities, that is, a reduction to the minimum of conflicts with the military. But this goal is, at least for a certain period, at odds with the reduction of prerogatives, to the extent that in many countries military opposition has halted reform. It is thus useful to analyse the two dimensions together: the reduction of military prerogatives – or autonomy – and the development of military opposition. Stepan does this through an analytical model that we will fine tune in order to include a line on politics and other dimensions relevant to our analysis, thus expanding its ability to explain issues.

Stepan combined the two dimensions of civilian control of the military in a hypothetical new democracy, resulting in the graph that is reproduced in Figure 3.2.

I have retained Stepan's terms for the four corners of the square, although I think only two are possible in a process of transition. In effect, although it is not a constant, the lower right-hand corner position is possible in the first stages of a transition when the military keep all their privileges from the previous authoritarian period and the conflicts inherent in democratic change have yet to arise. If the process duly advances, then the lower left-hand corner position will also be reached, that is a democracy that has resolved the military problem. Consequently, in the terrain of real possibilities, I think it is more likely that the area where prerogatives–autonomy and conflict–opposition come together is likely to be in the band indicated in Figure 3.3 that does not include the extreme positions of considerable military privileges with conflict or high-level conflict with a military that no longer enjoys the prerogatives that belong to periods of authoritarian rule. These extreme hypotheses are practically impossible in reality and are incompatible with democracy, however young.

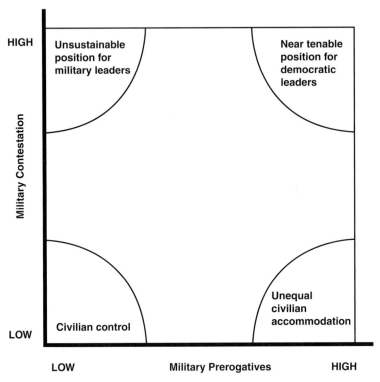

Figure 3.2. Alfred Stepan's proposal: the relationship between prerogatives and contestation

This figure can be compared with Figure 3.4 that was established by Stepan in order to include some of the cases he studied. Many other countries could be added, although none would exceed the limits of the band in Figure 3.3.

One way to develop this analytical model is to combine it with the stages of the reduction of the reserve domains we described previously and represented in Figure 3.1. This leads to Figure 3.5, in which the different stages in the reduction of military interventions and autonomy are represented along the *x*-axis.

This figure synthesizes a panorama of democratic reform of the military during which the government in charge puts the necessary legal changes and political measures in place that will allow it to progress to the beginning of the horizontal axis. Such sweeping legal

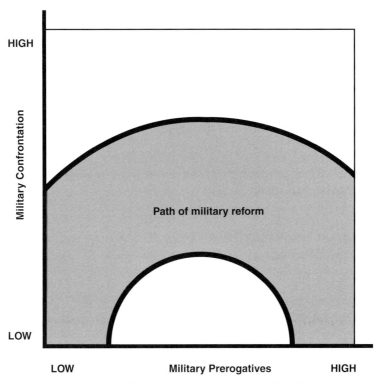

Figure 3.3. The relationship between prerogatives and confrontation: the path of military reform

changes can lead to the writing of a new constitution or decisive political measures that can include the separation of the armed forces and the forces of public order. At the same time, nonetheless, the reforming government must be sensitive to levels of conflict that, although this is not a transcendental factor, are not only controlled through the management of the pace of change indicated by the horizontal axis, but are also affected by factors not usually controlled by the minister of defence and sometimes not even by the government itself as a whole. These factors relate first to the overall progress of the transition process and the increase in the regime's legitimacy. Other relevant factors may include the consensus among political forces or support from other countries and international bodies.

In this way, a programme of democratic military reform would consist of a study of all the factors that allow one to advance along the curve

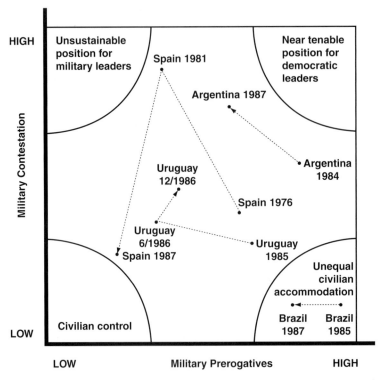

Figure 3.4. The relationship between prerogatives and contestation: paths to military reform in several countries

drawn in Figure 3.5. However cursory our analysis of concrete instances in the third wave of democratizations, it will soon become apparent how incomplete this approach is. To shift the armed forces from the first or most interventionist positions to the final, most democratic points on the horizontal axis, presupposes changes within the military community that impinge on the very definition of the military profession and its attitudes towards society. It is not merely a question of controlling the military or reducing their previous prerogatives. One must define its tasks in the new democratic context and its role in the new state administration. It is necessary, then, to add a new axis to our figure for military reform: the professional transformation axis. Given it involves a major development in the model we are analysing, this requires some reflection.

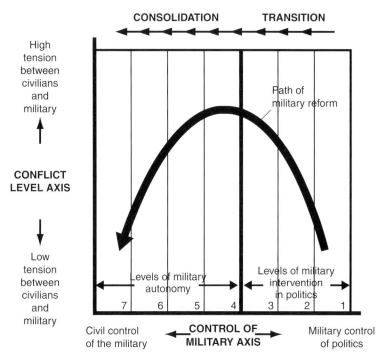

Figure 3.5. The process of democratic military reform: two dimensions

The military profession and the democratic system

Samuel Huntington's *The Soldier and the State*, published in 1957, is the first serious attempt to define the military profession after the Second World War, and has inspired a significant body of research. From the very beginning he states his basic thesis that the modern soldier is a professional and that this professionalism is what distinguishes today's soldier from a warrior in other eras.

To define the content of the profession, Huntington employs Harold Lasswell's expression: the administration of violence. According to Huntington himself, the defining features of the military profession are its professional qualifications, responsibility and corporate identity. It acquires its professional qualifications only through extended training and experience. Its responsibility to perform its functions when society requires them gives it its essential general nature, together with the fact that it holds a monopoly on its expertise. Its corporate identity arises from the sense the members of the profession have that they constitute an organic unity, and their awareness that they represent a group that is separate from civilians.[14]

Huntington's aim in his magnum opus is to demonstrate that when the military profession effectively defends national security, it is incompatible with 'the American mental attitude that tries to impose liberal solutions on military matters, as it does in civilian life'. Consequently, in order to be controlled and effective, the army must remain isolated from civil society and from the world of politics. He believed that the involvement of officers in politics undermines their professionalism, reduces their professional competence, divides the profession against itself and replaces the values of the profession with values that are alien to it.[15]

This position leads Huntington to idealize elements of the military profession and to deem it immutable in relation to changes in society when he proclaims: 'the military ethic is concrete, permanent and universal'.[16] Huntington suggests a definition of the military profession that implies that subordination to the civil power is a characteristic inherent in the profession, which allows him to claim considerable autonomy for this group.[17] He sees no other way to make military values compatible with the inevitable advances in technology than their isolation from civilian values. However, armies who think they foster permanent values are a real danger to democracy, since it is just one step from permanent to higher values. And military that believe they possess these higher values inescapably and see themselves as the guarantors of these, readily convert them into national essences. This is at the core of the armies–institutions concept we shall examine later and which readily spawns the idea of the internal enemy, as demonstrated by the application of the Doctrine of National Security in Spain and many Latin American countries.

Almost immediately afterwards, Morris Janowitz published his work that vied with Huntington's in its influence on later literature. Janowitz's concern was quite different since, rather than walling the military off from external influences, he tried to analyse a route-map of an inevitable development of the military profession after the Second

---

[14] Huntington 1957: 7–11.   [15] Huntington 1957: 71.

[16] Huntington 1957: 89. Another quotation corroborates this: 'Only if they are motivated by military ideals will the armed forces be the obedient servants of the state and will civilian control be assured' (p.74).

[17] There is a more detailed discussion of Huntington's position in relation to civil control in chapter 7 of this book.

World War. His contribution has a clearly voluntarist – as well as futurologist – component as he coined the concept of 'constabulary force' to describe armies as police forces dedicated to resolving international conflicts. He begins by considering, among other changes, those made to the authority of the organization: from authoritarian domination to conduction and persuasion; advances in the reduction of differences between civilian and military elites when these later techniques in organization and negotiation are adopted; and reforms in the indoctrination and training that supply the military professional with opinions on political, social and economic subjects, opinions they now need as a result of their new tasks.[18]

For Janowitz, the profound changes in the basic features of the profession, the fruit of openness not only to civilian knowledge and techniques of organization, but also to public administration and politics, have impacted on those values that were considered central to the armed forces. He does not consider that values such as honour, loyalty, or duty will disappear, but believes they will have a different weight in the future profile of the profession. For him 'the military profession comprises a mixture of heroic leaders, military, managers and technical specialists, and an officer can come to embody diverse combinations of these elements'. At another moment he declares 'in a democratic society it is highly inappropriate for honour to be the sole, or even the dominant, value of the professional military cadre. Honour comes to be combined with and dependent upon public prestige and popular recognition'.[19]

Years later, Janowitz saw a need to review the positions he considered to be linked to a mass or conscript army, when his country decided to suppress compulsory military service and rely entirely on volunteer, paid, armed forces. But, in any case, like Huntington, he not only pioneered a strand of scholarship – that of the evolution of the military profession – but also of ideological positioning, in this case favouring the opening up of the military profession to the values of civil society.

Amos Perlmutter's contribution followed similar lines when, some years later, he tried to show that corporate behaviour and orientation is not the basic feature of the military profession properly speaking, and that the factor pushing the armed forces to intervene in politics is their corporate spirit and not a correct definition of the profession. Clearly in favour of accepting an evolution in the profession, Perlmutter

---

[18] Janowitz 1960: 7–13.   [19] Janowitz 1990: 45 and 1960: 225.

states: 'historically, the most important attributes of the professional soldier have been valour and discipline. But today's professional must be an administrator as well as a hero. Consequently he needs to assimilate modern techniques of management and administration, as to be applied to strategy. Independently of the loss of the traditional soldier's romanticism, corporate professionalism has broadened the political and social horizons of the military.'[20] Perlmutter argues that a change had taken place in military values and that the old virtues of valour and discipline had been replaced by technical expertise in leadership and strategic thinking. He also comments on Huntington's claim that professionalism included subordination to the civil authorities: 'A professional attitude in itself does not avoid intervention, just as a corporate orientation does not necessarily provoke it.' In this matter, Perlmutter distinguishes between the effects of changes on the military profession in a democratic situation and in a situation that cannot be considered so: 'The fusion of the administrative and the professional in non-praetorian states implicates the military in politics, whereas in praetorian states it impels them into politics.'[21]

In the context of these reflections it is useful to focus on the approach begun by Charles C. Moskos whereby he presents two models: the armed forces as an institution or as an occupation, as descriptions of the social organization of the military. For Moskos, the army as an *institution* gains legitimacy in terms of values and norms, and its ends transcend individual interest in favour of the pursuit of higher goals. Its values can be summed up by expressions such as 'duty', 'honour', and 'fatherland'. Its members are seen as followers of a vocation and consider themselves different from society in general, a view mirrored by society's own perspective. The remuneration of its members is usually lower than in the marketplace, but they enjoy a series of social benefits linked to the institution. If they have complaints to voice, they do not organize themselves in interest groups, but rather voice them individually, which means they accept the paternalism of the institution. For Moskos, armies have traditionally had institutional features, such as, for example, being available for service twenty-four hours a day, frequent transfers with their families to other postings, a rewards system that includes considerable non-monetary perks such as accommodation, cut-price shops or retirement benefits.

[20] Perlmutter 1982: 3.   [21] Perlmutter 1982: 5 and 393.

In contrast, an *occupation* gains legitimacy in terms of its ranking in the marketplace, where financial reward prevails over everything else, employees have a voice in terms of their working conditions and trade unions are a common way to articulate interests within the industry and administration.

Moskos believes that the armed forces have tried to avoid the consequences of the occupational model, and gives as an example their resistance to the principle of equal pay for equal work when they give higher pay to married than to single personnel. In real terms, however, no army can or could be classified completely by any one of these models, since it will always contain elements and features of both. Even so, the distinction makes sense to the extent that a gradual erosion of the institutional model and an evolution towards the occupational model are perceptible; an evolution encouraged by the United States, among others, when it eliminated military conscription in 1973, gradually accepted racial equality and felt the impact of the Vietnam War on military organization and habits.[22]

In my view, the expression 'occupational' is misleading, but scholars have accepted it for some time and it would only create confusion to use another word. One must take the terms of the so-called Institutional/Occupational Model (I/O) as tendencies and not as concepts with clear-cut boundaries, although it is clear that a shift towards an army as institution would represent a divergence from the way society is evolving, whereas a change towards an army as occupation can be considered as convergent with the way society is heading. In this sense, Huntington's definition of the profession fits with the concept of the army as institution, while Janowitz's vision is closer to the army as occupation. In other words, Huntington tries to define the essences of the military profession in a changing world, whereas Janowitz tries to define the way the military profession must change when challenged by the international order and its own society.

Calculating the extent to which an institution depends on its own values raises questions as to its social usefulness, when these values emerge as distant from those generally embraced by society. Experience shows that the greatest differences between the values of

---

[22] Moskos outlines his thoughts in two short articles published within ten years of each other. See Moskos 1977 and Moskos 1986. Moskos can also be read in Spanish in Moskos 1985.

the armed forces and those of society as a whole are usually in the area of religion, family, gender equality and sexual freedom. When the Spanish transition began, the military community believed that the Catholic religion was a constituent element of its military ethos, condemned abortion and divorce, considered that women formed part of the military community as officers' wives, not as a potential members of the community in their own right, and punished homosexuals and conscientious objectors. From my point of view, these issues marked the difference in values between the military and civil society more than those related to political positions or the acceptance of democratic freedoms. They were important as elements giving coherence to the military institution, one of whose *raisons d'être* derived precisely from these differences with society in general, since it was the duty of the military to nourish and defend these values that were being eroded in society with the passage of time. It is only a short step from defending traditional values deemed to be permanent to defending and preserving national essences, particularly for a community raised under the slogan 'Everything for the Fatherland'.

The fact that an army has predominantly institutional or occupational features is very important in the processes of democratic transition and consolidation. Although Charles Moskos had initially thought of his I/O model in relation to the situation in the United States, he later commented: 'an institutional military organization can develop antidemocratic values in societies that have a fragile civilian culture, thus tearing the basic tissue of civil supremacy'.[23] The military interventionism in politics I described in Figure 3.1 always occurs when the armed forces have a strong collective feeling as an institution that their own values are superior to those of society as a whole, when its ability to organize usually outflanks the civil administration's and its internal discipline gives it enormous potential to act as one in the face of the administration and society.

Historical evolution can add to the institutional features we have described, the military's feeling – and legal recognition – as guarantors of constitutional order, as happened in many countries in Latin America, or, as happened in Spain, as guarantor of the authoritarian regime that existed prior to the transition. The same problem occurs even when actions by the army – or part of it – provoke or begin the process of transition, as was the

[23] Moskos 1985: 152.

case in Portugal. The institutional feeling of the Portuguese army favoured the creation of the first democratic institutions, in which the military granted themselves a tutelary role over the new regime.

In each of these cases the extreme institutional character of armies represents a serious problem for the process of democratic transition, inasmuch as there can be no settled adjustment by the armed forces to a democratic regime unless their nature shifts from deeply institutional positions to others that are more occupational, to borrow Moskos's terms. The process of integrating the armies into a democratic regime implies that they are incorporated into the democratic administration of the state as an intrinsic part of it. That process is practically impossible if the military feel they belong to an institution that is not integrated, but rather dialogues and negotiates with the administration of the new state. Consequently, the advance from institutional to more occupational positions is a vital factor in every process of democratic reform of the military.

But that is not an end to the problems and the relations between the military profession and democratic consolidation, because we must consider the changes being wrought in the tasks and professional content of the armed forces. We again have recourse to Charles Moskos for a description of this process in his suggestion of three models of military organization, made with the United States, and to a lesser degree the states of Western Europe, in mind. These three typologies refer to twentieth-century armies before the Second World War (the modern military), to the period of the Cold War (the late modern military) and those after 1990 (the post-modern military). Moskos sums up their features in the Table 3.1.[24]

The perception of threats, structure of the armed forces and definition of the main mission are the three factors that unleash the process of change and drive the changes of the remaining features that, in this sense, we can consider as consequences, although they may be more visible. Moskos's table is a clear continuation and refinement of Janowitz's pioneering work. With greater hindsight, it clarifies the features that mark out the transition after the Second World War that Janowitz had already signalled, and puts into relief his accurate intuitions, since when he describes the post-modern armed forces he confirms many of the features Janowitz foresaw twenty years before the fall of the Berlin Wall.

It is evident that Moskos's latest contribution does not follow the line of his I/O model previously described. But it is also clear that the two

---

[24] Moskos 2000: 15.

Table 3.1. *The armed forces in three periods: the United States*

Forces Variable	Modern (Pre-Cold War) 1900–1945	Late modern (Cold War) 1945–1990	Post-modern (Post-Cold War) After 1990
Perceived threat	Enemy invasion	Nuclear war	Sub-national (e.g. ethnic violence, terrorism)
Structure of the force	Mass army: Conscription	Large professional army	Small professional army
Definition of main mission	Territorial defence	Support for the alliance	New missions (e.g. upholding peace, humanitarian acts, etc.)
Dominant military	Leader in combat	Manager or specialist	Soldier–statesman; soldier–academic
Public attitude towards military	Support	Ambivalent	Indifferent
Relationship with media	Incorporated	Manipulated	Taken into account, favoured, courted
Civilian employees	Minor component	Average component	Sizeable component
Role of women	Separate of excluded units	Partial integration	Full integration
Role of wife	Integral part	Partial involvement	Uninvolved
Homosexuals in the army	Punished	Tolerated	Accepted
Conscientious objectors	Restricted or banned	Routinely permitted	Taken into civilian service

assessments are complementary. In the first place, the three stages are more clear cut in the United States than in Western Europe, where they are more easily identifiable than in non-democratic or developing countries. On the other hand, an army that is classifiable at a particular stage may be more or less institutional, although it is evident that evolution over time tends to reinforce the occupational aspects of the armed forces.

This all implies that in a process of military reform, when a government is attempting to adapt the armed forces to a properly functioning democracy, it must also promote the professional transformation required by changes in the international order, the security needs of countries and the role of states as actors on the international stage. Consequently, we are not dealing with contradictory approaches, but two complementary tasks in a process of adapting the armed forces to new times: an adaptation to the changes required by democratization, and, one must add, to the changes necessary to respond to globalization.

This leads us to look afresh at the relationship between professionalism and the tendency of armies to intervene in politics. Rather than resolving this problem, Huntington avoided it by postulating that true military professionalism involves implicit subordination to the civil authorities. Such key analysts as Finer and Abrahamsson disagree with Huntington's view that greater military professionalism brings greater civilian control.[25] However, scholars of civilian–military relations in Latin American countries have pointed out that greater military professionalism, especially when it is the result of corporate design, normally brings a greater likelihood of intervention in politics.[26] In one of the most penetrating studies of civilian–military relations in Latin America, J. Samuel Fitch made it clear that it is an illusion to hope that professionalism will lead an apolitical military to civil control. Consequently, 'the challenge is to design professional norms and institutional norms for civil–military relations that are not only consistent with democratic principles, but also adapted to the Latin American context. Neither modernization nor greater professionalism has resolved the problem of military intervention in politics'.[27]

A second approach to military reform

The conclusion from these reflections on the military profession is quite clear: it is not enough to reduce privileges or prerogatives; it is necessary to redefine the tasks and nature of the armed forces. That is, the adaptation of the armed forces to a democratic context will not be an enduring process if changes are not made to the definition of the profession in the

---

[25] See Abrahamsson 1972 and Finer 1976.
[26] An example of that is Frederik Nunn's historical study of civil–military relations in Chile. See Nunn 1976: 85.
[27] Fitch 1998: 35.

double sense of moving it towards terrain favouring an occupational army and adapting it to the new needs of a world that has changed.

To return to our model for military reform, we must, as I pointed out, add a new dimension to the model, in which we encapsulate the process of professional change on two fronts.

In Figure 3.6 I have added a new horizontal axis, representing the evolution of the 'army as institution' to 'army as occupation' or transformation of the profession. A successful process of democratic reform thus implies simultaneous progress on the two horizontal axes, reducing to a minimum the level of conflict produced by previous transformations. In Figure 3.6 this implies starting from the situation I represent with the letter A, where the armed forces are hugely interventionist and institutional with no tensions with the civil authorities, and moving to situation B, where the army has moved to the occupational sphere, there is civilian control and a low level of conflict. The shift from A to B will normally involve, as I have reflected in Figure 3.6, more or less parallel

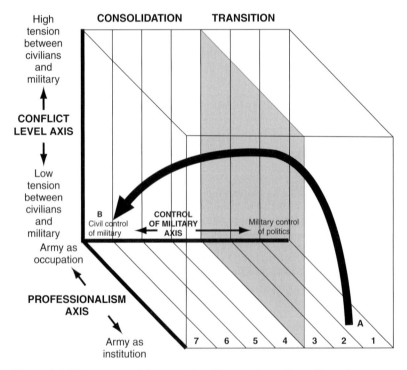

Figure 3.6. The process of democratic military reform: three dimensions

advances along the two horizontal axes and will experience some conflicts or tension in civil–military relations.

One must take into account the fact that it is very difficult to contemplate a process of reform so thorough that it is possible to cover the distance separating positions close to the points A and B. It is impossible for a programme of reforms to take us at one stroke from a military dictatorship, for example, to a stable democracy. I know of no instance when that has been possible. In the case of Spain, the coordinated implementation of measures on both horizontal axes in order to reach the sphere of a consolidated democracy lasted at least thirteen years. Consequently, for any reform measure, we would start by deciding which point on the curve A to B has been reached, which is approximately the same as deciding the level a country undertaking reform is at, in terms of the degree of political intervention or autonomy, in Figure 3.1. Next we must establish how far we can advance the cluster of measures on the prerogatives axis and, in terms of the professionalism axis, what is feasible at a given moment, taking into consideration the possible tensions with the military community represented on the vertical axis. Figure 3.7 shows a hypothetical case in which the reform moves from point X1, very close to the beginning of the transition process, to point X2, on the boundary of the period I have termed consolidation.

In other words, the democratic reform of the military – or at least part of it – is the combined total of possible actions at a given moment on the two axes which we use to sum up military policy, while paying due attention to the vertical axis, that is to the gradual acceptance by the military community of the new situation that is being created. I must insist again on the need to get the order of the actions to be taken right, the coordination of the three axes – that are not static – the pace and upper limit of the reforms underway and, above all, the overall development of the transition process.

Once we move on from our consideration of an explanatory model on three axes, which allows us to study the possibilities and programme for more substantial reform, we can then attempt to establish some ground rules in order to evaluate how the approach could be fruitfully applied to individual countries in turn. I am not advocating establishing general laws on the basis of explanations of what happened in Spain and a few other countries: that would be absurd. I am simply suggesting a series of norms that could help guide a reform of the military, particularly if it fits the suggested model.

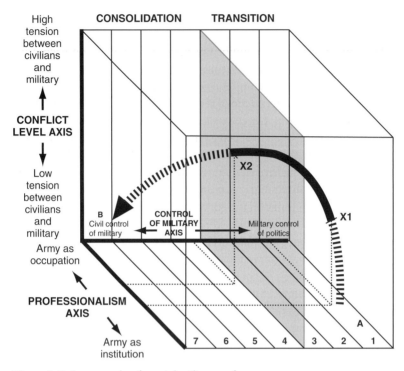

Figure 3.7. An example of partial military reform

The first of these norms, one we could call the law of interdependence, establishes that it is impossible to make progress if all efforts are concentrated on a single axis. A government wishing to consolidate advances in the control of its armed forces through more democratic legislation will see that whether the outcomes are lasting or not depends as much on political events in their country as on managing parallel changes in the military's professional profile or activity. Curtailing actions on one of the horizontal axes or setbacks in the political arena or reductions in the government's available instruments for controlling conflict levels will bring the whole process grinding to a halt.

The second norm indicates the need to evaluate carefully the potential for conflict, as well as for support for reform within the more general processes of democratic reform. We could call it the constraint imposed by the political frame at a particular moment. Before undertaking a process of reform, one must study and define both departure point and destination in terms of the political situation at the start of the reform and during its implementation.

The third norm is the equilibrium between advances on each axis. This is important in order to take advantage of all the possibilities offered by each political conjuncture and avoid hold-ups or difficulties in the overall process of reform. It is very difficult to carry a process of reform to conclusion if it develops without any prospects of continuity, until civilian control of the armed forces has been established. One should anticipate that advances, however significant, will be stunted until results are consolidated and political conditions allow the process to make another spurt. If this rather 'stop–go' process occurs, and one of the axes shows a greater increase than the others, we can expect to see a strong tendency for it also to stall, and this stalling will be consolidated more in line with the axis of less progress than with the one that shows the most movement forward.

The fourth norm – on limits to the modernization of the military profession – alerts us to the difficulties that exist when making significant changes to the profession's profile and ideology if a general process of modernizing ideas and habits in the general ambience of the society as a whole has not taken place, or is not underway. This is another example of the close connection between what happens on the vertical axis and the model's second horizontal axis.

4 | *The component parts of military reform*

In the previous chapter I tried to develop a diagrammatic model of a process of military reform as part – or partial regime – of a process of transition to democracy.

The next step must be to establish the discrete steps to be taken, together with a more detailed analysis of the actions and policies that comprise the process of reform as articulated on the three axes. We have already indicated in preceding chapters that both the goals and the means are different in the periods of transition and consolidation. Consequently, I have divided the description of the measures to be implemented into these two periods.

Military reform in the period of transition

In this period, actions must concentrate on preventing the armed forces from intervening in politics, reducing conflict levels and preventing possible coups.

T.1 *Factors that influence conflict levels with the military or its acceptance of the process of reforms (vertical axis)*

T.1.1 Legitimizing democracy

As I have indicated, civilian–military relations in this phase are shaped by the general process of transition to democracy. The greater the effort expended on transforming the institutions left by the authoritarian regime, the easier it will be to carry through a parallel military reform. Similarly, weaknesses in the functioning of the newly installed democracy will slow down or impede the processes whereby the armed forces come under civilian control.

In the Spanish case, the pace of reform, the swift, transparent organization of the first elections and the impact of the transformations framed by the new Constitution, were factors pushing in the right direction. The situation in most countries in Latin America has been quite different, since the slow pace of some processes, the lack of successful measures to improve citizens' level of wellbeing and evidence of widespread corruption have undermined the credibility of the executive and the democratizing processes. On top of that, we must add the lack of interest shown by the political elites and groups holding economic power when it comes to ensuring the normal functioning of democratic institutions, an attitude that represents one of the greatest problems, if not the main one, in democratizing the armed forces. When public opinion loses faith in the political system and its leaders, it is impossible to undertake a process by which civil society asserts control over the military.

Consequently, progress in the democratic process, the establishment of new institutions and advances in giving these legitimacy in civil society (a legitimization that is both a result and synthesis of the whole process of political transformation), constitute the set of factors that can contribute significantly to the acceptance of reforms and the reduction of unease and conflict levels in civilian–military relations.

T.1.2 The existence of internal conflicts

When there is open conflict within the country that requires action by the armed forces, the potential and limits for military reform must be assessed very carefully. Internal armed conflict that has necessitated army intervention, whether ongoing or recent, places the military in a position of strength in relation to a civil government that, precisely because such conflict exists, cannot have firm foundations. Events in such different countries as the Balkans, Turkey or Colombia are very instructive in this respect: it is almost impossible to advance along the axis of legal reform and reduction of the ability of the armed forces to intervene in political life and along the axis of professional change if society is torn by serious conflict.

It seems clear enough that without a political resolution of the Kurdish problem and of Islamist threats to the lay republic, it will be very difficult for Turkey to make definitive progress along the axis of institutional reform, even though the perspective of negotiations with the European Union has already led to changes, which, though formal in nature, should not be at all underestimated. Indeed, the process of integration into the Union, if this advances, may constitute an element of stability that could help diminish the tutelary role of the armed forces and overcome the internal conflicts I have mentioned.[1]

In the case of Colombia, the open struggle against the guerrillas is an almost insurmountable hurdle to proper subordination of the armed forces to the government, and may explain situations like the army's control over the police. On the other hand, initiating a new offensive against the guerrillas without increasing democratic control of the armed forces is a burden that undermines the whole effort, diminishes potential outcomes and over time makes it impractical. In this sense the attitude of the United States is unhelpful because it does not insist that a process of democratization of the armed forces is a prerequisite for the support it provides.

T.1.3 External influences

There is no consensus among scholars as to the role external influences can play, either in terms of their importance or the direction in which they might be pushing. The second half of the twentieth century offers examples of experiences that lead in every possible direction. Laurence Whitehead has stated 'in peacetime external factors can only play a secondary role in redemocratization'.[2] His approach is heavily influenced by developments in Latin America where the influence of the United States has been negative in terms of democratization in many cases and ambiguous in most.[3] In contrast, the support of democratic European countries, the help they have given, even as civil societies, and the fact they constitute obvious beacons to follow, were crucial factors in the transitions in the three southern European countries in the 1970s. This is undoubtedly one of the factors that helped these three processes to successful completion in countries that are now consolidated democracies.

The existence of the Atlantic Alliance was a relevant factor, although the process of the political construction of the European Union was more decisive, particularly in the early stages, because, among other reasons, this was the goal desired by citizens in these countries and

---

[1] Güney and Karetekelioglu 2005.   [2] Whitehead 1986: 20.
[3] An assessment of the role of the United States in the processes of political change in Latin America can be found in Whitehead 1986. For a comparison of US and European influences, see O'Donnell 1997b: 230.

involved joining the Alliance.[4] The 1980 and 1982 programmes of the Greek and Spanish Socialist parties both contained respective demands for withdrawal from NATO. The entry into the European Economic Community of Greece in 1981 and Spain in 1986 meant these positions had to be reviewed.

T.1.4 Coherent government action

At this point I want to detail the necessary attitude of government leaders, who must espouse military reform as a priority in their programme of political measures, and the coordinated action of an executive that must take this on in a coherent manner. The minister for defence, who should be driving the reform, clearly cannot usually control factors influencing conflict levels with the armed forces. On the other hand, these can be tackled more easily by the government as a whole. This is why policy for military reform should not be seen as an isolated issue, but as part and parcel of a government's overall policy for reform.

In the case of Spain, the appointment by President Adolfo Suárez of a military commander as government vice-president gave public recognition to the importance of the issue and was a way to integrate it into the government's raft of actions. Later on, now in the process of consolidation, Felipe González visibly integrated defence, foreign and general government policies in the so-called 'Decalogue' he put before Parliament on the eve of the 1986 referendum. These are quite different examples, but both follow the direction that I want to highlight in this section.

T.1.5 The behaviour of key political actors

This is a complex factor that can either lead to advances in the process and a reduction of conflict, or to difficulties and an increase in tensions between civil society and the armed forces. It is, moreover, a factor that is completely tied to the features in each particular country and which makes blanket generalizations futile. In terms of the Spanish transition, we should refer to at least two well-known developments.

---

[4] The case of Turkey illustrates this. Turkey has belonged to NATO for many years but that has never led to any demand for reform. In contrast, the prerequisites of the European Union for conversations about integration to begin have already provoked considerable reforms, albeit partial ones, in the ability of the armed forces to intervene in politics.

One is the dialogue between opposition and government, the search for consensus, equally with civil society, on issues that are considered vital for the smooth unfolding of the transition. That is why the Moncloa Pacts gave such a huge fillip to the process as described by Alfred Stepan:

At strategic moments, the opposition in Spain managed to alternate skilfully demands and transactions, and thus the democratizing process went from a modest 'reform' begun by government, to an 'negotiated reform' with the democratic opposition and a 'negotiated break' with the past, also agreed with the opposition. This collaboration between government and opposition in the transition reduced the potential for a military reaction.[5]

Another crucial factor to be highlighted in the case of Spain, and one specific to that country, is the attitude of King Juan Carlos. I am not referring as much to his intervention in the February 1981 coup, as to the continual support he gave to the military policies of the various governments, especially during the initial stages, when the armed forces considered him the legitimate heir to their previous commander-in-chief and, consequently, someone they now had to obey.

T.2 Measures to reduce the capacity of the military to intervene in politics (first horizontal axis)

We will now detail two developments within a process of military reform designed to reduce intervention by the armed forces in politics and strengthen civil control at this stage: legislation on national defence and the reduction of the military presence in civilian spheres in the administration.

T.2.1 Legislation on national defence

Basic defence legislation has to be reformed since all countries in transition have inherited a legal structure that requires modification. Obviously, this issue is closely related to all other legal reforms, particularly if a new constitution is being drawn up. The case of Chile is a clear example of how the reform of defence laws depends on a necessary reform of the constitution. At this stage the issue must be tackled of whether a law should be drawn up and passed in the full knowledge

---

[5] Stepan 1988: 120.

that it cannot be applied in its entirety. Although it is true laws exist to be respected, the principal concern at this stage in the reform process must be to ensure legislation is properly thought through and defines the direction to follow. One must ensure that no agreement with the military or its constraints, whether explicit or not, leads to formulations inconsistent with the levels of democracy already achieved or the reinforcement of reserve domains of the armed forces. In such cases, it is better to delay passing new legislation. Differences between countries notwithstanding, a list of tasks to be tackled could run something like this:

- Defining the nature of the control wielded by the democratic civil institutions over the armed forces. This is a simple matter on paper in the case of presidential republics in Latin America. In the case of Spain, there was the complicating factor of a head of state, the king, who in the pre-constitutional period exercised all the competencies of the commander-in-chief of the armed forces and then enjoyed those of a parliamentary monarch after the Constitution was approved in 1978. Although it may appear of little consequence, I would like to point out that it is a good idea to hold in reserve the title of Commander for the head of state or president of the republic, and to use the titles of Chief of Staff for the commanders-in-chief of the armies of land, sea and air. As there is an overall command of the three armies in Spain, the common European title, Defence Chief of Staff, was employed.
- Special consideration should be given to the minister for defence, a figure who does not usually have a powerful profile in authoritarian regimes. It is advisable to strengthen this role legally, as well as de facto, in order to fight against the tendency in all armed forces to seek direct links with the president or head of state, given that such connections increase the forces' potential to reinstate their autonomy. One possible formula consists in granting the minister for defence a number of the president's roles, which the latter simply delegates to him.
- The creation of a National Defence Council, or similar body, to demonstrate that the democratic government is interested in finding out about, defining and directing the country's military activities.
- The conversion of any joint military decision-making body, if such exists, into a consultative body that reports to the president, government

or minister. Joint bodies are not helpful in an organization that should base its discipline and efficiency on a hierarchical chain of command that brings with it clear individual responsibilities. On the other hand, joint bodies are usually created in periods when the military holds political power and, if maintained in democratic contexts, they usually turn into instruments which the armed forces use to defend their corporate interests or strengthen themselves as institutions opposed to the new system. We have already seen how vital it is to shift the military from an institutional to more occupational stance if the process of military reform is to be consolidated.

- The definition of defence and military planning procedures. This is an issue that cannot be tackled properly until it is possible to delineate the military policy. However, it is necessary to establish a democratic mechanism to formulate these policies as part of the initial legal reform process, even though the resolution of these issues will have to be left to a later stage.

- The creation and organization of a ministry of defence as a department that will gradually grow to resemble those in the consolidated democracies of Europe. As with the previous point, this belongs to the phase of democratic consolidation, but effective implementation will be much more feasible later if it is included in the initial legal reforms.

- The delineation of systems of state and military intelligence ensuring civil control. In some countries this is clearly a priority issue: for example, Peru after Fujimori and Montesinos, and Serbia-Montenegro after Milosevic. But this is a question to be addressed in every case during the initial stages of military reform. Armed forces with independent access to information on internal matters are also incurably inclined to intervene in a country's internal affairs. In this situation, moreover, their institutional potential for dialogue with other institutions of state is reinforced. In the case of Spain, the transformation of the intelligence services of the military and the previous regime into CESID, an instrument serving the democratic government, was a discrete, lengthy operation and the central role it played in consolidating democracy has not been sufficiently recognized.

- Essential reforms to the military justice system. The adaptation of a military justice system to a democratic one is a lengthy business and not a swift, sweeping reform that belongs to the transition. Nevertheless, and depending on the situation in each particular country, it will probably be necessary to implement an urgent reform that will not resolve the problem definitively but will, for example, put an end to situations in which military tribunals can try civilians and prevent treatment of conscientious objectors that conflicts head on with democracy and affects public opinion. In each case one must carefully review the content of that initial reform and trim it to the context, since it is unlikely conditions will permit the whole-scale insertion of the system of military justice into a single democratic judiciary. In Spain, the Moncloa Pacts between the government and opposition evoked more urgent issues that were the object, if quite late in the day, of the initial legal reforms. The existence of an independent system of military justice is a powerful factor in reinforcing the armed forces as an institution. In non-democratic situations it is normally used as an instrument of political repression and a mechanism for maintaining public order. For this reason, it is a situation which must be reformed as far as is feasible during the first phases of the transition. But a military justice system is also an instrument designed to safeguard military autonomy, and uphold distinct values and criteria that are even opposed to those of a society in transition to democracy. Nonetheless, reforming this situation can be extremely problematic, which is why it should generally be left to the stage of consolidation. Experience in a number of countries shows that the military try to maintain an independent system of justice in order to guarantee immunity for their previous behaviour, as a way of camouflaging actions that represent an abuse of human rights, or simply as a means to grant themselves a different status and privileges in respect of civil society. In each case a programme of legal modifications must be drawn up that is consistent with the process of transition and other features of military reform.

T.2.2 The reduction of the military presence in essentially civilian sectors of the administration

Periods of dictatorial rule lead to a substantial presence of members of the armed forces not only in the political decision-making process and government posts, but also in public service spheres that are quite outside the remit of the armed forces.

T.2.2.1 *Police and public order*

The most usual sphere is the police and other forces of order. An essential step in the process of bringing the military under control is turning the police into a civil body. Keeping the police in military hands in Colombia, for example, does not guarantee greater effectiveness, but it is a prerogative the army retain in the special circumstances in that country. In terms of Spain, the operation to remove the police from military control and prevent it becoming an additional area for the employment of the military was executed relatively easily. It also formed part of a broader strategy to change the image of the Francoist police (*los grises*) and included changes to their uniform and public image. Removing the police from military control has been an essential feature of peace processes in several countries in Central America. At the present time, in many countries where there are high levels of corruption in the civilian police, there is a strong temptation to hand these tasks and responsibilities over to the armed forces. Nonetheless, the consequences of using the army rather than tackling police reform can have serious implications for the development of a working democracy.

T.2.2.2 *Other parts of the administration*

Other areas of the administration exist that are normally linked to air and maritime transport: ports, airports, air-traffic control, meteorology, etc. It is less urgent or less crucial to make them civilian. One must realize, however, that this makes integrated management of certain areas of the administration difficult and usually nurtures elements of prerogative that belong to previous eras, including uncontrolled income and clear opportunities for the armed forces to have access to corrupting mechanisms.

T.2.2.3 *Information services*

In this period, the issue of control of the information services should also be tackled as part of the programme that reduces the capacity of the military to intervene in politics. This is an area we mentioned in the section on legal reforms and which is often the key to sustaining dictatorial regimes. There are no simple or blanket solutions to this problem. One should point out, however, that linking these activities directly to the president of the republic is, in many cases, a way for the military, who may still be in charge of these services, to nurture their autonomy.

As a general rule, a first step may be reducing the range and size of these services. It is also advisable to create several, and to locate one, for example, under the direct control of the defence minister and the other under the control of the interior minister.

T.3 *Measures for transforming the profession (second horizontal axis)*

Action in this area is more appropriate in the stage of democratic consolidation since this type of measure requires that the civilians responsible for carrying them out have a minimal knowledge of military ethos and that they have familiarized themselves with their procedures and training arrangements, amongst other things. On the other hand, these measures do not usually have an immediate effect and the difficulties are not so much to do with formulation as with implementation, because they demand a mixture of firmness and skill. In short, time and persistence are needed, and these are features that belong to the period of consolidation, and not to the period of transition.

But measures must indeed be taken during the transition to bring the military community towards values and principles that are closer to those upheld by civil society. One could mention others of a more symbolic nature and which encourage the military to stop interfering in politics (extrication). We could include:

- Regulating the situation of military staff who attempt to participate in politics from elected posts or through membership of a political party. A clear-cut separation of political life and the military profession.
- Introducing the study of human rights into the curriculum of military academies and, at the same time, more and more demanding to see these rights being respected in practice, particularly in situations where conscription exists.
- Introducing criteria of lay values and/or the tolerance of different religions.
- Gradual elimination of the previous regime's symbols from officers' quarters, barracks and training centres.
- Encouraging interaction with armies in democratic countries and participation in regional security bodies, that is, direct contact with more occupational armies.

- Reducing in most cases the size of the armed forces, independently of the fact that larger changes – impacting on the pyramid of officers and generals or structure of the force – are left to later.

As well as implementing measures such as these, we should expect a new democratic government to confront the difficult problem of human rights violation or abuse during the previous authoritarian regime, so common under dictatorships in Latin America and more recently, to mention a quite different example, in the countries of former Yugoslavia. One cannot generalize or invent universal solutions in this respect. A study of countries in Latin America shows that managing the problem is hugely complex and that granting truces or amnesties, as in Argentina or Uruguay, or accepting demands for impunity, like those from the Chilean army, may have avoided greater conflict with the military in the short term and even prevented coups. However, these issues will inevitably resurface with time, because a democracy will not become stable if they are not resolved. This is borne out by the fact that truth commissions have had to be set up in these three countries and the power of the judiciary is eroding the areas of impunity that were created.

The experience of transition in 'third wave' countries seems to confirm that it is very difficult to resolve these questions satisfactorily if the conditions are not in place to do so in the first months of the transition. On the other hand, it is strongly advisable to avoid any ideologically motivated purge of the military; on the contrary, it is better to focus on cases of blatant corruption.

When formulating and implementing policies to transform the profession, one must assess the impact of such actions on the other two axes of our model. The reform of the military justice system to prevent its ability to try civilians not only eliminates a reserve domain and adapts the situation of the military to the needs of democracy, it also sends a clear message to the military concerning society's demands for changes to the profession. Similarly, we should bear in mind the fact that in situations of high conflict levels between civilians and military it is all but impossible to introduce fruitful changes to the profession.

Reform during the stage of democratic consolation

I defined the stage of democratic consolidation in chapter 2 from the perspective of civil–military relations, as that during which the elected government establishes military and defence policies and gives leadership to the armed forces, once the military's interventionist attitude towards politics has been neutralized. As in the previous section, I will analyse the measures and actions pertinent to this stage based on the three axes of our model for military reform.

C.1 Factors that impact on conflict levels with the military or on its acceptance of the reform process (vertical axis)

The ordering of these factors could be similar to the period of transition, whereas the biggest changes relate to the way in which they influence events. The period of consolidation is not one of big, quick changes, but of prolonged change, of adaptation to new procedures that are consistent with democracy. In these contexts, the behaviour of the relevant actors, coherence in the actions of government and even international influences assume a less decisive, but more sustained character.

In terms of international influences, there are always possible ways to improve relations with neighbouring countries in the defence field, to gradually apply measures to increase confidence and give new significance to relations between the nation's army and others. Joining alliances and security organizations will eventually convince armies that democracy is the internationally accepted system and, by the same token, that military interventions in politics will not tolerated. On the other hand, working with military from other countries represents a challenge and an opportunity in the strictly professional field for members of the armed forces. That is obvious in the case of the Atlantic Alliance, but although they do not have the benefit of an organization of this nature, the countries of Latin America, through the Organization of American States (OAS), have signed binding agreements condemning any anti-democratic changes in the hemisphere.

We must also take into account that if the process of consolidation advances, then popular support for the government of the moment will be more decisive than the new regime's legitimacy. Certain measures or reforms will become possible in situations where there are strong governments with popular or parliamentary support. The Spanish transition is a perfect illustration of this when the drive to reform was given a terrific boost by the convincing socialist victory in the 1982 elections.

Finally, mention should be made of the decisive factor ensuring that the reduction of conflict with the military is sustained: there must be a substantial reduction of the army's institutional character, and changes in the values and principles cultivated by the military profession, so they are more consistent with democratic pluralism, tolerance and a system based on freedom, and closer to those held in esteem by the rest of society. This is an example of the need, included in my model, to coordinate advances on the three axes. That is to say, there can be no civil supremacy in the long term if this does not become a principle accepted and felt to be necessary by the military as a professional body. To that end, important changes must be achieved on the axis I have labelled 'professionalism'. Felipe Agüero wrote that in the case of Spain there was a critical moment of inflection – one he locates in 1982 or soon after – when the military realized there was no possibility, even in the terrain of their own professional interests, of progress outside the democratic regime.[6] Military policy must reach this point in the area of reshaping of the profession. From then on, it is very unlikely the problems represented on the vertical axis will be repeated to any significant degree.

C.2 Measures to reduce military autonomy (first horizontal axis)

As we saw in the previous chapter, the process of military reform in the consolidation stage can be measured by the progress made in reducing the autonomy of the military. The crucial factor in the whole process is for the government to be able to develop and implement military policy. To that end, it is very likely that new legal reforms will be necessary to spell out what civil supremacy means and enable the process to go forward.

C.2.1 Legal reforms to consolidate democracy

Although other sections also require legal reforms, here we are only concerned with the reforms designed to remove obstacles on the government's path to the assumption of full responsibility for delineating military policy. The laws regulating these areas are usually drawn up during the period of transition in a negotiating framework imposed by the military, or at least highly pressurized by them. This should not happen in this phase and consequently it may be the case that some laws should not be a development or continuation of those from the previous

---

[6] Agüero 1995b: 138.

phase, but in fact should improve on and rectify concrete points in laws already passed by elected governments. In some instances, as in the case of Portugal, these changes take place because reserve domains, as defined in the initial Constitution, are removed. In Spain, the 1984 Law modified ambiguities and other obstacles to the rule of the government that it had been impossible to avoid in the 1980 Law, promulgated by the elected parliament after the Constitution had become operative.

C.2.2 Drafting military policy

First of all, it would be a good idea to define the content of this concept. Following Fitch, I see military policy as 'the entire set of government policies that deal with civilian–military relations, that is to say, the relationships between the armed forces, the state and the rest of society'.[7] To express this in other terms, it is the sum of actions and measures with which the executive directs the military within the administration of state and in its relations with society. Military policy is obviously different from defence policy, the goal of which is to provide the country with security against any present or future threats it might face.

As I have defined it, the content of military policy is different from and broader than that encapsulated in Spanish legislature and legal thinking. Following the 1980 Law, an attempt was begun to clarify these terms and the following definitions were thus included in the Introduction to the Report from the Ministry for Defence 1986–1989:

Defence policy is defined as an integral part of the general policy that determines the objectives of national defence and the resources and actions necessary to fulfil them. Military policy is an essential component of defence policy and determines the organisation, preparation and realizing of military potential, as basically constituted by the Army, Navy and Air Force, taking into account the national resources in relation to defence. The President of the Government is responsible for defence policy and, by delegation, the Minister for Defence. The Minister for Defence draws up and implements military policy.[8]

I am not using the idea of military policy as part of a defence policy, the part, that is, corresponding to the military, but in a broader sense, as a policy that creates the conditions and drives a particular model of

---

[7] Fitch 1998: 134.   [8] The Ministry for Defence 1989: 23.

civilian–military relations. When policy aims to successfully integrate and adapt the armed forces to a democratic regime that is being constructed or consolidated and to ensure democratic control of the armies, then democratic military policy is the order of the day, and this description would not make sense in the stricter, more technical concept used in Spanish legislative thinking that I have mentioned. Nevertheless, this definition requires a political actor to define and drive it, even though it will go beyond his competencies in many respects. This agent must be the minister for defence who, in order to play this essential role, must be a civilian.

C.2.2.1 The Minister for Defence

The civilian minister must be seen, above all by the military, as a necessary factor in creating and maintaining defence policy and military policy in the present international context. Consequently, the minister should stay in post for the length of the presidential mandate and avoid short periods in the post which mean that he has no time to gain minimal knowledge of the situation, let alone take decisions of any transcendent significance.

When I say that the minister must be seen by the military as a necessary factor, I mean that some of the post's functions are particularly vital today, even from the perspective of the corporate interests of the military, and must be given emphasis. Five of these stand out as most relevant in the light of the experience in Spain:

1) An irreplaceable presence as an actor in the field of international relations, both in terms of organizations and bilateral activities with other countries.
2) To make the connection between defence policy and the legislature, which is a crucial factor in consolidating the partial regime of civilian–military relations. Experience indicates that the post cannot be held by a military in active service.
3) To arbitrate between the forces in their disagreements over budget allocations or over the different approaches to what should constitute a policy of joint action.
4) To encourage an interest in and knowledge of military matters on the part of academics, parliamentarians, journalists and society in general, in order to create a space for debates on defence questions in society at large.

5) Finally, it should be emphasized that the civilian minister must assume the task of defending the legitimate professional interests of the military, to counterbalance restrictions in terms of their right to form associations and trade unions.

The civilian minister must be very clear that the fundamental issue at stake in civilian–military relations is power and that as minister he must hold the reins in terms of power. The Spanish military, like those in many countries, when defending the separation of military and political–administrative chains of command, believed that the role of the latter was to 'support' the forces and certainly not to direct or give them orders. There can, however, only be a single chain of command if the goal is civilian rule. The president of the government and the minister must have 'command' of the armed forces and not simply 'support' them in their functions.

For all these reasons, it is essential that the government president liaises with and supports the minister in a period of military reform. The military community must be aware of this understanding and realize that a very important part of the minister's authority derives from the fact he is exercising attributes delegated by the president. They must also be aware that the minister is highly respected within the government, where he exerts considerable influence.

C.2.2.2 *Strengthening the Ministry of Defence*

After a civilian minister of defence has been appointed, the second requirement is the creation of a ministry with real power to manage military policy, one that, according to the circumstances in each country, is equivalent to those in consolidated democracies. Latin America provides many examples of processes that have ground to a halt at this point, since nearly every country today has a civilian minister of defence, but in most cases, these ministers do not have the legal, administrative and political means necessary to lead military policy, that is to say, they do not have a true ministry of defence.

The creation of a ministry of defence is an arduous process of abrogating areas of decision making the armies see as properly their own. That is why it requires at least two stages. The first is the creation of an initial nucleus around the minister who must try to determine defence policy priorities, liaise with the media, and control the intelligence services directly dependent on his office. At the same time, this nucleus must include a mechanism for asserting gradual control over the budget. The second stage is the creation of a ministry that can carry out the four competencies that should characterize a comparable ministry. These functions are, in the order that they should probably be put into practice: budgetary tasks, weapons and matériel, the definition of military missions and policy in respect of personnel.[9] Arrangements establishing the functional dependency of army bodies on the appropriate parts of the central apparatus of the ministry can be put in place later.

C.2.2.3 *Integration in overall government policy*
It must be made clear that defence policy is conceived as part of overall government policy, taking advantage of every opportunity to show how it is coordinated with foreign policy and with policies of other relevant departments. The integration of defence and foreign policy must be led by the president of the republic or government, according to the nature of the democracy involved. This issue has increased in importance over recent years now that armies are being honed into instruments of foreign policy, especially in its multilateral dimensions. This new situation, which occurs at a time when the need to defend the territories of the nation in the classic sense of the term is diminishing, affords the army a new mission that is compatible with democracy.

C.2.2.4 *Relations with parliament*
The involvement of the legislature in the task of military reform must be guaranteed, at least in two ways. On the one hand, control must be gradually asserted over the allocation of resources to defence and the implementation of the budget. On the other, parliament must not only rubberstamp but also participate in drawing up basic elements of defence policy and military policy in the way we have outlined here.

In order to help bind military reform to parliament, one must bear in mind a factor that is valid in other fields: a policy of transparency facilitates civil control of the armies. It is necessary to combat secrecy, the holding back of information, even of an economic nature, as this is something that cannot be justified today. More transparency, more information and more accountability also represent an increase in civil control over the military.

[9] On this issue see Bruneau and Goetze 2006.

In terms of these previous tasks, one should note that most countries in transition lack politicians and civil servants with an expertise in security matters. This is one of the most crucial gaps to fill if civil control of army affairs is to progress. Moreover, civil posts in the area of defence are not valued because they do not usually help the individuals who occupy them up the ladder of promotion.

Once again, the appointment of a civilian minister will be the first step to take, followed then, for example, by an energetic policy of dialogue with the legislature to encourage the training of members of parliament from all political formations, the promotion of security studies in universities and the opening of centres of advanced military training to civilians.

C.2.3 Eliminating military prerogatives

In this section, once the problematic presence of the military in areas of the administration outside its competence is resolved, two other tasks must be tackled urgently: the reform of the military justice system and the status of groups of companies under army control.

C.2.3.1 *Reforming the military justice system*

As far as military justice is concerned, adaptation to working within a democratic system requires a series of adjustments that are difficult to meet in their entirety in countries in transition to democracy. The following are essential:

- Military justice must not be applied to civilians.
- It must deal with military crimes and not with crimes of all kinds committed by military. Otherwise, this becomes a corporate preserve and privilege.
- It must be integrated into a single judicial system and should not constitute an isolated or independent sphere of jurisdiction.
- It is necessary to separate out the penal code, applied by judges, from disciplinary legislation, enforced by military command.
- The military command cannot exercise any sway in the judiciary, that is, its members cannot be judges, preside over or be involved in tribunals, validate sentences, etc.

The adaptation of military justice in many countries runs up against the serious problem of establishing accountability for the crimes committed during the years of military dictatorship. Nonetheless, these issues are normally resolved by civil courts and even in some cases by international courts. The defence of human rights in these circumstances means the military justice system must be reformed and subordinated within a single judicial system.

C.2.3.2 Companies owned by the armed forces

There are two types of companies controlled by the armed forces: companies related to arms manufacture and those the forces manage in order to get additional resources.

In the present situation, it makes no sense to militarize companies that manufacture arms or equipment, even though there might be a wish to sustain some kind of national industry in this sector, since in all probability, that will require others kinds of management. In some countries this issue can be tackled in the context of a broader programme of privatization, although the evolution of Eastern European countries shows that military enterprises remain in place even after the general process of privatization has been finished. Consequently, the path taken in Spain is not one that can be followed elsewhere: there the companies under army control were transferred to the National Institute for Industry that owned and managed all the industrial enterprises in the public sector, in order to proceed to privatization years later.

For a variety of reasons – Cuba, for example, is a very different case to Honduras or Ecuador – armies in most of Latin America own companies. A very common situation – and the one most difficult to administrate – is that where the companies owned in order to create the resources necessary to pay military pensions are in serious economic difficulties. In such cases, the best policy is to proceed as soon as possible to an analysis of the financial state of these companies and the payment of pensions and then draw up immediately a mechanism to incorporate the latter gradually into the civil service pension system. This is a delicate matter impacting on the most sensitive corporate issues, but a well-administered solution can bolster mechanisms for asserting civilian control over the armed forces.

C.3 Measures to change the profession (second horizontal axis)

The set of measures necessary to move the armed forces from a highly institutional to a more occupational position must be at the heart of military reform policy in this period. They are not, however, easy to classify or sum up, given their complex, heterogeneous nature. Therefore no strict order for implementation can be established. In each case it will be necessary to assess military sensitivities to the changes being introduced and external factors supporting the need for change, which may be a great help here.

As I have explained, an increase in professionalism does not suppose the democratic normalization of civil–military relations as such, although in many cases of military reform, modernization and improvements in technical capabilities will necessarily be on the agenda. Progress must be made on the road to improved professionalism, that is, democratic professionalism that accepts that every soldier's duty is to embrace loyalty and subordination to the democratic civil authorities. It is impossible to reach this level of professionalism if the armed forces have an area of autonomy that exceeds the one granted to them by the civil powers, or if they cling to values and beliefs far removed from those of the society they should serve.

Civil control of the armed forces at this stage requires action in relation to the very idea of what constitutes the military profession, something that ceases to be defined exclusively by the military themselves and has to be adapted to the new circumstances via a policy expressly applied by government. The incorporation of new tasks, as we shall see, that give the armed forces more reasons to exist, can contribute to changes in the content of the profession that are necessary if civilian–military relations in a democracy are to be placed on a stable footing.

We shall now examine a set of measures I have categorized in three groups.

C.3.1 Defining new missions and the ensuing need for organizational change

The definition of missions to be carried out in the present context is a pressing issue since the new international situation, whereby conflicts between states are practically a thing of the past, has thrown into crisis the missions traditionally pursued by armies in most countries. This has led to a situation of confusion and uncertainty in which many armies have looked to internal activity to justify their existence. The risk that armies will occupy areas of power is heightened considerably in such a situation. One only has to think of the activities linked to internal security or the struggle against drug cartels that many Latin American armies are engaged in, as encouraged by the United States' policy of providing them with matériel and equipment.

Consequently, the definition of new missions requires political debate and cannot be rushed. The 'Strategic Concept' approved in 2003 in Spain shows the road travelled in this country, focusing on only three missions: defence of territorial integrity within the parameters of the EU and NATO; contribution to international peace operations; and collaboration deemed necessary in security operations such as maritime control of boats that may be transporting drugs, rescue operations, natural disasters, etc.

In any case, the executive must decide the missions with the support of the legislature, whenever possible. Missions linked to internal security should be short lived, not permanent, supported by the police, carried out under civil control and subject to civil legislation.

If the armed forces must of necessity collaborate in internal security missions, the boundary that must never be crossed is that of undertaking actions requiring or justifying internal intelligence, surveillance or information on the citizenry.

The change in missions will generally imply processes of modernization and changes in the size and operational scope of the armed forces. It is opportune if measures such as reducing manpower or disbanding units that are no longer operative are implemented in the light of a previous raft of directives on new missions for the forces and if the changes are a result of the latter. In practice, however, almost all such processes are gradual and must be carried out with no exact idea as to how the situation will finally end up.

C.3.2 Measures impacting on the forces as a career

These are very important measures or policies that must be carefully prepared and require a detailed knowledge of the context and a precise definition of the goals to be achieved. We can highlight the following:

- Modifying the system for promotion. This is a controversial area in Spain and many other countries, since the abandoning of strict criteria of longevity has historically led to arbitrary actions and conflict between the different sections of the army. However, the system must be changed and criteria introduced that reward better professional qualifications and encourage an attitude of continuous training. This reform can be gradual, and can start with the participation by the minister in the process of selecting those to be promoted to the rank of general and the promotion of generals. It can then be extended to the regulation of other areas of the military profession.

- Controlling the organization of military training. This reform requires careful preparation, to the point that in many cases it is advisable to proceed gradually. The crucial issue is the ability to convince the military over time that the definition of their profession, including the moral values and principles to be fostered, is not an internal matter for the military themselves but that society, through its elected representatives, must have the decisive input. Military policy must include a definition of the military profession that is thought to be appropriate at each given moment.
- The opening up of the military profession as a career for women. This reform is supported by the experience of a great number of countries, in particular, western democracies, that have gradually accepted women into the ranks of their armed forces. Such an innovation has a dramatic impact on such a highly institutionalized body, given that it goes against the grain of the education received by the officer class in almost all countries; an education that cultivates principles such as bravery, valour and even comradeship and that was seen as unable to include women. Consequently, it is a step that can be applied very easily and lead to extremely psychologically beneficial changes to the military community.

C.3.3 Changing the quality of life in the military
There are various changes that can both improve quality of life as well as enhance the integration of the military community into civil society. They include:

- Policy on military housing encouraging the military to live in urban centres instead of isolating them in barracks. This measure is facilitated if it is part of a broader programme of the sale of military land not needed in present circumstances.
- The elimination of cut-price supermarkets and other non-salary benefits. These changes can be pursued if accompanied by a policy to increase pay to bring it into line with civil service levels. On the other hand, all non-salary benefits must be eliminated – such as those that involve employing soldiers to carry out services of a domestic, family or personal nature.

- Changes in working hours. These can be brought closer to civilian working conditions, especially if the military are not engaged in missions that will increasingly be carried out abroad.

C.3.4 Other measures to be taken to change the profession

I detail here measures that cannot be grouped in previous sections but that are worth highlighting:

- The need to defend human rights should be introduced into all training programmes. In other words, the dignity of the individual should predominate over other considerations that have historically militated against this being considered a priority.
- Practical mechanisms must be put in place to improve the way soldiers are treated and to protect their rights. This is vital if conscription is maintained. There must be a department in the structure of the ministry, and not just in the armed forces, dedicated to this end.
- International cooperation must be established with other countries, above all with international defence and security organizations and the United Nations. A presence in these bodies presupposes a degree of civil leadership which simultaneously strengthens this leadership overall, as well as involving the military in missions that will become more and more common, linked to international peace keeping and operations of a humanitarian nature.

There can obviously be no movement towards what we have called a *democratic professionalism* if these issues of modernization and moves towards a proper professionalism are sidelined.

The stage of consolidated democracy

At this stage, the content of civil control centres on the definition of a suitable area for autonomy by each government and on equipping the armed forces for a reality that is undergoing constant change domestically and internationally. As I pointed out, civil control of the armed forces cannot be resolved properly if treated as a problem between two players. If we do not gain society's support for progressive formulas that implement democratic normalization, then no lasting framework can be established to solve the problem of controlling the military. Defining missions that are accepted by society at large is another important challenge. To this end, the creation of an international profile or degrees of trust with neighbouring countries becomes a normal element in the management of military policy in countries that have entered this phase. The acceptance by the military of new missions endorsed by civil society may very well give rise to issues of control, on top of the changes in organization and thinking these missions also imply.

5 | Transition and military reform in Spain

The Spanish armed forces at the start of the transition

Before examining the process of military reform in the period of the Spanish transition along the three axes into which I have divided it, I will sketch out the state of the Spanish armed forces at the time of General Franco's death. The intention is not to provide a detailed analysis or fully balanced description; what is important here is to highlight features of the Spanish military that might have conditioned or entered into conflict with the process of democratization that was undertaken. What should be emphasized is the way the Spanish armed forces were positioned in terms of the model we have developed, that is, the way they fit within the framework of a democratic state. Then we need to evaluate their location on the institutional–occupational axis and measure the levels of conflict throughout the process, as explained in chapter 3.[1]

Some relevant features for the military control axis

In relation to the axis that reflects the adjusting of civil–military relations to a democratic framework, one must mention, in the first place, a feature that stands out even to non-specialists. I refer to the over-manning of the three forces, and in particular to the gross size of the army that, on top of an endemic excess of officers, had to cope with the vast numbers recruited because of the conflict in the Sahara.[2] In 1982,

---

[1] The best descriptions of what the army was like at that time is still the one by Busquets 1984. See also Payne 1968, Olmeda 1988, Lleixà 1986 and Losada 1990.

[2] Even General Franco recognized this fact. In his memoirs, Francisco Franco Salgado-Araujo records a remark made by the dictator: 'there cannot be a well-paid officer class, unless we reduce the military staff, that is today in excess of our needs'. Franco Salgado-Araujo 1976: 450.

the year marking the end of the period of transition, the army had 960 colonels, while the legal staffing quota, which was still far too large, represented a total of 600. Consequently, the colonels' periods in command of a regiment had to be very short so that a good ratio, though not all, had an opportunity to have that experience. This created huge unease and forced the three armies to control other fields of activity in order to have posts that could be occupied in dependent activities. The Civil Guard and police are a good example of this. On the other hand, excess size meant that the military budget was almost entirely spent on staff costs, and an inevitable shortage of equipment and matériel ensued. One should not underestimate the important of this factor, since it was this that most decisively helped to create the belief among the professionals that things could not stay that way indefinitely and that, as we might now say, the model inherited from the Franco era was not sustainable, especially in terms of the army.

As well as the excess number of chiefs and officers, we must also consider the fact that the command cadres were on average much older than their colleagues in armies in the West, which meant that a policy to rejuvenate the officer class was a priority. One example of the state of play, although it may seem a very marginal one, is the fact that at the end of the period of transition in 1982, every single member of the Higher Council of the Army had fought in the civil war. For these and many other reasons we will examine, military reform had to go hand-in-hand with a complete modernization of the Spanish armed forces.

The second feature we must highlight, in terms of this chapter, is the political power the military sphere wielded, one symptom being the fact, mentioned by Robert Graham, that 40 of Franco's 114 ministers were military.[3] Juli Busquets adds that there was a very high number of military in the regime's legislature, given that 955 of the almost 4,000 procurators in the Cortes that existed over the ten legislatures were also military.[4]

This invasion of the political arena took place first in issues related to public order. The Director-Generals of the Civil Guard and National Police were military, and both bodies routinely became a place to post army officers, since they were considered to be part of the armed forces. For this reason one can say that, in times of need, the defence of order within national borders was in the same set of hands: the army's.[5]

---

[3] Graham 1984: 195.   [4] See note 1.4 in Busquets 1996.
[5] Fernández López 1998: 52.

A powerful weapon enabling the military to control civil society was the 1945 Code of Military Justice, which allowed civilians to be tried by the military courts on the basis of articles with a very broad remit punishing anything regarded as insulting to the armies, and open to very loose interpretation. If that were not enough, the military ran the Public Order Tribunals over long periods. In the middle of the transition, after the first elections of 1977 and when the government of the Generalitat had been reinstated in Catalonia, Lieutenant General Coloma Gallegos, the Captain General of Catalonia could still bring Albert Boadella and Els Joglars to court over their play *La Torna*. It would perhaps be the last case when the army was judge and interested party and directly decided the punishment for would-be insults or lack of respect towards the military authorities.

It is also worth reflecting on the economic privileges of the military under Franco: he left armies that were very badly paid. True enough, a large number of generals held posts in the administration and in state enterprises, but this fact did not affect the majority of the armed forces. On the other hand, the real perks and privileges enjoyed by the military did mark a difference with other professions and the middle classes in the post-war years of hunger, penury and rationing,[6] though this was no longer the case after the economic growth in the 1960s, when they became elements that encouraged social isolation and small-time fraud. By the mid-1970s, the armies strongly believed that the economic situation of their officers did not correspond to their social status.[7]

Finally, a decisive factor in the transition was the existence of three ministries: one for each army. This allowed the navy and air force in particular to have influence and occupy posts in straightforwardly civilian areas related to maritime transport and ports and air travel and airports. The existence of the three ministries fostered a special corporate mentality in each army and prevented the creation of a mechanism for organizing the joint actions that are essential if the armed forces are to be effective. This reality was the major reason

---

[6] S. G. Payne says: 'even lower-ranked officers could, for example, get supplies in the well-stocked cut-price military supermarkets, that were the only places where decent, reasonably prices food products could be found at that time' Payne 1968: 370.

[7] In the Annual Report for 1979 of the Information Division of the General Staff of the Army it says literally: 'It can be seen that the economic position of the cadres is not in line with the social category they belong to.'

why establishment of a genuine ministry of defence was such a difficult and prolonged business.

The situation on the professional axis

The army as institution

Javier Fernández López[8] suggests that at the beginning of the transition the army could be split into three large ideological groups: recalcitrant Francoists, out-and-out defenders of the values of their victory in the civil war and opposed to all far-reaching changes; those in favour of limited reforms, who were the most numerous; and progressive-minded military in favour of an evolution to a European-style democracy. I share his opinion that most of the armed forces were not reactionary at the time of General Franco's death, but I think that even those in favour of – or amenable to – limited reform defended a political stance defined by three main features that were obviously more marked among the recalcitrant Francoists:

- They considered themselves to be the guarantors of the 'institutional order' as set down in the 1967 Organic Law of State.
- They maintained 'unbreakable' loyalty to the head of state, Francisco Franco and his heir-designate, Juan Carlos I.
- They believed they must act as defenders and repositories of patriotic values that were not shared by civil society or, at least, were not defended within that society.

Their mission as guarantors of the institutional order was described in Juan Carlos I's first message to the armed forces on the day he was proclaimed king. He told them: 'You are the repositories of the highest ideals of the Fatherland and the safeguard and guarantee of the fulfilment of all that is laid down in our Fundamental Laws; a faithful reflection of the will of our people.'[9] And over a year later, in January 1977, in his speech addressed to the king on the occasion of the Military New Year celebrations, Gutiérrez Mellado still emphasized the same idea when he said:

We want, Sir, your Armies, the Armies of Spain, to fulfil their constitutional mission, as servants of the State and guarantors of the permanent values of the

---

[8] Fernández López 1998: 49.   [9] The full text can be read in Platón 2001: 366.

Fatherland, cooperating in the achievement of the great aims of the nation.
We believe that in this way the Armed Forces constitute a huge factor for
stability in all circumstances, especially in times of deep social and political
evolution. They safeguard the State, and guarantee that each necessary development is legally enacted.[10]

Another sign of the extent to which the military high command felt
obliged to defend the need to abide by the laws of the dictatorship is
the statement by Admiral Pita da Veiga, then Minister for the Navy, when
the 1976 Law of Political Reform was voted in: 'My conscience is clear,
because democratic reform will happen from within Francoist legality.'[11]

Puell de la Villa has explained how the military internalized the
slogan 'After Franco, the institutions'.[12] Probably only the most extremist minority thought Francoism would be viable without Franco, but
even those who accepted that the institutions should evolve to a degree
had been brought up to scorn what they dubbed inorganic democracy,
political parties, trade unions, so-called atheist liberalism: all necessary
elements in any process of transition to democracy.

The appointment of General de Santiago as military vice-president in
the first government of the monarchy, and the maintaining of three
military ministries as well as military command of the National Police
and Civil Guard were factors that also favoured, or at least did not
undermine, these missions to guarantee the preservation of the previous
legal order.

Loyalty to the head of state went together with defence of the regime
that had been born out of the Francoist army's victory in the civil war
and was a cornerstone upholding the ideology distilled by the officer
class during the Franco dictatorship.

The defence of patriotic values was a key topic taught in military
academies and proclaimed by the military high command in the period
prior to and immediately after Franco's demise. Admiral Pita da Veiga
formulated the principle in a speech in October 1975: 'we stay rock-
hard so the politicians can make their policies. We are vigilant so the
fatherland is secure and its essences, of which we are the repositories,
remain unchanged.'[13] General de Santiago himself, in a press release
published in 1967 to belie some press versions of the nature of the
meeting between President Suárez and the Higher Councils of the

---

[10] Gutiérrez Mellado 1981: 64–5.   [11] Martín Villa 1984: 134.
[12] Puell de la Villa 1997: 187.   [13] López-Ramón 1987: 213.

Armed Forces, reiterated the idea that the latter were the 'permanent guarantors of the values of the Fatherland before the people, from which they proceed and which they serve'.[14]

The journal *Ejército*, the official organ of the army, printed articles that defended this mission, some even post-dated the approval of the 1978 Constitution. As late in the day as January 1978, a lieutenant colonel wrote in its pages, rejecting the subordination of the army to civil powers on the basis that the 'defence of the integral existence of the nation' was the preserve of the former. Consequently, 'the Armed Forces will always veto decisions taken by the civil powers that dangerously unbalance the great needs of the nation's destiny'.[15]

The strength of this principle of the defence of values superior to those nourished in civil society was such that even democratic generals like Díez Alegría or Gutiérrez Mellado remained ambiguous. Díez Alegría, who was the first high-ranking military to uphold, even in Franco's lifetime, the subordination of the army to the civil powers, affirms in the same text:

But without neglecting this primordial mission, and in many cases as a continuation of that same mission, it also assumes its historic duty as the guardian of national traditions and values that must endure at the moment of crisis we now face. Similarly, it assumes its moral duty to uphold the highest virtues of the nation, to be exemplary in renouncing material gain and devoted to the service of the Nation.[16]

Nevertheless, the general dared open a crack in the immutable nature of these principles: 'the military spirit must be able to incorporate, without weakening its heroic qualities, others that are equally enhancing in terms of administration and technology'.[17]

We should note that Gutiérrez Mellado was one of the first generals to introduce nuances in this terrain. In his General Report for 1976 as Head of the Joint Military Staff, he accompanied these nuances with rigorously traditional declarations:

The Army is ready to expel from its ranks those who become entities alien to our collective spirit because of ideas or attitudes that go against the discipline, hierarchy and permanent ideals that figure in our ordinances and decalogues, although this does not imply that these should not be corrected and

---

[14] Platón 2001: 397.   [15] López-Ramón 1987: 236.   [16] Díez Alegría 1972: 44.
[17] Díez-Alegría 1972: 80.

modernized in many respects and very urgently, in accord with the social evolution that has been taking place over recent years.[18]

A year later, in a lecture to the armed forces in Seville, he said: 'Let us not forget that we military don't have sole rights on love for our country.'[19]

The great risk with this kind of thinking is that it necessarily nourishes the idea of the armed forces as an institution, as a power above politics and politicians who evidently do not defend these ideals or do so insufficiently. The idea of the defence of national essences is at the heart of the train of thought upheld by Spanish armies over the last two centuries, which portrays them as an institution independent of the political powers-that-be that can legitimately intervene on the political stage whenever the generals think it necessary.

The three features examined here – guarantor of institutional order, loyalty to the head of state and defence of patriotic values – are upheld and given credence. As we shall see later, they converge to foster the idea of the armed forces as an institution, independent of the political powers in the land, that sees itself as above politics and politicians, with values of its own that are vital for the nation's survival that consequently give legitimacy to military intervention when extreme circumstances or dangers to the fatherland make this necessary.

Alberto Oliart gives us a briefer definition of the ideological position of the military at the start of the transition, which is all the more vivid for being the fruit of his own personal experience: '[the military] had only two elementary political ideas: the first, that communism was enemy number one; the second, that Spain was different from other countries and democracy was impossible in Spain'.[20] It is a definition that does not set out to be all-inclusive but rather to underline the two features the author thinks most important. Indeed they must be grasped as such in order to understand attitudes that would reappear throughout the transition. The obsessive opposition to the legalization of the Communist Party, already voiced in the first meeting Adolfo Suárez held with general and admirals, is difficult to understand if one does not take into account an ideological position that also helps explain the military's double standards during the transition towards democratic military and the acts of indiscipline by anti-democratic military.

---

[18] Gutiérrez Mellado 1981: 53.   [19] Gutiérrez Mellado 1981: 85.
[20] Oliart 2002: 90–1.

Finally, we must point out that the use of the word institution to define the armed forces, so common in the late nineteenth-century Restoration, was also very present in the early days of the transition. The decree-law of February 1977 that regulated political activities embraced a clearly institutional definition of the armed forces: 'A substantive, fundamental institution in terms of the order, foundation and guaranteeing of the State, of its survival and its life, that is of institutional order and political activity'. Almost two years later, the first article of the Law of Royal Ordinances also used the same word: 'These Royal Ordinances constitute the moral rule for the military institution'.

The internal enemy

One must add to these ideological elements the notion that armies have to fight not only external enemies, but also the enemies within, an idea that gathered strength after the civil war because of Spain's isolation on the international scene, the military's role as guarantors of the regime's continuity and its awareness of its lack of capacity for other missions. S. G. Payne has written 'after 1945 the main function of the Spanish military was internal security rather than national defence'.[21] General Franco himself had said as much in a speech in the 1950s: 'The sacred mission of the armies of a nation is that of maintaining order, and that is what we do.'[22] This becomes quite obvious if one examines the location of military units across the country, with most not in barracks near the capitals, but right in the heart of the big cities. The most powerful units, namely, the armoured and parachute divisions, together with others that were less well equipped and served, were lodged in barracks on the outskirts of Madrid. In fact, the struggle against subversion was one of the four hypothetical war situations that CESEDEN (the Higher Centre for Defence Studies) studied in its courses in 1969.[23] Gutiérrez Mellado

---

[21] Payne 1968: 182. See also Iglesias 2001: 19.
[22] Quoted in González García 1977: 67.
[23] See Rodrigo 1989: 42. It was part of the 5th Lecture Cycle on National Defence and the four hypotheses under consideration were: 1) Subversive war; 2) Conflict in the north of Africa and Straits of Gibraltar; 3) Limited frontier conflicts; and 4) Widespread conflict.

also included internal subversion in his personal vision of the three major concerns of the military at the start of the transition.[24]

This was a somewhat traditional stance in the Spanish army. In reality, an implicit agreement was established between the army and ruling bourgeoisie from the beginning of the First Republic, by dint of which the former obtained its autonomy and prerogatives in exchange for guaranteeing order against the incipient working-class movement, especially in Barcelona. We can even say that the agreement was explicit if we consider, for example, the speeches of Antonio Cánovas del Castillo in the middle of the Restoration.[25] For many years the conditions obtaining in Spain were those defined as Brumairean moments by Alfred Stepan after Karl Marx.[26]

The first mention of the internal enemy of which I am aware is in the Constitution of 1812.[27] The text is repeated in the Law Constituting the Army in 1878.[28] The anti-protectionist Álvaro Flórez Estrada, author of what is considered to be the best treatise on economic theory published in Spain in the nineteenth century, in one of his frequent incursions into the field of politics, his 'Political Constitution of the Spanish Nation as Pertaining to the Military', had already advised 'limiting the use of the armies to the repelling of external enemies, punishing anyone

---

[24] In the conference he was about to give in Barcelona when he had the accident that cost him his life, Gutiérrez Mellado wrote: 'Before 1975 ... the professional cadres of the Armed Forces had the following basic concerns: the one that existed while the World War lasted, prompted by the possibility that Spain might get involved, and then extended by the Cold War; a possible substantial armed subversion, with or without foreign help; and the terrorist problem that culminated in the assassination of the President of the Government.' See Puell de la Villa 1997: 224.

[25] Payne quotes from a speech in the Ateneo in Madrid in 1890: 'The army will be for a long period, perhaps always, a robust pillar of the social order and an invincible barrier against the illegal activities of the proletariat, that will achieve but one thing with violence, the futile spilling of its own blood.' See Payne 1968: 55.

[26] Marx in his work *The Eighteenth Brumaire of Louis Bonaparte* describes how the bourgeoisie abdicates its control (through the National Assembly) over the army in exchange for the latter's protection. See Marx 2005 [1852] and Stepan 1988: 10–11.

[27] Article 356 says: 'There will be a permanent national force on land and sea for the external defence of the State and the maintenance of internal order.'

[28] Article 2 was written as follows: 'The first and most important mission of the army is to sustain the independence of the fatherland and defend it from external and internal enemies.'

who contravenes [this norm] even if it were by virtue of an order from the Monarch'.[29]

The concept of the internal enemy was connected to other ideological elements we have already mentioned and in particular to the task of impregnating Spanish society with military virtues in order to defend it from its worst enemies.[30] In this way, various elements of ideology gradually built up a complex profile, with component parts that became more powerful when joined together and that clearly opposed the transition from the Francoist dictatorship to a democratic state.

Religiosity

The religiosity of the armed forces was another feature that became institutional. Any festivity was unthinkable without a religious function or ceremony and the Catholic religion was a fundamental feature of training in military academies. Francisco Franco, in his farewell speech as Director of the Academy in July 1933, when it was closed down, was already telling cadets: 'we have tried to endorse our faith as gentlemen by maintaining a high level of spirituality among ourselves'.[31]

The insistence on religiosity in its profile – template, one might almost say – that the armed forces advocated was highlighted by the unprecedented episode in 1973 of the expulsion from the Infantry Academy in

---

[29] Flórez Estrada 1958: 363. The article 36 proposed by Flórez Estrada literally says: 'Use should never be made of those newly conscripted into active military service to any other end than the repulsion of external enemies or the manning of a frontier garrison. If such a fundamental law were contravened, even if it were by virtue of an order from the Monarch, the chief who led the troops and the minister through whose offices the orders were communicated, will be judged to be enemies of civil liberty and immediately it being proven that they have contravened what is laid down in this article, they will be declared unfit to hold any military or civil post, and to enjoy any of the rights of citizens.'

[30] General Iniesta Cano even said in 1972: 'We are in the line of truth. No doubt about this. This is not fanaticism or an excess of jingoism; it is pure, healthy patriotism ... We only want one party, one that stands for love for the fatherland ... We must achieve perfect impermeability against any infiltration by mean spirits who, futilely, try to undo this beloved union between men and the lands of Spain that our Caudillo commands and that our dead proclaim and command ... Francoism will never disappear from Spain and after Franco, Francoism will continue through the centuries, because Spain, that is eternal and has a huge universal destiny, will derive from Francoism social justice, the wellbeing of all Spaniards and the happiness of the fatherland'. López Ramón 1987: 213.

[31] The full text can be found in Ferrer Seguera 1985: 262–6.

Toledo of several cadets a few days before their graduation as lieutenants. It seems clear that this punishment was not decided in order to castigate any actions in particular, but to set an example and because of the panic in the military command at the time caused by fear that the army's monolithic unity might crumble as a result of the changes that Spanish society was experiencing. Nonetheless, among the charges levelled at them was one of 'Having had a religious crisis that led them to abandon the Catholic faith, although they remained Christians...'.[32] Catholic religiosity was a very powerful agglutinative agent in the ideological profile of the Spanish military at the beginning of the transition, to the point that ten years had to pass after the approval of the Constitution for it to cease to be compulsory for the military to go to mass in the ceremonies during military festivities.

The actions of General de Santiago exemplify the role that religion played in shaping and strengthening the ideological positions of many of the military high command. In the debate he had with Alfonso Osorio over the programmatic statement by Adolfo Suárez's first government, he explained that he was against saying that sovereignty resided in the people '[b]ecause as a man coming from the traditionalist camp he understood that if power comes from God it was difficult to accept this principle of popular sovereignty'.[33] In his infamous article in *El Alcázar* two weeks before the February 1981 coup, he urged, 'Spain will be rescued if we possess the spirit of Spaniards and believers'.[34] Religiosity was an element that was so rooted among the military community that even the progressive tendency, born with the name of *Forja*, so crucial in the inception of the UMD (Unión Militar Democrática, the Democratic Military Union), came from a movement that was originally Catholic.[35]

On the other hand, Catholicism came together with other ideological elements we have mentioned and, in this way helped seal this circle of ultra-conservative thought. Communism is the enemy of the Catholic Church, and therefore the enemy of Spain and the incarnation of the

---

[32] They were also charged because of 'friendships with university people, with whom they talk about aspects of society in need of reform; for reading magazines like *Triunfo* and *Cuadernos para el Diálogo*, and books by Enrique Tierno de Galván and Aranguren; studying economic matters in prejudice of strictly military matters; being on *familia* terms (using the '*tú*' form) with soldiers outside duty hours'. See Aguilar Olivencia 1999: 428. See also Fernández 1982: 15–16.
[33] Osorio 1980: 149.   [34] Agüero 1995a: 249.   [35] See Busquets 1999: 34f.

internal enemy. In this way religiosity reinforced among the Spanish military the idea that their main aim was to fight the internal enemy.

These features shaped a profile the hard-liners in the armed forces, headed by Carrero Blanco until he was assassinated, tried to ensure was uniform across the whole of the armed forces. This struggle to impose a monolithic view on the military explains the hostile reactions to Juli Busquets' sociological study published in 1967, the author of which was the object of a court-martial four years later, as well as actions like those taken in the Academy in Toledo, the reaction against the UMD and tolerance of acts of insubordination and indiscipline that characterized the first years of the transition. For those who defended this vision, the democratic wing of the military was seen as opposed to the unity of the military community and demands for unity within the armed forces were essentially a call for the imposition of this monolithic profile.

The most direct result of this attitude was to isolate the military from the rest of society, an isolation that was also fostered by the economic precariousness of the officer class under Franco. Juli Busquets described this reality very precisely in his sociological analysis of the military corporate body:

Scant intellectual life, the consequence of the education received in the academies, means that the military in general do not like reading the same newspapers as the rest of the middle class and thus, for example, rather than mainly reading *El País*, as this class does, they read *El Alcázar* and before that the now defunct extremist organs *El Imparcial* and *Fuerza Nueva*, all of which helps to give the military criteria, ideologies and value-systems that are different to those held by the rest of society, and that are generally much more conservative.[36]

The above features shaped a clearly institutional army as in our definition in chapter 3. In fact its institutional nature was reinforced by the history of relations between Spanish armies and civil power in the period between the two republics of 1871 and 1931. In these years a tradition of independence from government and links to the Crown was established. Suárez Pertierra considers that 'the idea of institution as applied to armies in its modern sense is born' in the 1876 Constitution and the 1878 Law constituting the Army.[37] The first article of the 1878

---

[36] Busquets 1984: 213. On the same page, Busquets points up the eight sociological reasons for this isolation.
[37] Suárez Pertierra 1988: 2366.

Law states precisely: 'The Army constitutes a special institution as a result of its aims and character'. Later, the 1906 Law of Jurisdiction would bolster this character of the armed forces as an institution independent of popular sovereignty. As we shall see later, academic and political discussion about whether the 1978 Constitution reinforced the army's institutional character cast a threatening shadow over the initial debates of the transition.

Finally, and within the relevant features on the professional axis, we should mention two additional characteristics. The first is the international isolation of the Spanish armed forces given that, at the time of General Franco's death, their closest international relations were with South Korea, Taiwan and a few Latin American countries. They had almost no relations with armies in Europe. The agreement with the United States slightly improved this situation but at the cost of accepting relations of dependence where there was no real cooperation and only an exchange of bases in return for help in the purchase of equipment. Although the accords with the United States led to extensive modernizing changes in the three armies, relations with the Americans were not easy and the Spanish armies always believed that the concessions granted in exchange for the use of the bases were mealy mouthed. Alfonso Osorio, minister in the first government of the monarchy, has explained the lengthy discussions in the Council of Ministers that, in January 1976, had to approve the renewal of the 1970 accords by giving them treaty status. Carlos Arias allowed the opinion of José María de Areilza, Minister for Foreign Affairs, to override the reluctance of the military that wanted to insist on more concessions.[38] Although it may seem anecdotal, another indicator of the type of international relations the Spanish armed forces were accustomed to is the fact that when Vicepresident de Santiago handed his resignation to President Adolfo Suárez, the army minister, Lieutenant General Félix Álvarez-Arenas, was on an official visit to Pinochet's Chile.

Finally, another factor should be mentioned that differentiated the Spanish forces from other democratic armies: the Spanish military were a priority target for terrorists. This fact had huge consequences in the

---

[38] Osorio 1980: 53 gives an account of the meeting of the Junta for National Defence on 7 January 1976 when this issue was on the agenda: some of the military were in favour of demanding more concessions from the American government in return for the bases and a reduction in flights over national territory of fuel tankers for American military aeroplanes.

first years of the transition, particularly because the reactionary military used this, together with the creation of the Autonomies, as the pretext for their activity and appeals for support. But we will examine that when we look at the evolution of civil–military conflict in this period.

Legislative and institutional reform

The axis for institutional reform is the one on which measures to reduce military autonomy are implemented or, as seen from the other camp, mechanisms are put in place to assert democratic control over the military.

Spain passed through the stages described in chapter 3. The military's ability to intervene in politics was largely determined by the evolution of the overall process of transition. During the first government of the Monarchy, presided over by Carlos Arias Navarro, when political dynamics centred on the struggle between defenders of the status quo and reformers, the Spanish military assumed their role as guardians of the essences of the nation.

Contributing factors were the development of events in the early phase, and individual acts like the King's speech to the armed forces on 22 November 1975 and Arias Navarro's continuation as president of the government. Also significant were the speeches of General de Santiago praising General Franco when he took up his post as government vice-president and the article he published on 1 April 1976 ('Victory Day' under the previous regime) where he referred to the 'unforgettable Caudillo', the decree 3269/75 that placed General Franco as the head of the hierarchies in the three armies for perpetuity and other events that allowed the military to think that it was possible to perpetuate the previous regime.

After Adolfo Suárez's appointment as government president, the central political dynamics shifted to the relations between reformers and those who wanted a clean break with the status quo. In this situation, the Spanish military entered the next stage, that of trying to decide the drift of those political dynamics. A good example of this is the meeting that Adolfo Suárez held in September 1976 with the Supreme Councils of the three armies, two days before the Council of Ministers approved the Law of Political Reform, so they could have prior knowledge of its content, and during which they warned the president of the government of the consequences of legalizing the Communist Party.

Other examples are General de Santiago's resignation from the government vice-presidency in September 1976, Admiral Pita da Veiga's in 1977 and the pressure put on those drawing up the constitution. We shall examine these issues in due course.

When the process of democratization was quite advanced, that is, after the 1979 elections, and the Spanish military entered the phase of defending their organizational and operational autonomy, the political dynamics in the country became the struggle proper between parties. The subsequent steps in the process were now firmly framed by the consolidation of democracy.

It has to be said that the military had been assiduously digging the trench of their autonomy from military power for a number of years before Franco's death. Analysing the situation in 1974, General Baquer wrote: 'The temptation of the moment was – and this is no exaggeration – to establish an autonomous military power-base outside the government. To that end it was prudent to weaken the influence of the three military ministers on the Armed Forces and devalue their role in the Council of Ministers. That was exactly what was pursued.'[39]

General Manuel Díez Alegría was the high-ranking soldier who most clear-sightedly pursued a line of modernizing and reorganizing the armies in the final moments of the Franco regime. Already in 1968 he had begun to put forward reforming, modernizing plans, and to suggest a basic law that outlined an obvious reform from a professional military perspective, that is, the need for joint action by the three armies. He also went so far as to propose the creation of a general secretariat for defence that would oversee the administrative management of defence policy to be recommended to the president of the government. Navy opposition was total and in line with its corporate interests: it not only vetoed these proposals, but drew up and managed to get approval for the 1970 Organic Navy Law that protected it against any measures attempting to integrate it into the other armies.[40] Nonetheless, the organization of the navy notwithstanding, the 1970 law represented an evident improvement in the organization of the other two armies, to the extent that the first reforming decrees implemented by General Gutiérrez Mellado at the end of 1976 and beginning of 1977 were those to 'institutionalize the figure of the Chief of Staff' in the armies of the

---

[39] Alonso Baquer 1996: 14.
[40] For a description of the process see Puell de la Villa 1997: 165f.

land and air, rather than to create the Joint Chiefs of Staff, as in the Díez Alegría proposal that had been withdrawn. In this way the three armies were put on a level organizationally before being articulated in the Joint Chiefs of Staff.

General Díez Alegría's ideas and proposals, as well the vicissitudes suffered by various pieces of draft legislation after the 1966 Organic Law of State, are described in the lectures he gave in the Royal Academy of Political and Moral Sciences, in February and March 1975, by which time he had been sacked from his post as Head Chief of Staff (*Jefe del Alto Estado Mayor*), and in the draft law that was withdrawn from the Cortes.[41] In these, he defends, among other things, the view that 'the Army is subordinate to the political powers, and consequently, cannot take on those powers itself' and establishes the distinction to be con-solidated in later legislation between defence policy and military policy. He also suggests that there should be a distinction between the over-seeing of these policies and the deployment of the armed forces or the command of the latter. The overseeing of policies should be the preserve of ministers, although he recommended the creation of a single ministry of defence. In terms of the command of the armies, he advised against a collegiate solution – which was imposed from 1977 to 1984 – and advised that there should be a Head Chief of Staff with the Chiefs of Staff of the armies as adjuncts.

Although many of these criteria were diluted or suppressed in the draft law published in Official Bulletin of the Spanish Cortes on 23 April 1974, the text was a clear step forward to the articulating of the armies within the executive, in anticipation of a separation of functions and expansion of the remit of the government president that would take place after Franco's demise. Thus, the draft law established that both the leadership of defence policy and military policy should be in the hands of the president, and the Joint Chiefs of Staff that should be set up would report directly to him. Moreover the project contained yet another innovation: it referred only to the three armed forces and nowhere mentioned the Civil Guard or the National Police. It went even further than this when in article 22 it stated: 'the Armies of Land, Sea and Air represent fundamentally the means of defence against external action. In situations of internal emergency they will act within the framework that has been established legally.'

---

[41] Díez Alegría 1975: 24ff.

This series of innovations, obviously directed at professionalizing the military, was too ambitious in terms of what army leaders were prepared to accept. In a way that was unusual in the Francoist Cortes, the draft law became the object of a large number of amendments aimed at every single reforming move, until the government finally withdrew it in January 1975.[42]

General Franco sacked Díez Alegría from his post as Chief of Staff with the passive support of Government President, Arias Navarro. His sacking was accompanied by an unusual note that made mention of his political contacts in Romania (presumably with Santiago Carrillo, the then-exiled General-Secretary of the Communist Party) that clearly brought dishonour upon General Díez Alegría. Several years later, when Adolfo Suárez held the presidency, General Gutiérrez Mellado managed to persuade the Army Chief of Staff to issue a note putting things right and defending the good name of the fired general. In my view, a pretext would have been found, sooner rather than later, to relieve him of any opportunity to take leadership of the military at the time of Franco's death. Díez Alegría realized that the model established in the long period of Francoist dictatorship could not possibly survive after the dictator's demise. His knowledge of the reality and organization of armies in other countries convinced him of that. He believed he had no choice but to implement reforms to the profession from within the corporate body, thus allowing the army to move closer to those in neighbouring countries. To that end, it was necessary to reduce its size, endow it with better resources, spend less on personnel costs, prepare it for joint actions and connect it to a strong defence industry. As we have indicated, such a conception was incompatible with the views of the immense majority of the military command and was consequently impossible to implement from within the forces.

These ideas were shared by Gutiérrez Mellado, who was linked to General Díez Alegría from the time of his promotion to the rank of general in 1970, first in CESEDEN (the Higher Centre for Defence Studies) and later in the Military High Command (*Alto Estado Mayor*). Thus, the work in CESEDEN, created in 1964, and the text of the draft law that was thrown out were major influences on the first steps in Gutiérrez Mellado's reform, namely, the 1977 and 1978 decrees. These

[42] For a description of the vicissitudes suffered by the draft, see Rodrigo 1985: 152ff.

related to the creation of the Joint Chiefs of Staff – the JUJEM – and also influenced the 1980 Organic Law, although Gutiérrez Mellado included a decisive measure that Díez Alegría had suggested but of which there was not even a hint in the 1974 draft law: the creation of a ministry of defence.

There was intense legislative activity aimed at reforming the armies and articulating them within a democratic state in the period of transition and, in some cases, it was implemented from other areas via legislation prompting the police to begin its demilitarization. In terms of the democratic articulation of the armed forces, we must underline four fundamental innovations: the creation of the JUJEM, the writing of the Constitution, the creation of the Ministry of Defence and the Law of Basic Criteria for National Defence. In relation to the reduction of privileges, the reform of the Code of Military Justice was the most important step taken. We will examine the other aspects of legislative reform along the axis of the transformation of the profession and its values.

The creation of the JUJEM

General Gutiérrez Mellado tackled the setting up of the Joint Chiefs of Staff (JUJEM) only a few months after his appointment. The 23 December 1976 and 8 February 1977 decrees paved the way by creating the posts of Chief of Staff in the armies of land and air. Now that the three armies were equal in this respect it was possible to set up an instrument for joint action that was indispensable for making efficient use of military capabilities: the Joint Chiefs of Staff or JUJEM. Although Díez Alegría had rejected the formula of a collegiate command, this was the one inscribed in article 2 of the decree-law: 'The Joint Chiefs of Staff, politically dependent on the President of the Government, constitutes the highest collegiate organ in the Armies' military chain of command.' Puell de la Villa has shown how these reforms were accepted by a military high command that anticipated that in the near future the military portfolios might be assigned to civilian ministers.[43] A line of

---

[43] He quotes from the script prepared for Vice-president Gutiérrez Mellado's address to the Defence Commission of Congress on 19 January 1978: 'The joint presence of political–administrative functions and the Military Command in the Ministries of the Army and Air-force is not recommended in the near future, when one must anticipate that the entrance onto the scene of political parties will produce governments of different tendencies, with the possibility that civilians may be designated to take on military portfolios.' Puell de la Villa 1997: 208.

action was being fleshed out, as described by General Alonso Baquer, that tried to create an area of military autonomy from the division between military command and political–administrative functions.

The importance the military gave to the existence of a supreme organ of command is highlighted by the fact that they fought hard for it to be included in the Constitution of 1978. On the other hand, already in 1977 *El Alcázar*, one of the outlets for the hard-liners, used the same argument that many military leaders were happy with at the time: 'The Ministry of Defence does not represent the Armed Forces, whose sole voice belongs to their line of command and their supreme institutional organs.'[44]

For military autonomy to exist or be consolidated, it does not have to be defined or guaranteed by legislation. The law need only be ambiguous. In the case of Spain, the greatest risks of an evolution that would de facto consolidate military autonomy came from ambiguities in law – including the constitution – where a distinction between the line of command and the political–administrative line could be a way of putting a brake on the integration of the armed forces into the administration apparatus of the state. The decrees of 1976 and 1977 represented huge steps forward in the modernization of the armies but at the same time opened the way to a real possibility for the demarcation of a reserve domain in the new organization of the military.

Drawing up the Constitution

After the first democratic elections in June 1977 and the opening of the constituent phase, one can point to two dangers in terms of the correct wording of the articles devoted to the armed forces in the new constitution that was being drafted.

First, the danger existed that they would err on the side of the army as an institution that tried to link itself directly to the people or the Crown. In that sense, the real risk came from locating the armed forces in the Preliminary Section of the Constitution and not in the sections set apart for the administration of the state or government. There was also a possibility that a direct connection would be made to the Crown, if article 62h of the Constitution was interpreted as defining the king as the non-symbolic head of the armed forces.[45] Both measures risked

---

[44] *El Alcázar*, 20 September 1977.

[45] Article 62 of the Constitution reads: As corresponds to the King: h) The commander-in-chief of the Armed Forces.

placing the military in the democratic framework as an institution that was claiming and consolidating its autonomy from the government.

Secondly, there was the tendency mentioned in the previous section to want to distinguish and separate out the line of military command from the so-called political–administrative line, which meant the former was outside government control. This approach led to more restricted autonomy, but one that that effectively allowed the armed forces to maintain control of internal operations, organization and educational policy, i.e. the military's cultivation of the values and ideology it considered appropriate.

Consequently, this process has to be scrutinized in detail, starting from the basis that even when the rules of the Constitution signalled clear progress, such as the separation of the forces of public order from the armed forces, it was ambiguous in other respects and could not act as a strong, unproblematic reference point for the process of military reform.

The location of article 8 on the armed forces in the Preliminary Section was the first dangerous step to opening the way for the army to develop as an institution. The drafting committee was in fact in doubt about where to locate the article well into their final working sessions. It was very far from being a minor issue, since its location provoked a debate that lasted until quite recently.[46] The inclusion of the armed forces in the Preliminary Section devoted to the institutions or powers of the state, encouraged all those who conceived of the armed forces as an institution above parties and politics, an institution that dialogued with other institutions and centres of power of the state.

It is worth noting that the committee's doubt was not about whether to locate article 8 in the Preliminary Section or Government Section. It was a doubt about whether to include it in the Preliminary Section or the one specifically devoted to the armed forces, the forces of public order and states of emergency.[47]

In any case, the final words in the Constitution in this regard must be studied from a political perspective. A strictly legal or academic focus

---

[46] One can cite among the abundant literature on this topic López Ramón 1987, Suárez Pertierra 2004, Mozo 1995 and Cotino 2002.

[47] Fernández Segado 1996: 14: 'the Section that concerns the Government of the nation was never considered as a possible place for regulating the Armed Forces when the constitutional Commission was unclear about what to do in this respect.'

that tries to say exactly what the commission was hoping to achieve through its final version is inadequate, since the drawing up of the Constitution was the result of a political compromise in which caution towards the armed forces played a decisive role. It did what was possible in very difficult circumstances.[48] Miguel Herrero de Miñón's chronicle of the labours of the drafting Commission describes how true this was.[49]

The actual content shows how difficult it was to introduce changes in this terrain, since it was largely a copy of article 37 of the 1967 Francoist law, probably as a result of JUJEM pressure on Gutiérrez Mellado, who was their interlocutor – and adviser – on this issue. Nonetheless, I have already pointed to a very different, crucial feature in the text of the Constitution in this respect: the separating out of the armed forces from the police and civil guard. This step may relate to the decision to include article 8 in the Preliminary Section. One of the first drafts (the one leaked to the magazine *Cuadernos para el Diálogo* and published 22 September) included a section focusing on 'The Armed Forces, Forces of Public Order and states of emergency'. This section disappeared from the first draft to the Commission that clearly separated the armed forces from the forces of public order. Manuel Ballbé has explained this:

In effect, article 8 of the Constitution in relation to article 104 has a primary aim: to demarcate the Armed Forces clearly from the Forces of Public Order, now known as Security Bodies. This arrangement was completely contrary to the one in place up until then, because, let us remember, article 37 of the 1967 Organic Law of the Francoist State declared that the Armed Forces were 'constituted by the Armies of Land, Sea and Air and the Forces of Public Order'. The model in the Constitution is in clear contradistinction to this.[50]

---

[48] Mozo 1995: 623: 'We believe that the only possible conclusion to be drawn in respect of the present article 8 of our Constitution is that that it is the result of purely political reasoning, that is, it is what the drafters considered to be (politically) opportune and convenient.' He quotes Martínez Sospedra who believed that the reasons for the location of article 8 may be: 'first, the importance of the missions assigned to the Armed Forces; second, a political quid pro quo for introducing the term "nationalities" into the Constitution in article 2; and third, politics again, the drafters' wish to bring the Armed Forces round to democracy.'

[49] Herrero de Miñon 1993: 144 explains how a mere display of military documents classified as 'secret' was enough to obtain the agreement of nationalists, Communists and Socialists.

[50] Ballbé 1983: 460.

The drafting commission and the Suárez government must have thought that the separation of the armed forces and security forces was a radical enough change without going so far as to include the armed forces in the section related to the government, which is exactly where they put the forces of public order and security bodies. They must have considered that including the armed forces in the Preliminary Section was the least bad option.

One must emphasize that a large part of the debate addressed the attempts by Alianza Popular and military senators to re-establish Francoist parameters for the armed forces, or at least their efforts to ensure the final document did not separate out the civil guard.

The other essential feature for the viability of the reform process was the need to avoid granting constitutional validity to the JUJEM as a collective organ of command. The commission received a text approved by the JUJEM that it had submitted to the president of the government via the conduit of the recently created Ministry for Defence. This formed the basis for the draft outline of the articles referring to the armed forces.[51] When he became aware of the way the commission's work was progressing, Gutiérrez Mellado drew up an official letter stating his own position, one that clearly aimed at moderating the JUJEM's position, a letter he sent to the president of the government on 14 November 1977 and that was decisive in the drawing up of the final text for article 8. He wrote: 'no reference is made ... to the paragraph relating to the said Junta, because we understand this is not a matter for the Constitution but should be the object of a Law regulating the Defence of the Nation'.[52]

This was the way Spain avoided what might have become the greatest obstacle to subsequent military reform, since if the Constitution had

---

[51] In the first draft it was article 123, that later became article 8 in the next draft:

1. The Armed Forces, constituted by the Army of Land, Navy and the Air Force, have as their mission the guaranteeing of the sovereignty and independence of Spain, the defence of its territorial integrity and protection of its constitutional order.
2. An organic law will regulate the basic principles of military organization in line with those of the present Constitution and the composition and functions of a Supreme Junta, as the Government's consultant body in matters related to Defence, as well as the Joint Chiefs of Staff, as the supreme collegiate organ of the military command of the Armed Forces.

[52] I owe this information and access to the relevant texts to Miguel Herrero y Rodríguez de Miñón, who was a member of the drafting commission.

included a definition of the JUJEM as a collegiate command, it would have encouraged the military in their desire to create an autonomous space in relation to government and, as we shall see, would have prevented the core of the 1984 reform from becoming a reality. It would have been impossible to modify such explicit criteria in the Constitution at a later stage. We only have to remember how difficult this was in democratic Chile in relation to the institutional aspects of the armed forces that General Pinochet wished to leave sewn up in the Constitution.

Lastly, I have already noted how the final wording of article 8 was very similar to article 37 in the 1967 Organic Law of State that focused on the armed forces, except for the crucial difference that it did not include the forces of public order, and that it replaced the expression 'the maintaining of institutional order' by 'the defence of the constitutional order' and the removal of the mission of being guarantors of the unity of Spain. The fact that it was largely a copy of the Francoist law, although clearly a copy more in appearance than in substance, brought an accompanying risk: that it gave sustenance to the theses upholding the belief that the Constitution 'accepted' or 'blessed' the military as an institution shaped by the previous regime.

The debates over the Constitution in the Cortes Generales did not broach directly these issues or dangers. Although López Garrido has written: 'An examination of the process by which this precept was drawn up in the work of the Constituent Cortes is very little help when it comes to probing its legal or political meaning',[53] an analysis of the parliamentary debates of the Constitution reveals the political difficulties involved, the risks at stake in agreeing to wording that implied limiting civil control of the military and the fact there was widespread support in the Cortes for many of the theses defended by the Francoist military.

Two positions on the issues under analysis were reiterated during debates in the Congress and Senate: the first upheld the idea that the armed forces were above political parties. If that is the case, it seems logical enough that they must not only obey the government that reflects the parliamentary majority at a particular time, but must defer to the king, who is a more stable element than majorities produced by successive elections. Even the Socialist Party expressed itself ambiguously on

[53] López Garrido 1983: 949.

this point. One spokesman, Enrique Múgica, quoted approvingly a high-ranking officer who had recently told a meeting: 'The Armed Forces are subordinate to civil power, but their mission, quite above vying political opinions...'[54] He then repeated this in a plenary debate:

And finally, the previously mentioned military view voiced in a recent meeting of the Military General Staff to the effect that the Armed Forces are subordinate to the civil power which they respect as an expression of the popular will; but that their mission, quite above vying political opinions, cannot remain aloof from the problems of the community that are the focus of politics at the highest level, that preserve the essence of the Fatherland and guarantee the survival of the State.[55]

Admiral Gamboa repeated this in the Senate:

The nature of the military's mission locates the Armed Forces above political options, makes them neutral in terms of political parties and subordinate to civil powers, within a profile safeguarding permanent values. This neutral role in what is contingent and a profile safeguarding what is essential is precisely the best guarantee of peace and security for the citizenry, the basis of harmony and justice in the community of the nation served by the said Armed Forces.[56]

The second position maintained that the armed forces are 'rather more' than the public administration. If this thesis is accepted, the next logical step to defend is that the armed forces do not solely depend on the government that is in charge of public administration. Obviously, if what is at stake is dependency on an institution other than the government, it can only be dependency on a direct link to the Crown.

This was the argument forwarded by Miguel Herrero in Congress and by González Seara in the Senate, adequate proof that this was a party and not personal position. González Seara stated in the Senate: 'The Armed Forces are part of the State Administration, but the Armed Forces are rather more that the mere administration of the State and a good, clear testimony to that is the fact that the Constitution makes the King Commander-in-Chief of the Armed Forces.'[57]

Fraga Iribarne also used this argument in the same debate: 'the Armed Forces, as obedient as they must be, are not the same as a section of the

---

[54] Diario de Sesiones del Congreso de los Diputados. 1978. Tomo I: 921.
[55] Diario de Sesiones del Congreso de los Diputados. 1978. Tomo II: 1973–74.
[56] Diario de Sesiones del Congreso de los Diputados. 1978. Tomo IV: 4571.
[57] Diario de Sesiones del Congreso de los Diputados. 1978. Tomo III: 3295.

Home Ministry or some other department of local administration'.[58] At
different stages in the discussion of the Constitution, Fraga made many
declarations that could be described as highly institutionalist. In the plenary debate of article 8, for example, he justified including the latter in the
Preliminary Section with this kind of argument: 'at the present time Army
and people are the same thing, as in the times of ancient Rome'. At an early
point in a transition it is a serious error to relate the armed forces directly to
society, because that weakens their relationship with the state itself.[59]

In short, one can say that the debate over the Constitution managed
neither to clarify nor to get a proper hold on the issue of the institutional
nature of the armed forces. As a result, the text left unresolved the
question of whether or not the latter were an integral part of the
administration or 'rather more' than that. The time was still evidently
not ripe to deal definitively with such important issues as the relations
between the armed forces and the Crown or the effective subordination
of the former to the civil power established through the ballot box.

Apart from that, the debate included opinions that, even in the
context of the transition, can still be considered as supporting a concept
of armed forces that enjoy a degree of autonomy from government.
These views of the armed forces as the right arm of the state or the
backbone of the state, expressed by leading members of Alianza
Popular, undoubtedly reinforced the institutional inertia of the armed
forces. Extolling the armed forces is not a good way to encourage the
military to submit to the civil powers.[60]

Finally, the wording of article 97 of the Constitution[61] is also open to
different interpretations about whether the armed forces, the term used

---

[58] Diario de Sesiones del Congreso de los Diputados. 1978. Tomo I: 918.

[59] See Suárez Pertierra 1988: 2375.

[60] The categorizing of the military is a recurrent issue in Spanish history. Both
      speakers used expressions from the debate over the armed forces from the Second
      Republic. In his speech to the Congress of Deputies on 6 November 1934 José
      Calvo Sotelo had said: 'the Army is the very honour of Spain'. He later added:
      'Mr Azaña said that the Army is only the arm of the Fatherland. False, absurd
      sophistry: the army has now been seen to be much more than the arm of the
      Fatherland; I won't say it is the brain because that it should not be, but it is much
      more than the arm, it is the backbone, and if it breaks, if it bends, if it cracks,
      Spain breaks, bends and cracks with it'. Lleixà 1986: 182.

[61] Article 97 of the Constitution: The Government controls domestic and foreign
      policy, the civil and military administration and the defence of the state. It
      exercises the function of the executive and power of rule in accordance with the
      Constitution and laws.

in article 8, are something different to what is meant by the term military administration in article 97 and if this is also something different to civil administration. The first legal refinements excluded the armed forces from the area of military administration. This is the raison d'être of the distinction between the forces and political–administrative branch. And although political dependency on the government was always made explicit, ambiguity in wording and the definition of the JUJEM as the 'highest collegiate organ in the military chain of command', created, as I pointed out, a certain 'reserve domain' in relation to the armed forces, to employ J. Samuel Valenzuela's expression as explained in the previous chapter. The expression 'political dependency' was the subject of debate in relation to the 1980 Organic Law of basic criteria for national defence, with amendments from both the Socialists and the Communist Party, which shows how, at the time, that ambiguity was seen as something that should be corrected.

A gradual way out of this confusion was found in the concept of national defence and in the creation of a ministry of defence with a real capacity to work out and implement defence policy. To this end the armed forces were integrated into the ministry's structure and concepts of command and political dependency were brought together. Processes of military reform cannot be limited to legislative reform. Consequently, as we shall see, it was the creation and development of the ministry, and not any legal changes, that contributed to solving the ambiguities and errors. Later on, jurisprudence formulated the solutions from a legal perspective, to the extent that it is now taken for granted that the so-called military administration is a part of general state administration.[62]

The rest of the parliamentary debate of issues related to the armed forces in the Constitution was quite unexceptional. On the one hand, there were attempts from the left that was not party to the consensus to locate article 8 in the section relating to government, and the amendment from Raúl Morodo that wanted the armed forces to be described as agencies of the state. On the other, Alianza Popular and the military senators attempted to return to a Francoist integration of armies and forces of order and to include the defence of the unity of the Fatherland as appropriate missions for the armed forces.

---

[62] See Mozo 1995: 627.

The final drawing up of the Constitution in terms of establishing the supremacy of the civil powers was not ideal. An article in the Preamble to the Constitution was devoted to the armed forces and was not worded very differently from the 1967 Francoist law – except for the separating out of the forces of security – and dependency on the government was formulated ambiguously, allowing leeway for potential anti-democratic arguments. It must be recalled that it was Vice-president Gutiérrez Mellado's intervention that meant the Constitution did not include the institutionalization of the JUJEM, a move that would have had serious consequences.

It must be borne in mind that these issues were not the only ones leading to a great disparity of criteria between the constitutional commission and the military. Others were the abolition of the death penalty,[63] retained for times of war, recognition of the right to objections of conscience, the independence of the military system of justice and the retention of Courts of Honour.[64] However, it was the matter of Spain's unity that caused most conflict. Spanish military recognition of the autonomies and of the regional systems of government created during the Second Republic implied a complete break with the institutional order of the previous regime. It was a point constantly hammered home by the extreme right-wing press that exerted such an influence in military quarters. A reliable indicator of the genuine importance of this issue is the way General Gutiérrez Mellado kept returning to it during the months of debate over the Constitution. He had already made it clear in his first General Report as head of the military general staff, in 1976, that a united, strong and self-confident army must overlook the development of the nation 'in every respect, including the political, always carrying out its duty and guaranteeing permanently, under the orders of the Government, that the unity of the Fatherland will never be broken, however many and however respectable the region-alisms that are accepted'.[65] He also used the verb 'to obsess' in relation to the unity of Spain in his first speech in the presence of the king on the occasion of the military new year celebrations in

[63] Article 15 of the Constitution says in this respect: 'The death penalty is abolished except for the situations covered by military penal law for wartime.'
[64] Busquets 1999: 257–63 relates the pressure exerted in respect of the cases for courts of honour and the death penalty.
[65] Gutiérrez Mellado 1981: 54.

January 1977.[66] In the same ceremony, in 1978, he raised his tone and used a threatening expression: 'Spain is one and we Spaniards will not allow it to be broken up.' A few months later, the unity of Spain was the only question broached during his visit to the emblematic parachute regiment, and led him to intensify the harshness of his language.[67] All this shows how the wording of the second article of the Constitution guaranteeing the right to autonomy of nationalities and regions and that includes the expression 'nationality', as well suppressing the mission of guaranteeing the unity of Spain as one of the duties of the armed forces, represented a formulation that brought high levels of conflict which heightened the existing tensions resulting from specifically military concerns. Two of the three military senators proposed amendments deleting the expression 'nationalities' and defending the unity of Spain as a mission of the armed forces in article 8. None voted in favour of the Constitution.

As with other matters, however, the Constitution deferred a characterization of democracy that was impossible in the early days of a transition that had been agreed, even though the accord was not explicit. Legislation and practice over time gradually allowed these democratic steps to be taken, which were permitted but not always defined by the Constitution. In fact, it was a substantial achievement, even in terms of military reform, to manage approval of a text that introduced democracy without serious confrontation with the military, even though no military senator voted in favour. The Constitution could not determine what autonomous communities should be created and yet the State of the Autonomies is one of its crowning achievements.

---

[66] The sentence in full says: 'The unity of Spain, respecting the variety of her regions, in the best tradition of our history, the legacy of which you are the executor, we are sure, Sir, obsesses you as one of your greatest responsibilities.' Gutiérrez Mellado 1981: 60.

[67] His 1978 New Year speech in Gutiérrez Mellado 1981: 140f. In the headquarters of the Parachutists Brigade the general said: 'I shall speak to you about only one [problem], and it is a fact that although in my New Year speech I said "that Spain is one and we Spaniards won't allow it to be broken up", there are certain sectors that cannot or do not wish to grasp my message. I will use this solemn occasion before one of the Army's most distinguished units to say they should be aware that the Government, the whole Nation and the Armed Forces are ready to show these are not mere words, but will become acts. And Spain will always be one.' Gutiérrez Mellado 1981: 175–6.

To make steady progress, those leading the process of military reform had to avoid open conflict with the Constitution and concretize its implementation on the basis of democratic common sense, comparative law and the status quo in other countries. This is not at all an exceptional situation. Even in the United States, where armies came into existence that were not led by aristocrats and where the debate on civil control of the military thus originated, the Constitution is hardly explicit on this point. Huntington believes that the United States Constitution 'despite the widespread belief to the contrary, does *not* stipulate civil control [of the military]'.[68]

Creating the Ministry of Defence

In the posts he held before being appointed Vice-president of the government, General Gutiérrez Mellado experienced how difficult it was to coordinate three ministries, about which he had already formed his opinion during the years he collaborated with General Díez Alegría. In the renowned lecture the latter gave in the Royal Academy of Moral and Political Sciences, he mentioned 'the aversion to a Ministry of Defence or to any kind of single command' as one of the hurdles to overcome in a necessary new regulation of defence matters.[69] It is not very surprising therefore that the documents his office prepared for the first meeting of the Commission for Military Matters set up by the government, held 4 January 1977, included 'preparations for a Law on Defence. The core of which would be the creation of a single Ministry.'[70]

It was undoubtedly a brave decision. In retrospect, it is clear it was the most important action taken by Gutiérrez Mellado in his ambitious reform project. Although the text must have been ready by that time, caution must have advised Adolfo Suárez to wait until important acts like the legalization of the Communist Party and endorsement in the first democratic elections were accomplished before taking the decision to create a single ministry, which is what he did when he constituted his government after the 15 June elections.

The strategy for reform had already been set out in the proposals from the time of Díez Alegría, and, in its way, the navy had started it off

---

[68] Huntington 1957: 163.   [69] Díez Alegría 1975: 23.
[70] Puell de la Villa 1997: 2005.

with its 1970 law: first, to give command to the Chiefs of Staff and then to create a ministry that was a political–administrative structure. In fact, as was the case with almost all the steps taken in this first phase of reforms, they stemmed from suggestions that arose and were developed from within the military itself and where the JUJEM always brought amendments, although, as we saw in the case of the Constitution, Gutiérrez Mellado always had the last word.

It is hardly surprising then that the Ministry of Defence should be born as a ministry where posts like the Under-Secretary of Defence, the Director of Armaments and Matériel, the leadership of CESID or the Office for Information, News and Public Relations had to be held by military.[71] In 1982, Alberto Oliart took the first steps to alter this situation by creating two under-secretariats, one with a remit for defence and manpower policy and the other with an economic remit, which meant that when the government decided the time was right, one of these posts could be given to a civilian.[72]

Initially, inertia from the three previous ministries set the pace and it was structured with one under-secretariat and three general-secretariats, one for each army. Then, the embryonic structure that was to become fixed was decreed, and divided the ministry according to functions or area, ignoring the lines of the three preceding ministries. When creating a ministry of defence, it must not be structured in terms of the three branches of the armed forces, because each one will just turn into the representative of the interests of each army, rather than being a leadership body working towards integrated activities.

Once divided into operational areas, the functions of the ministry were not clear to the military, to the extent that the necessary functional dependency of each area in the respective forces in relation to the same area in the ministry was created back to front in some cases. The DGAM, the body responsible for the department's weapons and matériel policy, had to carry out its functions 'in accord with the norms and specifications laid down by the Headquarters of each

---

[71] Articles 11, 17, 21 and 22 of Royal Decree 2723 on 2 November 1977.
[72] This refers to Royal Decree 252/82 of 12 February, article 4.1 of which says: 'The posts of Under-Secretary for Defence Policy and Under-Secretary for Defence will be held by Generals from any of the three Armies in active service, except in those cases in which the Government, at the suggestion of the Minister for Defence, considers that the post of Under-Secretary for Defence should be held by a civilian who could suitably give leadership.'

Army'.[73] Ten more years would have to pass before it was possible to establish the functional dependency of the organs of each army on the main departments within the ministry.

The ministry was set up cautiously and for almost eight years it had no building of its own, since the three armies retained the entities, buildings and bureaucracies each ministry had had up to then. Even so, the need for the ministry was clear enough when it came to the creation, for example, of the ISFAS, the Social Institute for the Armed Forces, the existence of which would have been unthinkable in the previous situation with three ministries. Consequently, the construction of a ministry on a par with those in neighbouring countries was a slow, difficult business that involved gradually taking resources and capabilities from the three armies.

Perhaps because of this slow pace, the establishing of the most important instrument for controlling the military took place without too much protest. Gutiérrez Mellado considered it highly important and had written in his lecture, published posthumously: 'in what relates to our Armies, the outstanding decision was the one to create the Ministry of Defence, in June 1977'.[74] Some people are of the view that it would have been prudent to delay the creation of the ministry,[75] but we believe it was right that the decision was taken in the first moments of the reform, although a price was paid for starting it in such a corporate fashion. If the ministry had not been set up in 1977, it would have been impossible to appoint the first civilian minister of defence in 1979 and the foundations for the next vital steps in the process of consolidation could not have been laid. If it had been set up much later than the JUJEM, practices would have been put in place which would have made the subsequent evolution much more difficult, since the JUJEM would not have had that single authority to which it had to defer.

The creation of a ministry of defence is crucial in the process of reducing military prerogatives inasmuch as it is the key means for establishing the supremacy of civil society. In that sense, General Gutiérrez Mellado was right to assert that it was the central plank in his strategy for reform. Predictably, the way the ministry began reflected

---

[73] See Iglesias 2001: 34 and article 17 of Royal Decree 2723, 2 November 1977.

[74] Puell de la Villa 1997: 221. Manuel Díez Alegría believed the fusing of the three ministries to be 'a colossal step forward'. See Díez Alegría 1979: 165.

[75] Fernández López 1998: 114.

both the origin and professional focus of the reform, as well as the enormous constraints of that period. That is why the dangerous distinction between the line for military operations and the political–administrative line was consolidated in the legal text. This danger was heightened by the fact that the military units were not integrated into the ministry's structure. Of the three component parts of each army, the headquarters, the forces themselves and their support structure, only the headquarters were integrated into the Ministry of Defence's organic structure.

Legislating the organization of the armed forces

Article 8 of the Spanish Constitution reads 'an organic law will regulate the basis for the organization of the armed forces in accordance with the principles of the present Constitution'. This mandate was carried out in the period of transition by two laws in the years 1978 and 1980.[76] Agustín Rodríguez Sahagún, the first civilian minister of defence of the democracy, introduced the second law.

The law of December 1978 marks an important step in defining the functions of the president of the government and the minister of defence in terms of defence policy and their relationship with the armed forces. The law follows the path begun by Díez Alegría's proposal in 1974 to give the president leadership in the development of defence policy and responsibility for the military's senior bodies and authorities and although it directly attributes responsibilities and roles to the minister, it stipulates that the minister's most important functions are carried out as delegated by the president, a formula that seems appropriate and that has remained in place until today, but one requiring concerted actions by the president and the minister that must be clearly seen to be such by the military. The draft 1974 law only mentioned the president, to whom it granted leadership of defence policy and military policy, and created the Joint Chiefs of Staff – the JUJEM – that was also dependent on him. It is a draft that at no point mentions the three military ministries that still existed. The 1978 draft law, on the other hand, includes the first

---

[76] I refer to Law 83/1978, of 28 December that regulated the different Higher Organs of State in relation to National Defence and the Organic Law 6/1980 of 1 July, which regulated the basic criteria for national defence and military organization.

legal definition of the responsibilities of the minister just over a year after the post was created. It devotes one article – the seventh – to defining his responsibilities as being 'in charge of leading and coordinating defence policy, as well as executing the corresponding military policy'. At the time, it was difficult to imagine, particularly for the professional soldiers who drew up the two laws, that the formulation of defence and military policy could become the responsibility of the minister and even of the government. For this same reason, these two laws gave this mandate to the National Defence Commission whose responsibilities included 'formulating and proposing military policy to the Government'. It has already been noted that the characteristic feature of the move from transition to democratic consolidation in the area of military reform is that the government takes responsibility for defence and military policy.

As well as defining the figure of minister, the 1978 law, unlike the 1974 draft, encompassed a definition of the National Defence Commission, since the one still in place came from the 1939 law on the head of state, although General Franco apparently never convened such a body. Care was taken in the description to ensure the number of civilian members was always visibly higher than the number of military. The 1978 law also took on board the recent decree-laws for the creation of the JUJEM and the regulation of the roles of the Chief of Staff of each branch of the forces, although in both cases it extended the number of competencies.

The 1980 law continued on the path of strengthening the role of the minister within the constraints of the period. The description of his responsibilities was refined in article 24, which granted the minister the power to decide the process for producing and supplying different types and systems of weapons and resources. It was, nonetheless, a restricted power, since the law added, 'in accordance with the needs and specifications formulated by the respective general staffs as coordinated by the Joint Chiefs of Staff'.

Another advance made by the 1980 law in this field was to make clear that in order to carry out his functions, 'the minister would have at his disposal the Joint Chiefs of Staff and organs of leadership in the military chain of command of each army', a wording that is coherent with the aforementioned non-integration of the forces into the ministry's structure, but which shows it was gradually becoming clear that it was not enough to link the JUJEM to the president, given his multiple responsibilities, and that this weakened unnecessarily the figure of the minister.

Similarly, the 1980 law took another step to articulating the military within the state administration when it organically framed the JUJEM within the Ministry of Defence. Decree 836/1978 to develop the decree-law creating the JUJEM simply stated, 'it would be attached to the Ministry of Defence, for administrative purposes'.

Progress was also clearly made in terms of previous legislation, with the inclusion of the Cortes Generales as one of the higher bodies for national defence, resulting from the debate on the Congress of Deputies, since the legislature was not mentioned in the draft the government sent to parliament. The article's wording opened the door wide for the legislature to take on the area of defence, and this constituted a real innovation: 'The Cortes Generales pass the laws relating to defence and the corresponding budget allocations and exercise control over the action of government and military Administration.' This necessary incorporation was, however, reduced by the following paragraph. The Cortes debated, but did not pass the general lines for defence policy and weapons programmes.

In short, this legislative reform of the organization of the military resumed the initiative that in Franco's final years abortively attempted to reform the profession, although there were two crucial, very palpable differences within the new framework of the process for democratic transition. The first was the separating out of the military and the security bodies as established in the Constitution. The second was the existence of the Defence Ministry, created under the first government after the first democratic elections. Following the reforming moves within Francoism, legislative changes were initiated through the creation of the figures of the Chief of Staff for the Army and Air Force and then with the establishment of the JUJEM, informed by an obvious desire to bolster military autonomy in the face of the inevitable advance of civilian government. The democratically minded military even thought that the solution would be to separate out a newly created political–administrative line from the military line of command, and to avoid one interfering with the other.[77]

---

[77] This is the expression used by General Gutiérrez Mellado in a lecture he gave in Seville in February 1977: 'We have tried in this way to put the Navy on a par with the other two armies and to differentiate clearly the two existing branches in each ministerial department: the political–administrative side and the purely military command side, that descends from the Supreme Head of the Armies, His Majesty the King, to the most rank-and-file soldier, so that in the future there can be no confusion or interference.' See Gutiérrez Mellado 1981: 73.

Nevertheless, the very existence of the ministry meant that previous approaches to organization, line management and responsibilities had to be revisited, all showing that the creation of the ministry of defence was essential as the basic instrument for the democratic reform of the military.

Legislative reform of the organization of defence in this period was thus a huge step forward and clarified thinking, although it did not entirely succeed in solving the issue of the autonomy of the armed forces and their relations with the government and the Crown. This was in part down to the fact that the reform was conceived and carried through by military who, though democrats, found it difficult to see beyond a professional vision of reform because it was impossible to consult civilians with any knowledge of the area. We must also bear in mind the enormous internal resistance to the reforms that General Gutiérrez Mellado was gradually putting in place. Evidence of this resistance was the resignation of the Chief of Staff of the Army shortly after the passing of the March 1978 decree that gave substance to the decree setting up the JUJEM. In the account of the reasons for establishing the latter it said, 'As for the Joint Chiefs of Staff's political dependency in respect of the President, it should be made clear that this works through delegation to the Ministry of Defence'. Although the same account also constrained the minister's range of power when it affirmed that the carrying out of the tasks assigned to him 'must be harmonized with the responsibilities that are the province of Joint Chiefs of Staff', General Vega Rodríguez still found this unacceptable and handed in his resignation.[78] In fact, the leadership of the armed forces believed for a long time that the JUJEM was something similar to the Ministry of Defence rather than subordinate to it.[79]

Conversely, the political parties were only just starting to study these issues and this explains why there was insufficient clear thinking to debate and modify projects that had been maturing for years on the most professional wing of the military. There are examples of

---

[78] Powell 2001: 258. There are other versions of this episode. See Fernández López 1998: 118.

[79] A member of the JUJEM, Admiral Luis Arévalo Pelluz declared: 'we have our mission and the Ministry of Defence has its and we each accept what we have. We soldiers like each to be in our rightful place … and to have sufficient freedom to act and, naturally, we do not interfere in the tasks of others!' Mérida 1979: 65. See also Agüero 1995a: 255–6.

this in the debates in parliament over the 1980 law. On the one hand, the amendments from the Democratic Coalition were asking for the JUJEM to be linked 'directly to the King, as Commander-in-Chief of the Armed Forces'. On the other, the spokesman for the socialists, probably because any formula seemed better that the Francoist division into three ministries, affirmed, 'we socialists are quite in favour of there being a collegiate High Command'.[80] All in all, these legislative reforms vigorously tackled the issue of civil power and, together with the changes in the military system of justice and those of a professional nature, mapped out a path to enable the military to fit into democratic structures and reduce their prerogatives. This amply fulfilled reform needs in what we have called the period of transition.

Reforming the military system of justice

The previous chapter showed that the reform of the military judiciary system must have a double focus: the system must not be allowed to become an instrument with power to intervene in political life (trying civilians) or a mechanism to strengthen military autonomy inasmuch as it helps sustain attitudes and values that differ from the ones upheld by the rest of society. As we shall see, in the case of Spain, the double standard of punishing UMD members for the would-be crime of plotting military rebellion and tolerating constant acts of insubordination against the government turned the military courts into an instrument that no longer served the democratic system and was unable to maintain internal discipline.

All in all, it was understandable that the greatest resistance of public opinion to the military courts was inspired by memories of the way they were used as weapons of political repression. Consequently, article 117 of the Constitution established that 'the principle of the unity of the legal system is the basis for the organization and functioning of the Courts. The law will regulate the exercise of military jurisdiction in the strictly military arena and in the event of a state of emergency, in line with the principles of the Constitution'.

---

[80] See Cortes Generales 1984: 60 and 1984: 187.

Prior to that, the Moncloa Pacts, signed in October 1977, included chapter 7 aimed at reducing the area covered by the military courts.[81] The law reforming the 1980 Code of Military Justice tries to comply with the Moncloa Pacts rather than with the mandate from the Constitution, as is evident from the fact that its final rulings called for the setting up of a commission to study and reform military justice, a reform that would be implemented five years later, in the period of consolidation.

Nonetheless, the 1980 law introduced three very important changes. First, it reduced the area of competency and almost entirely did away with the possibility that the military could try civilians. The majority of cases that were transferred to civil courts were those to do with so-called insults to the armed forces. Secondly, the law strengthened guarantees by increasing the role of military jurists in all trials and making the use of a defence lawyer obligatory. Examples of this are the removal of the military prosecutor, who was a combat officer and not a military lawyer and the replacing of the military by members of military legal bodies in the preliminary investigations in court. Thirdly, it established the right to appeal, not only before the Supreme Council for Military Justice but also before the Supreme Court.

In terms of making progress in the reform of the Spanish military, one of the most important consequences was that the law, backed by the weight of public opinion, put an end to the situation where the military was both judge and prosecutor in cases of conflicts with civilians, particularly journalists and critical intellectuals. This represents a big

---

[81] The content of this chapter, to be found in Cotarelo 1992: 490, was as follows:

VII. The Code of Military Justice. A revaluation of its limits in relation to the competencies of military jurisdiction:

1. In respect of crime: the resolution of the overlap between the Common Penal Code and the Military Justice Code, by restricting the latter to the area of military crimes.
2. In respect of location: the limiting of the competencies of military jurisdiction to acts committed in strictly military centres or establishments or places.
3. In respect of personnel: the reviewing of possible excesses and the terms in which competencies are resolved when military and non-military personnel are involved in similar acts that do not constitute military crimes.
4. Subordination to ordinary Tribunals of the Forces of Public Order, when they act to maintain the latter.
5. The strengthening of legal and defence guarantees in the procedures of military jurisdiction.

advance along the civil–military relations axis, implying a considerable reduction in the potential for military intervention in civilian life. As I have pointed out already, even after the first democratic elections in 1977, the Captain General of Catalonia could order the trial of a theatre company, *Els Joglars*, because the work they were performing in Barcelona was considered to be insulting to the armed forces. The apportioning to the civil courts of all crimes against the police and civil guard in the law of December 1978, also contributed to a drastic reduction of the opportunities military courts had to try civilians.

However, possibly the change that had the most impact on the adaptation of the armed forces to the democratic system was the one introduced by article 14 in the law that made a timid advance along the path to a single system of jurisdiction, as recommended by article 117 of the Constitution, when it allowed sentences given by the Supreme Council for Military Justice to be taken to appeal in the Supreme Court.[82] Blocking the opportunities of the military courts to intervene in civil life is a necessary first step, but putting an end to the autonomy of the military courts is also essential to guarantee advances in the democratic reform of the military. Juli Busquets has argued that the possibility that the public prosecutor could make an appeal to the Supreme Court was the law's key improvement since it allowed the Supreme Court to toughen the lenient sentences imposed by the Supreme Council for Military Justice on those involved in the attempted coup of 23 February 1981, thus avoiding 'the consequent collapse of the morale of civil society and a boost to the morale of the conspirators'.[83]

The experience in Spain, as well as in most countries of Latin America, demonstrates that wherever military jurisdiction exists, its reform and integration into a unitary legal system, even though this takes place gradually or in stages, is undoubtedly a key element in military reform and a necessary step in the democratizing of relations between the armed forces and the rest of the administration.

---

[82] A minor, but decisive, change in article 84 also contributed to this by affirming that the Supreme Council for Military Justice will exercise 'a high level of jurisdiction over the armies…' whereas the 1945 Code had 'the highest level of jurisdiction…'.

[83] Busquets 1991: 168–9. In relation to this issue, mention should also be made of the ending of the exemption from necessary obedience in the case of orders contrary to the Constitution that was included first in the Royal Ordinances of 1978 and then carried over to the reform of the Military Penal Code.

Events in the Spanish transition also suggest that it is necessary to take advantage of the potential given by partial reform. In the first place, it is hardly prudent to contemplate implementing such drastic reform all at once. In the second, partial advances make it easier to control the whole process and keep an even balance in terms of the three axes of our model, axes that represent interrelated lines of action. Judicial autonomy is a basic element in the concept of the army as an institution, and any reduction in the military's sense that they belong to an institution that can dialogue with the government and other institutions of state is an important step to reducing levels of conflict.

Reforming the professional terrain

The measures included on our professional axis are the most complex and heterogeneous. Legal measures are not enough, since the aim is to advance on the path via which the military can come to accept the new democratic situation. The governments that emerge in the new situation, as well as the lawmakers, must tackle this task with at least a minimal knowledge of the features, procedures and training that characterize the armed forces. For these reasons, and because the processes of assimilation require time, I indicated in the previous chapter that more vigorous advances along this axis can be made in the period of democratic consolidation, when the government can take the initiative in formulating defence and military policy rather than in the period of transition now under consideration.

In the case of the Spanish transition, the government concentrated on political reform and 'delegated' to General Gutiérrez Mellado the task of establishing the framework for military reform and, within that, to a greater degree, the transformation of the profession. Consequently, the military decided on the measures for transforming the profession, without any debate with civilians while they were being formulated, either within the government or the parliament. Of course, this fact would seriously curb the process of assimilation to the new democratic situation in the short term, but in terms of strengthening the transition it implied the start of internal reforms that the civilian members of government would have been unable to conceive or put into practice. The modernization of the profession undertaken by General Gutiérrez Mellado was pursued along five main lines of action: taking the military out of politics; passing new Royal Ordinances; ending the situation where officers had more than one job and improving living conditions; adapting military symbols to the new democratic situation; and attempting to reduce the size of armies as well as establishing mechanisms for promotion that added the criterion of training to that of length of service. Later on, under civilian ministers of defence, important measures such as the law on finance and entry to NATO would be adopted.

Taking the military out of politics

This measure was introduced by Decree-law 10/1977, on 8 February. Together with the creation of the JUJEM, it constitutes one of the first legal measures taken in the military field by Adolfo Suárez's government. It was a very strict measure that prohibited any political or trade-union activity within the armed forces and forced into retirement, with no possibility of return, any career soldier who joined a party, stood as a candidate for election or simply accepted a post in the public sphere or in the state administration.

After forty years of Francoism, in which it was the norm for high-ranking officers to hold posts in political life or public enterprises, it was necessary to send a clear message to the military and the whole of society that a radical change was being introduced. One may well ask if the new legislation should in practice have included all public posts, to the extent that General Gutiérrez Mellado and Minister Alfonso Osorio were asked to move to retired status. This deprived the new government of possible support from democratic officers. It also restricted the activities of more open-minded military than the ultra-reactionaries who collaborated and found support in the anti-democratic media such as *El Alcázar* or *El Imparcial*. If in a process of transition the anti-democratic military have sufficient support and space to spread their ideas, then forbidding political activities creates the risk that the more liberal factions of the military find their ability to spread their ideas is curbed.

The explanation of the reasons behind the Decree-law supports this impression, since it contains one of the most 'institutional' definitions of the armed forces published in the Official Bulletin of State: 'The Armed Forces are, then, a substantive institution fundamental to the order of society, cementing and guaranteeing the State, its survival and life, that is, the institutional order and political activity'. On the other hand, the rationale for the measure was not based on the need to stop those who have a monopoly on the use of force from participating in politics. The justification was very different and based on the need to maintain unity within the armed forces: 'serenely aware of their political potential, the Armed Forces and its members must maintain their unity in order to fulfil their exalted mission as best they can when that is what their constitutional duties require'.[84] The call for unity at that time was a call for ideological homogeneity around the values cultivated during forty years of Francoism and excluded the model of a more occupational army and the open defence of democratic positions. It was, nevertheless, a concern that General Gutiérrez Mellado himself had expressed repeatedly, perhaps influenced by the convulsions the UMD (Unión Militar Democrática) had provoked within the army. In his 1/76 General Report as Chief of the General Staff he had already said that 'among the causes that can bring disunity to our ranks, the one that may be the most dangerous, since it has already led to the splits I have mentioned, [a reference to the UMD] the one we must be rid of at all cost is the cause of politics'.[85]

A few months later, a Ministerial Order of 19 November on freedom of expression within the armed forces regulated the publication of articles, lectures or declarations, a regulation that insisted in practice on prior authorization in almost every case. In January of the following year an explanatory note was published reducing the need for prior authorization to cases 'that can damage national security or which use data that are only known because of a post or appointment held in the Armed Forces', wording that would be preserved in article 178 of the new Royal Ordinances. In any case, these were dispositions that put a brake on the spreading of democratic ideas in the Spanish armed forces rather than helping to change the values previously cultivated by them. As the next chapter will show, these dispositions were abrogated by the law on the status of professional military personnel that twelve years later established much more flexible regulations.

The separating out of politics and the military was a necessary step in those first moments in the transition and, if properly implemented, it remains the case for other consolidated democracies. It has similarly been and still is a key aspect of the processes of transition begun in the

---

[84] The quotation comes from the Preamble to the Decree-law.
[85] Gutiérrez Mellado 1981: 50.

1990s in countries in Central and Eastern Europe. Care has to be taken that the manner of implementation does not reinforce institutional aspects of the armed forces, although Huntington defended such a line of action more than fifty years ago. On the other hand, the unity of the military is necessary when they are the vital element propping up a dictatorship and can even become absolutely indispensable in ensuring that a regime continues. However, that is not the case if the armed forces display an attitude of constitutional loyalty, although one can understand that every corporate body aspires to the unity of its different component parts.

The Royal Ordinances

The other great contribution made by General Gutiérrez Mellado to transforming the profession and its mindset was to put in place new Royal Ordinances to replace those developed in the eighteenth century by Charles III and of which only one part of the second of eight treatises remained operative.[86] The idea was not new in itself and both the navy and army had already undertaken revisions. It was sensible to centralize all these efforts and guide them in accordance with a new ethical code consistent with the democratic system. These tasks were carried out during almost the whole of 1978, that is, in parallel to the drafting of the Constitution, although the debate of the draft law in Parliament was not delayed until the former was passed. The Royal Ordinances were ratified on the same day as the Constitution, 28 December 1978. Gutiérrez Mellado considered this matter to be the most important of all the issues he had to resolve. His desire to leave norms that would be long lasting is evident in the fact that the directive prescribing the drawing up of the Ordinances made the involvement of young officers in the drafting committee mandatory.[87]

---

[86] In a lecture given in Córdoba, General Gutiérrez Mellado mentioned the Royal Ordinances, together with the regulating of the Armed Forces Day, as being one of the two dispositions he was most proud of implementing. See Gutiérrez Mellado 1992: 164.

[87] Puell de la Villa 1997: 214 quotes the following paragraph from the directive: 'The commission must include young Chiefs and officers, who bring to their military spirit an open mind that allows them to intuit successfully what might be suitable norms not only for the present, but ones that will survive in the future.'

The first article defines the goal pursued in the drawing up of New Ordinances: 'These Royal Ordinances constitute the code of ethics for the Military Institution and the framework that defines the duties and rights of its members. Their main purpose is to require and foment the precise fulfilment of duty inspired by love for the Fatherland and by honour, discipline and courage.' Here again is that double-edged weapon found in other parts of the policy for military reform in this period, since if it is an attempt to modernize the military mindset, it is also a mechanism that reinforces the institutional feeling of the armed forces, favouring and strengthening the autonomy of all things military by defining from within the military body itself, the organizational model and set of principles and values that differentiate it from civil society.

Some have claimed that from a legal jurisprudence perspective the norm is unconstitutional since it restricts rights but does not have the status of an organic law. It is a fact that the constitution had to be up and running before the norm could be discussed and approved, although there was probably a desire to avoid opening a debate of its content and also to avoid a statute conceived from within the political arena, and that led to it being drawn up and negotiated very quickly in a way that really assumed the future existence of a democratic constitution.[88] More than twenty-five years have passed and nobody has ever objected to the constitutionality of what was done. Jurisprudence also advised that its content does not sit well with the form of law in which it was framed. In effect, the large number of the articles is an expression of moral convictions that are completely at odds with the normative nature of a legislative text.[89]

---

[88] See Suárez Pertierra 2000: 278–9.

[89] Suárez Pertierra 2000: 265 in this respect points to the mandates to the legislator (like those set out in article 176 that establishes that 'the component parts of the Armed Forces will be protected by the law concerned with threats, acts of violence, outrages or slander that are originated or caused by its military condition or activity') or ones that are impossible to fulfil since they depend on the behaviour of others (see art. 101, which asserts that 'the appreciation and trust of everyone will be achieved through its competence and discretion, thus fomenting a spirit of collaboration and initiative that will benefit the service'). However, the articles that are legally more difficult to fit here refer to ethical norms or precepts and constitute almost the whole of Section 1. Art. 25 is an example of this: 'In order to live the military profession one must have a consuming vocation, that will be developed through habits of discipline and self-sacrifice until the highest level of dedication to a career of combat is reached, the one the vocation itself calls for.'

Even taking into account all these circumstances, we can say that the Royal Ordinances represented a powerful mandate for adapting the armies to the new situation, once approved by the constituent parliament. Article 11, when talking about discipline, says, 'it is expressed overall in respect for the Constitution, to which the Military Institution is subordinated'. In turn, article 26 establishes that 'every soldier must know and fulfil the obligations contained in the Constitution'. Article 9 already anticipates participation in international peace operations. It would be some years, however, before this took place, the first occasion being The United Nations Verification Mission (UNAVEM) in Angola in 1989. Subsequently, participation in such operations remained intense and constant.

The best known innovation is the one referring to the concept of due obedience contained in article 24, because it was put into practice in the trial of the individuals implicated in the attempted coup d'état of 23 February 1981: 'When orders invite acts to be committed that are manifestly contrary to the laws and conventions of war, or constitute a crime, in particular against the Constitution, no soldier will be obliged to obey them, and will, in any case, be wholly responsible for his actions and errors.' The reform of the 1980 Military Penal Code in article 185 maintained due obedience as grounds for exemption from criminal responsibility, adding that it is considered that due obedience does not exist when the circumstances are as defined by article 24 of the Royal Ordinances already quoted. In this way, as has been noted, grounds for exemption because of due obedience could no longer be pleaded in the trial for the acts of 23 February 1981.

One of the major problems caused by the 1978 Royal Ordinances arises from the fact that no mention is made of the government of the nation which thus remains off-limits in terms of the behavioural norms democracy was legislating for its armed forces. Suárez Pertierra has indicated with great insight that this lack of reference to government and its handling of defence questions, may have helped create the advantageous situation where the Royal Ordinances were compatible with the laws defining the organization of the military in this period and also with the different, sometimes fundamental, advances achieved in the period of consolidation.[90]

---

[90] Suárez Pertierra 2000: 282–3.

The new Royal Ordinances were not well received by the military and while they were being drawn up rumours spread through the barracks as to the worst intentions of the new text being prepared, to such an extent that General Gutiérrez Mellado mentioned the matter as an example of rumours with which 'people look to damage our unity, besmirch the leadership and, in short, encourage indiscipline'.[91] The fact they were passed was proof that the reform that had been embraced was thorough and went far beyond what was strictly organizational. The new Ordinances did not attempt a radical change in the values that had been nurtured under Franco, because that was practically impossible at that time. They reveal the risks involved in changes to the military profession that are not led by a civilian government and where the goals to be reached are unclear. But they are also evidence of real progress being made on many fronts, especially towards the creation of a new political context that would demand profound changes in the military world, including in its code of behaviour.

Professional matters

We will now analyse measures taken against holding more than one job – *el pluriempleo* – pay increases and others factors that altered the profile of the military profession.

As far as the military and *pluriempleo* at the start of the transition is concerned, Julio Busquets supplies a figure showing that, according to a 1976 survey conducted by the ministry for the Army, 27.4 per cent of its officers admitted they followed this practice and never asked for previous authorization from their commanding officers before taking on other jobs. The real figure was probably even bigger. *Pluriempleo* was a common phenomenon in the Spanish labour market in the 1980s. On the other hand, from the perspective of the government's reforms and modernizing policies, an officer who had more than one post was incompatible with the professional profile it wished to enforce.

General Gutiérrez Mellado tackled this problem in tandem with the process of raising salaries to the level of those in the civil service. An idea of the importance he attached to this question can be gauged from the

---

[91] His speech at the Artillery Academy on 4 December 1977, Gutiérrez Mellado 1981: 133f.

fact that he referred to it when he appeared before the Congress Defence Committee in January 1978. He did so pragmatically:

I want to touch on another custom that also must disappear, namely *pluriempleo*. One issue is that this has been an extended practice over many years and cannot be axed overnight, but we must be in no doubt, and the majority of us are in no doubt, that it cannot continue, that this must disappear, albeit gradually and respecting rights that may exist in critical, very difficult situations, since what we need is full-time commitment.[92]

The improvements in pay – on average increases of over 20 per cent – were handsome despite difficult economic times. The increase was greater for lower than for higher ranks, which meant that when it was deemed necessary years later to put salaries on an equal footing with the civil service, the percentage hike for higher ranks had to be greater. The regulation of the incompatibilities of holding other posts besides military ones and the application of a pay system based on a working day extended to 5 pm, completed the raft of measures to put a satisfactory end to *pluriempleo* given the crisis in the economy during the transition. It sent out a clear message about the need to establish a dignified profile for the profession and break with the habits from the previous period.

Others changes drove home this message. One was the regulating of promotion procedures in the Navy and Air Force, so that this would depend solely on available vacancies and proper selection mechanisms. In the case of the Army, over-staffing and the very different situations between the various bodies and levels meant that rapid regulation was impossible: a study commission was set up and its proposals were concretized in a legislative package that Minister Rodríguez Sahagún brought to the Cortes in April 1980 and which was passed over the next two years.[93] There were three laws regulating the classifying and promotion of commanding officers, the creation of an active reserve and reorganization of the ranking of petty officers. It was impossible to implement these laws in this period and they were passed gradually during the phase of democratic consolidation.

These dispositions tackled serious problems with innovative solutions, such as the creation of the active reserve, formulated from the perspective of professionals preoccupied by two issues: the need to rejuvenate the officer cadres and the lack of consistency in career

[92] Gutiérrez Mellado 1981: 216.   [93] Rodríguez Sahagún 1986: 193.

prospects between different bodies and levels. However, no attempt was made to tackle the thorny question of the reduction in size of the armed forces, in particular, the Army, a line of action that had to be pursued if real progress was to be made on these two fronts. The reduction in size of the army was an issue that could not be contemplated at that time if we consider the hostility, rumour mongering and outcry with which most parts of the armed forces greeted any incursion into military policy by Adolfo Suárez's government. Such positive measures as the creation of the ISFAS (the equivalent of Social Security for the armed forces) were only implemented in the teeth of intense resistance from the three armies.

Armed Forces Day and the changing of symbols

General Gutiérrez Mellado found an ingenious way round the Victory Parade that was held every year on the Sunday closest to 30 May. He kept the date but transformed it into an Armed Forces Day, decreed that it should rotate through the different military regions and added homage to the Spanish flag to the parade.[94] This was a change that the military who were not ultra-conservative found difficult to attack and which made it abundantly clear that Franco's army was one that should belong to the past. While a civilian minister could obviously have implemented this set of measures with a broader focus, in this case, as in others, it was very useful to have an officer showing the way to go.

In two other areas, exceptionally, initiative for change came from parliament. The first was the modification of the wording of the oath sworn to the flag and was prompted by an initiative by parliamentarian Julio Busquets, a former soldier sentenced as a member of the UMD, who presented it in May 1979, though it was not approved until December of the following year. It involved including a defence of the constitutional order in the oath sworn by soldiers doing their military service and also in the oaths sworn by those graduating from military academies. The second was the change to the Spanish coat-of-arms, an initiative taken by Luis Solana. Legally passed in October 1981 by the government of Leopoldo Calvo Sotelo, this measure was to be very important in the military arena a few years later, when it became possible to change the flag used by all units.[95]

[94] Royal Decree 996/1978 12 May.
[95] On these two issues see Busquets 1999: 280–1.

It would have been wrong to underestimate this kind of reform or to have set it in motion without considering whether the armed forces were in a fit state to accept them, given that they set great store by such issues. In terms of the oath to the flag, the reaction against the changes made by a general who was firmly committed to democracy, gives some idea of how great an allegiance this was.[96] On the other hand, it was the right decision to stagger the replacing of the previous regime's flag by the constitutional flag in the various units until well into the 1980s. These were necessary, opportune changes and the fact they were initiatives taken by parliament and not by the Ministry indicated that the first elected representatives were taking an interest in such matters, and at the same time that the military were being required to adapt formally to the democratic system.

The military finance law

Law 44/1982 was introduced into parliament by Alberto Oliart, the civilian Minister for Defence in the first government of the democracy that did not include any military. It guaranteed the three armies resources for investment over eight years with an annual 4.5 per cent increase in real terms, on condition that there was a reduction in personnel costs, since total expenditure could not grow at an annual rate higher than 2.5 per cent. It was not a completely new initiative, since there were precedents under the previous regime, the last being the 32/1971 budgetary law for National Defence, a law General Gutiérrez Mellado was quick to extend to 1982 via Decree-law 5/1977. Inflation, non-meeting of budgets and a relative inability to spend drastically reduced the effect of this legislation. Although there could clearly not be a further extension and it was necessary to rethink the whole area, the law was also conceived as a peace gesture towards the military after the 23 February coup in the course of the trial of those implicated. The consequences of this law were far reaching, although its effects were not visible until the period of consolidation.

---

[96] General Sabino Fernández Campo described his disgust at this measure and even stated, 'I was quite upset when no high military authority expressed in a respectful and disciplined way his disagreement, or even had the courage to make his protest by resigning from post'. See Fernández Campo 2003: 202–3.

First of all, the law forced the three armies to plan their expenditure, and this implied a more rigorous discussion of their goals and clearer thinking in terms of each army's options. However, more than anything it placed on the agenda the issue of the coherence of the demands from all three, and created a real basis for the planning of joint actions. Lack of openness in terms of the use of resource allocations or a refusal to give proper accounts is an inherent feature of military autonomy. Increase in parliamentary control is a way to reduce that reserve domain, but efficient control can only be achieved through the gradual creation of a ministry that can plan and hold the three armies to its plan. The military finance law opened the way for such planning and rationalization.

Secondly, the law empowered the ministry in relation to the three armies, and decisively strengthened the role of the minister as arbiter in relation to the demands from the three branches of the armed forces and the conflicts between them that these brought with them. The civilian minister could take the final decisions on the aspirations of the three forces, as he belonged to none. The minister can only have this powerful arbitrating role when such planning exists and resources become an overall defence issue and not a question to be resolved by each of the three armies.

Spain's entry into NATO

This was debated by parliament in the second half of 1981 and approved by the Congress of Deputies on 19 October by a straight majority of 186 votes in favour and 146 against. It was a controversial decision that prepared the way for the 1986 referendum, to which the Socialist Party was committed from its time in opposition during the debate on entry. Any debate of its political timeliness or of the lack of consultation with the opposition on this question is neither here nor there because the passage of time has shown that the decision was a correct one. Nonetheless, it is worthwhile emphasizing how important this decision was for the subsequent transformation of the military profile of the Spanish armies and modernization of their thought, jurisprudence and organization. In terms of entry into NATO the Spanish military did not display a homogeneous attitude. Both the Navy and Air Force were in favour of entry. The Army was less favourably disposed. If the statements made by various commanders in 1979 are analysed, one can see hostile or unfavourable attitudes on the part of two lieutenant generals, and positive views expressed by others.[97]

In effect, independently of the fact that it was a crucial decision in terms of domestic and foreign policy, entry into NATO constituted a powerful instrument of military policy, and pointed the way to an opening up internationally and to establishing connections with armies in democratic countries. In a period when Spain's armed forces had to digest frequent political changes that were contrary to their way of thinking, it was vital to endow reforms with a professional and technical content that could not be questioned, particularly in relation to the Army.

In this context the debate about whether entry into NATO or into the EEC was more important makes little sense. It is more than likely that if the Spanish transition had headed towards a semi-democracy, it would have been compatible with continued membership of the Alliance, as attested by the examples of Greece, Portugal and Turkey. In this respect, Spanish democracy became solidly rooted when Spain joined the European Community. On the other hand, membership of the Atlantic Alliance was what most influenced the professional profile of the military by providing reference points for modernization and giving anchorage to current and future reforms.

The transition and conflict with the military

In one of his comparative studies of Spain's transition to democracy, Juan J. Linz describes three features as being specific to this process.[98] First, the restoration of the monarchy; secondly, the transformation of the unitary state into the State of the Autonomies; thirdly, the need to open up a constituent period in the strict sense of the term by previously dismantling all the institutions of the dictatorship, a task Adolfo Suárez performed with real vision and effectiveness.

These three features greatly influenced the process of transition and also, although in unequal fashion and sometimes indirectly, the levels of conflict between the armed forces and the civil government. In other

---

[97] Similarly, the odd high-ranking officer spoke of the need to ask for compensation in exchange for joining the Alliance. See Mérida: 1979: 143, 200 and 269.
[98] Linz 1992.

countries, for example Greece, the period of military dictatorship was one when democratic freedoms and the democratic constitution were suspended. It was enough to re-establish these freedoms, allow political parties to operate and hold proper elections, to reintroduce a functioning democratic system.

This was not the case in Spain. The period of forty years was too long and the Second Republic was a too short and unruly democratic period in which to establish solid democratic institutions that functioned.

Consequently, and because the Francoist regime had established a series of institutions (the Cortes, Municipal Councils, the Movement, the Single Trade-union), a real constituent process had to be opened up that acquired its own content (monarchy and the state of the autonomies), and the impetus from this would be decisive in helping to consolidate the process, precisely because it was so wide ranging. The forces of reaction, who wanted to put a brake on the transition to democracy, had to confront a process that contained elements that were innovatory yet tangible for most citizens, who could see that what was being built was not 'a' democracy but 'our' democracy. No matter that the latter included elements that challenged the standard military ideology head on, an ideology that had gelled in the years of the dictatorship and was taught in military academies. I am obviously not referring to the monarchy but to the recognition of pluralism as represented by the State of the Autonomies and the legalizing of political parties.

Most leading military cadres found these two elements, which shaped the first years of the transition, at least to the end of 1982, the most difficult to accept.

I agree with Linz that the transition did not develop out of a totalitarian regime, but out of an authoritarian state that from 1959 had set in motion a process of economic liberalization producing high growth in the 1960s, and accelerating the process of urbanizing Spanish society and the creation of a middle class that would be essential for stability and the moderate nature of the process of the transition.

Under Franco, power was not institutionally in the hands of the military, although the military obviously believed they were the guarantors of the continuity of Francoist institutions. For these reasons, the military could not themselves take the decision to open the way to democracy and etch in its features. The protagonists at the beginning of the process were politicians and sectors that had hitherto benefited from Francoism but who now thought it would be impossible to preserve the system and that a move to democracy was necessary. They came together in the Unión del Centro Demócratico (UCD), and counted on the support of the king who kick-started the transition by sacking Arias Navarro as government president and choosing Adolfo Suárez as his successor in 1976.

In any case, although the military in Spain, unlike the situation obtaining in some dictatorships in Latin America, could not begin or sustain the process, they had to accept it and assimilate the various phases of the transition. The dialogue conducted by Suárez with the military high command was very difficult, based on mutual distrust and conditioned by a factor I see as key that I will later analyse: the civil powers did not control the armed forces in any real sense until the mid-1980s. This factor, together with the gradual weakening of the UCD government, marked the relations between the civil powers and the military during the years of transition. It is worth repeating that the degree of conflict between the democratic institutions and the military did not arise from an erroneous policy towards the military, but from the difficulties the military had in assimilating the changes brought by the transition.

Three forms of conflict

Once Adolfo Suárez had been appointed president and begun the process of political reform, the armed forces took shelter behind blanket rejection of the democratic transition, and nourished their position by reading *El Alcázar*, *El Imparcial* and *Fuerza Nueva*, the section of the press that was opposed to the government but, most of all, opposed to democratic institutions and values.

At the beginning of the process and in line with their role as guarantors of the continuity of the previous institutions, the military attempted to determine the process by only accepting reforms that came from the previous legal status quo, which was always in fact the case. However, they were quick to reject the results of such an evolution, even though it took place 'within the law', and the initial conflicts that arose at this stage were always between the government and the military high command. The most significant were the resignations of General de Santiago as government Vice-president in September 1976 because of the legalizing of the trade unions, and of Admiral Pita da Veiga as Minister for the Navy in April 1977, when the Communist Party was legalized.

Throughout the process there were numerous attempts to modify, limit or veto changes brought by the transition to democracy. We have pointed out ones made while the Constitution was being drawn up, and in relation to the amnesty for members of the UMD, the pressure brought was such that it managed to halt the measure from 1977 to November 1986.

There was also resistance to internal changes within the military sphere when traditional practices were challenged. General Milans del Bosch's angry opposition to the promotion of Ibáñez Freire to Lieutenant General[99] and the decision to promote all the generals preceding him on the scale when José Gabeiras was promoted from divisional general to a chief of staff of the Army, testify to the military's collective resistance to the introduction of criteria other than length of service when deciding promotions. The resignations of two chiefs of staff, Admiral Buhigas in November 1977 and General Vega Rodríguez in May 1978, also show the difficulties that were straining the relationship between the Ministry and the JUJEM, and how difficult it was for the military to accept orders from someone of similar rank, particularly at the top of the hierarchy. Even so, when Alberto Oliart, as a civilian minister of defence, decided in the autumn of 1981 to revamp the JUJEM, he met with flat opposition from the Navy's Supreme Council based on the so-called inability of the Navy Ministry to contemplate such a change.[100]

It became evident with the passage of time that these reactions from the military created difficulties and affected the process but did not stop or change it significantly. Two other more serious kinds of conflict came to the surface: visible expressions of indiscipline and opposition to the government on the one hand, and reaction or subversion on the other. The attempted coup d'état of 23 February 1981 showed how these two lines of conflict finally came together because the instigators in both camps were practically the same people. The most serious acts of indiscipline were aimed at General Gutiérrez Mellado when he went on a tour of the military regions to explain the Constitution to the armed forces and also, a few weeks afterwards, at the burial of General Ortín. The subversive acts that are public knowledge go from Operation Galaxia to the attempted coup of 23 February. These have been analysed from a variety of

---

[99] Fernández López 1998: 97–8.   [100] Oliart 2002: 104.

perspectives.[101] I wish to analyse their features and possible policies to underline reactions against the process of democratization pinpointed on the so-called conflict axis.

The rejection of the process of transition and related military policies was widespread among the military. The inflammatory campaign led by *El Alcázar* and *El Imparcial* stirred up reaction among the majority of the armed forces because, with very few exceptions, they were the only newspapers that made their way into the officers' quarters.[102] The hatred and contempt harboured towards General Gutiérrez Mellado as the scapegoat behind the whole process, was of an intensity that is hard to grasp in retrospect. I will revisit this point later, but the general clearly paid a very high price for his acceptance of the need for the transition rather than leading the military's resistance to the latter.

Secondly, though it is obvious that some aspects of military reform conflicted with the practice of the armed forces hitherto, the fundamental reason for the unease was undoubtedly the move towards a lay society and a democracy with political parties that was diametrically opposed to the model of society being defended in the military academies. The question put to General Gutiérrez Mellado at the meeting in Cartagena with officers from the three armies that triggered off the act of insubordination by General Atarés is symptomatic of the lack of understanding with which the military viewed the political changes that were underway. The question came from the captain of a corvette, a rank roughly on a par with a major, and was in this vein:

Vice-president, sir, what are the government's grounds for thinking that the principles behind the lay, liberal Constitution that is going to be put to a referendum will bring peace, prosperity and justice to Spain, if, when governed by those principles from 1812 to 1939, Spain suffered five civil wars, three dethronements, endless spilling of blood and misfortunes that led our Fatherland to a degree of decadence and prostration it had never experienced before?[103]

It would be hard to find a more precise summary of the reasons for rejection of the process of transition being inculcated by a curriculum in military academies that was militantly set against a lay, liberal society.

---

[101] For example Agüero 1995a, Fernández 1982, Fernández López 1998 and Platón 2001.

[102] To borrow an expression used by Busquets 1999: 356f.

[103] I have taken this statement from Platón 2001: 462.

Almost two years later, Milans del Bosch, then captain general in Valencia, encapsulated the attitude of the extreme right in the armed forces after the Constitution had been passed: 'Objectively speaking, the balance-sheet for the transition – so far – is hardly in the black: terrorism, insecurity, inflation, economic crisis, unemployment, pornography, and, above all, a crisis of authority.'[104] Clearly, the examples given are of extreme cases, but they represent fairly accurate snapshots of the general outlook in the armed forces at the time. The big problem was always politics rather than military reform.

Thirdly, terrorism was an element that was stirring up military discontent. In the period of the transition, ETA seriously thought it could impact on the democratic process by mounting terrorist attacks against the military. In my view, these attacks cannot be seen as *the* cause of military discontent, since if they had taken place under Franco, they would only have helped to maintain unity among the military. However, in the context of the transition and, in particular, given the way the extreme right used the funerals of military victims to publicize their views, ETA terrorism served to galvanize an attitude across the armed forces against the evolution of the political system. The protests against General Gutiérrez Mellado were not provoked by the horrific terrorist acts aimed at the military, but by the difficulties, that were insuperable in the short term, of the move from a Francoist to a democratic army and, to a lesser, but nevertheless related degree, of the problematic shift from an institutional to an occupational army.

Fourthly, it is worth noting the tolerance displayed by the leaders of the armed forces and military courts towards acts of indiscipline and insubordination at the time. It is not just that there was a double standard in terms of expressions of support for democracy from within the forces: attitudes of indiscipline and even of rebellion from the extreme right were treated lightly and covered up. It is evident that military courts and channels of discipline were used to punish democrats and protect the extreme right. What happened to coup-leader Tejero is ample proof of that. In January 1977 he sent a telegram to the Minister for the Interior telling him how to deal with the Basque flag; in October of that same year he issued orders to break up a demonstration in Málaga calling for the right to vote at eighteen, one that had been authorized by the civil governor. In August 1978 he dared to publish an

---

[104] Mérida 1979: 197–8.

open letter to the king that seriously infringed usual military practice for communicating with higher-ranking officers. Finally, in November 1978 he participated in the attempted attack, known as 'Operation Galaxia', on the offices of the government president. In every case, he got away with the most lenient of sentences. He was imprisoned for seven months for attempted conspiracy against the government, a sentence that can be contrasted with the severity of the eight years imprisonment meted out to those involved in the UMD, curiously enough both deemed to be guilty of similar crimes.[105] The military justice system was so corporate it could not even help rid the armed forces of their undesirable members.

General Atarés, who had gravely insulted General Gutiérrez Mellado and attacked the Constitution, was let off scot-free. The only disciplinary course of action left open to the Vice-president was to sack people, since the officers subordinate to him shared the same lax attitudes as the military as a whole towards indiscipline from the extreme right. This attitude can only be explained by the fact that, broadly speaking, opinions across the armed forces were against the political developments that were being introduced. What might be called 'institutional feeling' increases the possibility of conflict with democratic institutions and makes them more violent. The first sanctions given out for an act of indiscipline were in response to the so-called 'manifesto of the hundred', signed and made public by a hundred young officers – petty-officers and captains – in support of the military involved in the 23 February coup attempt. Although this came after the failed coup, the Minister, Alberto Oliart, had to intervene directly to ensure the military high command changed their traditional attitudes of protection and tolerance.[106]

After this summary analysis of conflicts during this period, some conclusions can be drawn as to the policies and tools necessary to handle such problems. These are highly conditioned by the Spanish context and may be of little help in other scenarios.

The previous chapter showed that the most important factor in terms of resolving conflicts with the military is the strength of the general process of transition in itself. That is true in the midterm, since in the short term the pace of the transition may be a source of conflict when it happens at a rate the military cannot handle. The absence of inner tensions was also mentioned. It is clear that ETA terrorism sharpened

[105] See Fernández López 1998: 132.　　[106] Oliart 2002: 102.

hostility towards the process of democratization, but it should also be borne in mind that the most crucial factor was the need to agree entirely new forms of coexistence within a plural Spain, through the creation of the State of the Autonomies and that this concept conflicted head on with Francoist concepts of the nation. In the case of Spain, a series of factors helped reduce the level of conflict, such as entry into NATO or consensus with the opposition over issues that were central to the transition but which are unlikely to be found in other countries. It is also true that the factors that reduce conflict usually kick in during the middle term, while those that heighten conflict levels do so in the short term.

As pointed out in the previous chapter, the king's role in keeping these confrontations under control was central. It is not just that he acted decisively on the night of the 23 February, but that he acted as a unique, continuous brake on positions contrary to the process through the support he gave to the legitimate government.[107]

Another very specific feature of the Spanish situation is the role of General Gutiérrez Mellado as the irreplaceable initiator of reform – no civilian would have been able to implement this as extensively and as knowledgeably – but which made him the target of all resistance to the transition from within the armed forces. The general's actions were providential because he deprived the armies of a member of the government they could rely on to represent their attitudes of opposition to democratic change.[108] He was always a military member of government who took on the difficult task of initiating military reform, and was never a military representing the armed forces before the government. Moreover, he introduced a programme of reforms that, as he always explained in advance, was about 'remilitarizing' the military, although he obviously never used this expression or the word 'reform', preferring to talk about modernization. A civilian could never have conceived or carried through such a raft of reforms. It meant he aroused anger and

---

[107] A good example of this is his speech on the occasion of the military new year ceremony in 1979 when he made a vigorous call for discipline in the wake of the incidents at the funeral of General Ortín.

[108] When General de Santiago resigned he sent a note to several military commanders-in-chief explaining that when he rejected the legalization of the trade unions 'neither my conscience nor my sense of honour allow me to take responsibility and even less implicate the Armed Forces via the representative role they grant me' See Platón 2001: 404.

hatred throughout the entire military, but we must repeat that military policy was only a pretext, and that the armed forces were above all reacting to the way the political situation was evolving. After the 1979 elections, it became clear that a civilian minister had to be appointed.

Alberto Oliart has pointed to three measures he took to restore discipline and calm in the armed forces after 23 February.[109] First, entry into NATO, secondly, the change in the membership of the JUJEM and thirdly, sensitive handling of all the problems related to the trial of those involved in the attempted coup. They were three necessary measures at that time, but experience in Spain demonstrates that the most important factor for controlling conflict with the military is the strength and legitimacy of the process of transition itself.

Backed by this, two lines of action suggest themselves. First, and in terms of issues linked to the autonomy of the military, especially those specified on the professional axis, it is necessary to undertake a process of gradual reform, as far as possible, in order to encourage gradual acceptance of the new contexts being created and to avoid forcing the military down a cul-de-sac in terms of what their mindset enables them to accept.

In terms of their prerogatives and ability to intervene in political life, on the institutional reform axis, it is advisable to act quickly. The sustaining of a centre of power like the Supreme Council for Military Justice is a good example. It hindered control of the process and opened the way to situations on the axis of conflict that were not nipped in the bud, due to the military leadership's lack of ability or will to impose discipline, and which would have been less likely to arise if that organ of power had been dismantled.

---

[109] See Oliart 2002: 103.

6 | *Consolidation and military reform in Spain*

The state of the military at the end of 1982

If we were to sum up the evolution of relations between civil society and the military from the beginning of the transition to autumn 1982, when democratic Spain experienced its first change of government, we could say that very considerable advances had been made in terms of military intervention in political life, the reduction of military autonomy and the establishing of normal, democratic relations. These advances, however, were made at the cost of a high level of conflict expressed in the attempted coup in February 1981, the subsequent letter dubbed the 'Manifesto of the Hundred', and another coup nipped in the bud by CESID that was being prepared for the day of reflection immediately prior to the elections on 28 October 1982.

If we continue with our graphic model of the process on the three axes introduced in chapter 3, the process at the end of 1982 looked something like that shown in Figure 6.1. Point X82 (autumn 1982) would be located on the line dividing levels three and four of military autonomy described in chapter 3, that is between the military's ability to determine and even prevent some government decisions on the one hand and the use of corporate energies to defend organizational and operational autonomy, on the other. In fact, the Spanish armed forces had been preparing their autonomy in anticipation of the new political situation that might arise after General Franco's death years before his actual demise, as seen in the previous chapter. The location of X82 in relation to the remaining axes is more subjective and debatable: although it is not easy to measure exactly levels of autonomy or the influence on political life of the armed forces, it is easier to gauge the situation in terms of the institutional reform axis than on what we have called the professional reform axis. Progress was less evident on the latter, as reflected in Figure 6.1. Finally, at this moment in time, the level of conflict between government and military was at its zenith, although

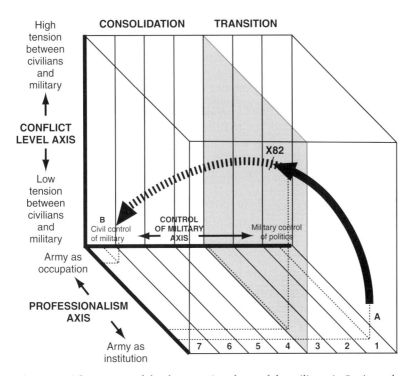

Figure 6.1. The process of the democratic reform of the military in Spain at the end of 1982

possibly beginning to decline. Given the existing levels of conflict, the great unknown factor then was whether elements within the military would try to sustain an insurgent position, by risking new coups, or whether the process of the democratic normalization of the armed forces would go forward.

Continued military reform involved a three-pronged operation. On the institutional axis, it was necessary to remove situations and ambiguities that could endanger consolidation and to proceed with the reforms highlighted in the previous period towards the goal of the supremacy of civil society. On the professional axis, the task ahead was complex because it demanded many very different actions in such distinct fields as allowing women into the forces or initiating missions abroad. Changes in mentality require time, suitable policies and favourable conditions. Finally, it was more difficult to programme what had to be done on the level of conflict axis. Fortunately, the government's

massive electoral victory gave it enormous strength and moral authority. Nobody could interpret the large-scale support coming from society
and the practical rout of the political forces from Francoist times as
anything but a call to complete the process of consolidation and open
out Spanish democracy.

As noted in the previous chapter, the process of reform (and the
Constitution itself) had not put the cap on certain issues. It had left
them defined in such a way as to make it difficult to bring the military
correctly within the state administration or at best was ambiguous in
this respect. Four issues had to be resolved:

1. The implementation of the commander-in-chief of the armed forces
   role the Constitution granted to the king meant it would be possible
   to think of a connection between armies and the state at this level and
   the subordination to the elected government would not yet be an
   intrinsic part of the relationship between armed forces and the state.
2. The creation of the JUJEM (Joint Chiefs of Staff) as an instrument of
   collective command, thus implying that the minister was not overall
   in command of the forces and therefore opening the way to the
   representation of corporate interests at this level.
3. The distinction drawn between military and political–administrative
   lines of command that led to a reserve domain for the military and
   one set apart from the politicians assigned to the area of defence.
4. The exclusion of the forces, that is the three armies strictly speaking,
   from the organic structure of the Ministry of Defence, which meant
   the armies could build an area of autonomy around themselves.

Obviously these four positions combined to bolster each other. In
more than one respect they received support in debates in parliament
from Alianza Popular, a party that encouraged attitudes in favour of the
autonomy of the military. *El Alcázar*, needless to say, went much
further and proposed the most extreme interpretation of the ambiguous
formulations referred to when it repeatedly denied any possibility that
the Ministry of Defence could represent the armed forces. This view was
probably the one preferred by the armed forces in the first years of the
transition. Consequently the four issues constituted a Gordian knot that
had to be tackled *en bloc* if they were to be resolved.

This equivocal situation could not last for long, and sooner rather
than later the situation would have to lean either towards consolidation
of an autonomous space for the armed forces or continuation along the

path of subordination to the civil powers. The democratic transition in Spain was developing too promisingly for a 'Turkish solution' to arise. By a Turkish solution, I mean one in which the military command is above the civilian ministry and the military 'institution' dialogues with the other political institutions of state and even arbitrates between them or acts as guardian to certain features of the Constitution.

The untying of the Gordian knot was the real challenge to be faced on the axes of institutional change or reduction of military autonomy. It was a task that was more difficult to implement than to imagine conceptually and was central to the continuation and conclusion of the reform undertaken in the transition. This view has been opposed by defenders of the 'two reforms' thesis. Ramón Parada, for example, has written:

[T]here was not one military reform, but two: the reform under the UCD government, piloted by General Gutiérrez Mellado, and the reform under the socialist government, led by Minister Narciso Serra, in which the norms for reforming the command structure of the Armed Forces, the judiciary and Public Service of the military were established. These reforms are not all on a par and the difference derives, in my opinion, from the fact that the first respected the concept within the 1978 Constitution whereas the second went against its wish for the institutional–legal profile of the Armed Forces to be maintained.[1]

This was not the only voice in favour of concluding the reform before military autonomy was reduced. However, it is essential to signal that there was no second reform, but rather a single process 'to embed the figure of the Head of State and the military apparatus emerging from Francoism in the explicit order defined by the Spanish Constitution of 1978'.[2] There were of course two clearly differentiated phases within the process, but in practice every reforming action taken in the stage of consolidation, and the measures then implemented, had been premised by the reform during the transition. An obvious example is the whole-scale reform of the Military Penal Code in the mid-1980s that continued what had been started in 1980. However, we must emphasize that the key reform in the period of consolidation, the 1984 Organic Law of Defence, was only possible because of General Gutiérrez Mellado's

---

[1] See Parada 1997: 10. A similar opinion is put forward in Platón 2001.
[2] See Lleixà 1986: 104.

decision to prevent the Spanish Constitution granting the JUJEM institutional status.

One can even divide this stage of military reform into two parts for the period of democratic consolidation: before and after the 1986 referendum on whether Spain should remain in NATO. In the first period, attention was primarily focused on internal issues and legislative reform. The second included the agreements with NATO, the Western European Union (WEU) and the renewal of the treaty with the US that led to a considerable reduction of its presence in Spanish bases. This was when the most important reforms were enacted on the professional change axis.

Nonetheless such subdivisions of the process that enable a better understanding of the goals and difficulties at each stage cannot be used as evidence to support the idea that two separate reforms existed in the transition to and consolidation of democracy in Spain. The democratic reform of the military can only be fully understood when grasped as a single process of evolution towards the proper articulation of the armed forces within the new Spanish political system. The process clearly continued apace after the elections as a result of the strengthening of the government's authority by the overall majority it won in both chambers through the ballot box. Felipe Agüero has underlined this fact by asserting that it opened 'the stage of the consolidation of Spanish democracy' and also that 'from 1982 there was no repeat of military political opposition to the democratic regime. From this moment, military opposition focussed strictly on corporate issues and attempts at resistance were transformed into strategies for adaptation'.[3]

This is accurate and distinguishes the features of this part of the process, although one factor that weighed heavily at that time must also be borne in mind: the memory of the attempted coup d'état in February 1981. The government and many citizens were obsessed with preventing any future coups, and that led to a focus on controlling the armed forces, hunting out and punishing every act of indiscipline, detecting all officers with anti-democratic ideological leanings in order to relieve them of positions of responsibility, etc. This obsession with avoiding another coup might have been an obstacle to reaching a correct perspective on reform, inasmuch as it encouraged police investigations and control of the activity of officers (speeches, meetings, etc.)

---

[3] Agüero 1995a: 301.

rather than concentrating energy on changing structures and creating a legal framework to shape army attitudes that would accept subordination to the civil power as the only possible situation in a democracy. Striking a balance between controlling the military and maintaining discipline on the one hand, and inspiring motivation and necessary collaboration in order to construct and apply a new framework of relationships on the other, is one of the most difficult challenges in a period of consolidation.

As stated already, concentration on the need for vigilance and control would have meant slowing down or paralysing the reform process. A more serious error would have been to embark on a process of cleansing the armies of members who might not be committed to democratic ideas. This would have provoked a corporate reaction and prevented the assimilation, however limited, of the aims of the reform. Besides, such an ideological cleansing was totally impractical. Minister Alberto Oliart told *El País*: 'I remember Raymond Carr, the historian, asking me a stupid question: "Why didn't you clean up the army?" "Because if I clean up the army on the basis of people's ideas, I'll be left with twenty soldiers"'.[4] Azaña had held a similar view forty years earlier. In his study of military reform during the Second Republic, Michael Alpert states: 'for him [Azaña], democratization of the officer class had more to do with laws, decrees and systematic endeavour by the intelligence services than purges of individual officers'.[5]

The government formed at the end of 1982 soon realized it was essential to clarify lines of command and the government's relationship with the armed forces if this problem was to be properly resolved. Two events of a different order, the first in the early days of Felipe González's government and the second a year later, reinforced the necessity for wide-sweeping reforms. The first was the need to decide a position in terms of the Atlantic Alliance a few days after the new government had been formed, given that the Atlantic Council (the meeting of NATO foreign ministers) had been called early in December. It was decided to put Spain's situation in the Alliance 'on ice'. As Spain belonged to almost all its bodies, that meant there was continuity in the form of association. It was clear that withdrawal from the Alliance would have mortgaged the continuity of the military reform process by depriving the armed forces of clear reference points in terms of modernizing and

[4] See Santos Juliá 1996: 354. [5] See Alpert 1982: 47.

openness and tackling new missions. This was a vital decision that
enabled the reform process to fulfil its goals for this period. It also
helped to highlight the need to modernize the armed forces, to start
work on the professional reform axis without delay and alongside
gestures such as the President's visit on 8 December to El Goloso, the
headquarters of the Armoured Division whose commander, General
Lagos, had been assassinated by ETA only weeks before, helped to
reduce – or stabilize – the levels of conflict that existed between the
military as a whole and the democratic government.

The second act did not become public knowledge or was not even
communicated to most members of the government: the decision – in
the end abortive – taken by the Supreme Council for Military Justice to
give a partial pardon at Christmas 1983 to those sentenced for their
involvement in the 23 February 1981 coup. The government prevented
the Council from taking this decision, although the government had no
legal powers in this regard at that time. A pardon, however partial,
against the wishes of the government would have led to a huge surge of
public opinion against the armed forces, and seriously undermined the
government's authority. The Supreme Council for Military Justice's
attempt to intervene pinpointed the problems still being created by the
areas of autonomy enjoyed by the military, and the fact that the elimination of these could not be rushed, although it was urgent to act.
Consequently, the reform of the military justice system was seen as a
priority in the first phase of the reform programme. In any case, by
taking every opportunity and creating new ones when necessary without any exposure in the press, when it was time to implement the phase
of the reform of military justice that closed down the Supreme Council,
those who had voted for the pardons were no longer members.

The reform continued, although the programme of measures and
actions that had to be taken was not worked out immediately or
planned before the elections by the Socialist Party. Details in the
Socialist Party programme pointed the way but did not amount to an
overall policy for reform: subordination of the armed forces to civil
power, a civilian minister, a reduction in the retirement age for officers,
reincorporation of the UMD soldiers who had been expelled and modernization of the armed forces. The 21st Congress of the Socialist Party,
in 1981, voted for proposals to rejuvenate the leadership of the armed
forces, modify criteria for promotion, incorporate civilians into the
Defence Ministry and to reject, although not entirely explicitly, the

line dividing the forces from the political–administrative area of state: 'Even today, the Minister for Defence is only secretary to the Joint Chiefs of General Staff'.[6] The materials that already existed and the work of the embryonic Defence Ministry were used to prepare a plan of action that was outlined to the Defence Committee in the Congress of Deputies in February 1983 although it was only completed ten months after the government was formed, that is to say, in September.

In retrospect, four features in the consolidation of civilian–military relations can be highlighted as being central to its success. First, the act of implementing a *general programme* that responded to the need to advance along the three axes, though not, as yet, at all in a conscious way. The speech introducing the Organic Law for National Defence in the Senate in December 1983 proposed a reform programme that included the Law itself, the creation of a genuine ministry of defence and the reform of military justice as measures we can include on the institutional reform axis. The programme set out also included laws on staffing levels (to reduce the size of the armed forces), a centralized setting of a project-oriented budget, measures to include on the professional reform axis, and proposed a new Law on Remuneration that aimed to reduce conflict and better integrate the armed forces into Spanish society.[7] The drawing up of a general reform programme is not a must in the transition period, but a global vision of the process is always a great help, and is a necessity in the consolidation stage. As the process advances along the three axes towards the area of democratic normalcy, the coordination of measures and proper sequencing of their implementation become more essential. If we think it necessary to advance more substantially along the three axes in order to reach the situation of democratic normality that prompted their existence, obviously only an overall programme can take this interrelation into account. It is much more difficult to act simultaneously across the three fields during the period of transition. Ministers Agustín Rodríguez Sahagún (1979–81) and Alberto Oliart (1981–82) had to devote the bulk of their time to managing the conflicts and tension then existing in the military. This kind of situation does not usually arise once a process of consolidation is underway.

The second feature is *the timing and sequencing of measures* in the programme. Changes cannot be made to the curriculum in military

---

[6] Agüero 1995a: 307–8. [7] See Cortes Generales 1984: 520–2.

academies, for example, if the subordination of the military to the government has not been established, nor can the issue of the functional dependency of the organs of the three armies be resolved before a ministry of defence has been created which has a minimum leverage to exert its control. In terms of sequencing, it is essential to set goals that can be reached within the not too distant future: for example, in the case of Spain, the four-year period of a legislature or the length of a presidency in Latin America. It must be understood that passing laws is not enough: one must be sure they are implemented before proceeding to the next measures. The order of measures will vary according to the features of each consolidation process, but in general the axis of institutional reforms must be given priority, given that the other two depend on its development.

Thirdly, an attempt must be made to develop defence policy and even military policy that are *policies of state* and not of the party that happens to govern at a particular time. Reform guidelines must be established that are uncontroversial, even from a legal perspective. Laws for reforming the organization of defence should be based on arguments taken from comparative law rather than through a debate on the correct interpretation of the Constitution. In the case of consolidation in Spain, another example of this attitude was the retention in post of individuals who had been appointed by the outgoing government even though it was a rival party, the UCD. Obviously the largest possible support in parliament must be sought, and an increasing number of elected representatives must begin to understand, knowledgeably discuss and support the policies that are being implemented.

Fourthly, both the reform programme and its implementation were very dependent on the government *taking the initiative* in the whole process. It is essential that government sets the pace and orders the process, while constantly revising, if necessary, the programmes that have been devised and ensuring that events themselves do not decide the agenda.

In fact, the process involves gradually moving towards a situation equivalent to well-honed democracies that have essentially identical problems in the field of civilian–military relations. What is at stake is the management of the area of military autonomy that has been decided or accepted by civil authorities: the control of the tensions arising between democratic government and a group with expertise in a particular area, on the one hand, and between government and a very specific part of the state administration, on the other.[8] The aim cannot be to reach a stage in which problems in civilian–military relations do not exist, but to achieve a situation in which civil supremacy is not questioned and problems are located within the parameters established in already existing democracies. This is why Schmitter believes that generalizations based on the different experiences drawn from concrete cases make more sense in the period of consolidation than in that of transition.[9]

In effect, Spanish experience in the area of military policy offers some elements from which one can generalize and bear in mind prior to embarking on similar processes in other countries, provided that factors specific to Spain are taken into account, some of which are unlikely to be present in other situations. The figure of King Juan Carlos is one such factor. We should recall that the interpretation of the expression 'commander-in-chief' in the Constitution was one of the cornerstones bolstering the vision of the armed forces as an institution that was not integrated into the state administration. In this respect, the great achievement of the king in the early 1980s was to ensure that this was not the case. If in the transition his endorsement strengthened the process in relation to the military, and if later on it was decisive in isolating and stifling attempted coups, from 1983 his contribution to democratic consolidation came from the support he gave to the reform programme and the subordination of the armed forces to civil power.

As in the preceding chapter, we will examine the process in the light of the three axes along which we have divided the policies that shape democratic reform of the military.

Legislative and institutional reform in the period of consolidation

We have seen that the crucial tasks on this axis in the period of transition centred on the reduction of the space for military autonomy and the integration of the armed forces into a democratic structure in their relations with government. The distinctive feature of the period of consolidation is the government's drawing up of military and defence policies. To that end the government must clearly set out the way it

---

[8] Bruneau and Tollefson 2006: 3.   [9] Schmitter 1995: 562.

intends to lead the armed forces, and provide itself with a ministry capable of formulating such policies.

In chapter 5 we saw that in terms of reducing military autonomy, once the problems of military intervention in politics have been resolved, the next task is to prevent the military establishing functional and organizational autonomy. In this sense I have described the three stages preceding what I call democratic control of the armed forces: the stages of organizational and operational autonomy, partial acceptance of civil supremacy, and retention of ideological control by the military. The basic legislative move in order to overcome the first was the 1984 Organic Law and the creation of a ministry; for the second it was the reform of the military justice system; for the third, the reforms of military education and criteria for promotions.

Thus the way forward on what we have labelled the institutional axis is as follows:

- Establishing efficient control mechanisms over the armed forces and taking charge of military policy.
- Defining military and defence policies.
- Integrating the armed forces into the state administration.

The most important acts in the first line of action were the changes to the 1980 Organic Law of Defence and the setting up of the Ministry of Defence; in terms of the third, it was the reform of the military justice system.

The Organic Law regulating the basic criteria for National Defence and military organisation (LODNOM 84)

This legal text was prepared in the first nine months of government to ensure that all the necessary elements were included to make it clear that the armed forces must be subject to the elected government. As Felipe Agüero has pointed out 'The government wanted to insert the Executive unambiguously in the chain of command and authority, and thus prevent the re-emergence of the autonomy that had traditionally informed the idea of "Military Power"'.[10] That is why the new law included the following five significant changes to existing regulations:

---

[10] Agüero 1995a: 309.

- Assigning to the president direct and effective leadership by ensuring he is responsible for defence policy and 'exercises his authority in order to phase, coordinate and lead the activities of the Armed Forces'. That resolved the ambiguities in previous regulations.
- Assigning these duties also to the Minister for Defence, but always as delegated by the president and by adding 'exercises the capacity to enforce regulations and discipline as assigned by law' in order to point to his role in maintaining discipline.
- Creating the figure of the Chief of Defence Staff, or JEMAD, as 'the Minister's main collaborator in establishing and implementing key aspects of military policy', emphasizing his organic, functional dependency on the minister.
- Transforming the Joint Chiefs of Staff, by changing its nature as the maximum organ in the chain of command established by the LODNOM 80 to that of consultant and adviser to the president and the minister for defence.
- Reforming the National Defence Commission (Junta de Defensa Nacional) by restricting its functions to those of advising the king and the president.

In terms of the president's responsibilities, the aim of the legal changes was to concretize his role as the true commander-in-chief of the armed forces.[11] As a result, apart from being in control in times of war, as stipulated in the 1980 law, the reform now gave him the leadership role in 'formulating policy for negotiations with foreign powers and defining the main lines of thought for strategy and military policy'. Finally, the law reiterates that the president 'defines key strategic goals, approves the plans that derive from this definition, the general disposition of the forces and measures established to provide for the needs of the Armies'. This concentration of power was criticized by Alianza Popular, who indicated that it corresponded more to the government as such than to the president.[12] However, in an effort to clarify the chain of command, by suppressing collective bodies and structuring it around individuals, it

---

[11] This is also the opinion of Iglesias 2001: 59, Lleixà 1986: 114 and Blanco Valdés 1988: 162, who declares that 'after the passing of Law 1/1984, 5 January, reforming the LODNOM, the President has now become the central state figure in the leadership of defence and military policies, that is, the key figure in national defence'.

[12] See Cortes Generales 1984: 466.

was necessary to follow the same route in terms of the government and the head of government. Clearly, this powerful formulation is incompatible with the demarcation between the armed forces and the political–administrative departments of government present within the process of the transition to that point. In this way, one of the most dangerous ambiguities in previous legislation was resolved without even giving it a mention, a change reinforced by the integration of the forces within the organic structure of the ministry that we shall examine in due course.

If the aim, in terms of the president, was to define him as the true head of the armed forces, then in terms of the minister of defence, the aim – and this was achieved – was to establish him as the key figure in military and defence policies and in the management of reform. That was why he was assigned leadership of the president's defence policy as delegated by him, and additionally that 'he oversees the training and operational effectiveness of the armed forces and carries out the legal and disciplinary responsibilities assigned to him by law'. The same article described much more precise and wide-sweeping competencies than those set out in the previous law, indicating that it is his duty 'To draw up, decide and implement military policy', responsibilities that are his own and not delegated by the president. One could say that defence policy depends on the president and military policy on the minister. The responsibility for 'formulating the Joint Strategic Plan and within that deciding Combined Goals for the Forces' that in previous legislation was given over the JUJEM, now fell to the minister in tandem with the former's new consultative role. The rest of the article lists requisites for the economic programme for defence, purchasing policy and leadership of military administration. It is worthwhile highlighting the definition of roles in terms of staffing. This was a particularly delicate question in terms of what had become one of the last redoubts of military autonomy. The 1984 law established that it is the minister's duty 'To direct, coordinate and control the staffing policy of the Armed Forces, by overseeing education and administering social policy therein.' It included, moreover, a mention of education in connection with the creation of an Educational Council, as anticipated in the decree reorganizing the ministry that was already written and that was approved immediately after the law was promulgated. The modification of military education is an issue we shall scrutinize in terms of the professionalism axis and is certainly not one to be tackled in the early stages of consolidation.

The creation of the figure of the Chief of Defence Staff or JEMAD was in line with the single-person chain of command that was being proposed and that clearly put Spain on the same footing as other democratic European countries and countries that belonged to NATO, with the exception of Turkey and, in part, of Portugal. In terms of his job description, it is worth underlining an issue that may be highly significant in processes of transition: caution must be exercised over new laws and they must only be introduced when their content is ready and guarantees exist that they can be implemented. Decrees, on the other hand, can reflect potential at a particular moment and can be changed as reality changes or when there is a realistic opportunity to adopt a specific policy.

This was the case with the definition of the roles of the JEMAD: after the 1984 law, his roles were spelt out in the Royal Decree once the ministry had been restructured, fine-tuned in the subsequent decree modifying the organization of the ministry in 1987 and in other decrees that culminated in the Royal Decree 265/1996 that gave him operational command of the forces that carry out missions established by the Joint Strategic Plan and also coordination of the armed forces' involvement in organizations or alliances of a military nature. The problems in deciding the JEMAD's roles were complex. From the start, what was envisaged was a head of operational command of the armed forces, but care was needed to avoid the creation of a post that could abrogate institutional representation of the armed forces or the corporate interests of the military as a whole. Consequently, the legal texts were written with great care, so there was no doubt about the scope for autonomy in the leading of military operations. A gradual process of development bound up with the change in the nature of military missions allowed the definition of his functions to be fine-tuned. The creation of the post of JEMAD was central to the reform process, not only because it contributed to the normalizing in a democratic sense of the relationship between government and the armed forces, but also because it was a powerful tool for modernizing military structures and putting them on a similar footing to other armies that became reference points in the period of consolidation.

The most radical change within the 1984 law undoubtedly centred on the JUJEM, which went from being a collegiate body of command to one with strictly advisory capacities. This meant that the minister frequently chaired it, a powerful public sign that areas of operational autonomy were unacceptable. Here one must reiterate the importance of General Gutiérrez Mellado's decision that the Joint Chiefs of Staff should not be included in the Spanish Constitution as a body with a leadership role. One must also reiterate the need to articulate the relationship between government and armed forces through a chain of command of individuals who answer entirely to their superior. It must then be made clear that the minister is the head of this hierarchy on every front. This is how one must interpret article 12 of the law that establishes that the Chiefs of Staff exercise the command of their respective armies 'under the aegis of the Ministry of Defence on which they are directly dependent'.

The 1984 law was consistent in relation to the National Defence Commission (Junta de Defensa Nacional) both in its focus, that opposed collective decision-making bodies, and in its wish to make defence and military policy entirely dependent on government. Consequently, in the list of duties of this committee it was no longer called on 'to formulate and propose military policy to Government and guidelines for possible non-military contributions to the overall defence of the nation'. That task was replaced by the call to provide advisory reports on issues decided by government. Under the new law those responsibilities now fell to the minister for defence.

These five briefly outlined elements created the structure necessary to manage the process of consolidation. The 1984 law, in fact, largely dismantled formulas and barriers put in place in the last years of the Franco regime to defend the military autonomy that had survived till then. Contrary to the opinion voiced by Michael Alpert in his study of Azaña's military reform that 'military reforms have been introduced in Spain through decree-laws or have not survived' (a decree-law becomes active immediately and may or may not then be passed as an ordinary law), the 1984 reform law was debated in both chambers, although it was dealt with as a priority. As far as possible, it is best if all laws, and even policies, in the period of consolidation go through parliament in order to link them to the reform process and give them maximum legitimacy, something that is rarely possible in the stage of transition. Only one of the eleven norms with the status of law promulgated in the area of defence in 1984 was a decree-law: the one that referred to the deferring of the retirement age of the Chiefs of Staff so they could stay in post for additional time, even though they had reached the statutory age for retirement. This was a disposition that allowed the JUJEM to keep its members for the duration of a legislature if such was the wish of the government. In 1985, only one of the six dispositions with legal status was a decree-law. It was the disposition that a year and a half later completed the elimination of the collective decision-making bodies and granted an advisory role to the Higher Councils of each branch of the armed forces.

The opportunity arose to do this when a Higher Council excluded an officer for ideological reasons from its annual listing of officers for promotion to general or admiral. If I previously suggested that it would be a mistake to embark on a policy of purges or for the minister to make his selection entirely on ideological grounds, it is similarly necessary to prevent the armed forces from reaching decisions purely based on ideology. A decision had to be taken whether to oblige the Higher Council to reconsider its decision or to eliminate the decision-making powers that some collegiate bodies still retained, and the second option was taken: within a week the government approved a decree-law that changed the nature of the Higher Councils by transforming them into collegiate consultancy bodies that reported to the Minister of Defence and their respective Chief of Staff. At the same time their decision-making capacities were transferred to the Chiefs of Staff. In the matter of promotions to the rank of general, the traditional shortlist of three was changed to a list of all the officers who in the qualifying year met or might meet the objective criteria for promotion, ones that specified the suitability or fitness of each individual candidate for promotion. In other words, it was made plain that the criteria for promotion to general was the preserve of the government, who would take advice from competent bodies within the armed forces, but with which it would not enter into negotiation over final decisions.

The First Law of 1984 had already modified another attribute of the Higher Councils by establishing that 'the Chiefs of Staff of the three armed forces will be designated by Royal Decree agreed in the Council of Ministers and proposed by the Minister for Defence after hearing the Chief of Defence Staff and the Higher Council of the respective army'. This modified the previous system under which the Councils proposed a shortlist of three from which the minister would choose, in favour of a mechanism through which the initiative remains the minister's without restrictions or corporate negotiations with the Supreme Councils. It is another example of the criteria that I believe to be essential for relations between government and armed forces: to always listen before taking decisions, but never to negotiate those decisions.

Apart from reaffirming the authority of the minister, both in its content and its provisional requirement that obliged the Higher Councils to accept the most recent modifications carried out, the decree-law of 10 July 1985 duly completed the task of reconfiguring the collegiate bodies with decision-making remits that still survived in the forces, thus bringing to a conclusion the action started by the 1984 law.

Finally, it is also useful to look at some aspects of the parliamentary debate around the draft law. The law was broadly accepted in the Congress of Deputies: Alianza Popular, however, tried to reduce the powers of the president and restore the JUJEM's commanding role and, in a lower key, the nationalist parties rejected the de-legalizing of military territorial divisions.[13] When the law was debated in the Senate, Alianza Popular joined the consensus and the law was finally passed with 282 votes in favour, 9 against and 2 abstentions. One of the reasons for this consensus was the fact that the law was introduced as a continuation of the reforms begun in 1977, as one more link in the chain of reforms begun at that time. It was also introduced as the product of common sense. The Report from the Ministry of Defence justified it by arguing the need to be able to facilitate joint action by the three forces and allow proper execution of military operations. Both the minister's speeches and those of Socialist Party spokesmen put the emphasis on comparative law, on the need to place the command structure of the Spanish defence system on a par with their neighbours, rather than invoking a debatable implementation of the Constitution.[14] In fact, the recourse to comparative experience supposed an acceptance of the way in which the project was developed, namely by reflecting on the difficulties surrounding the leadership of the armed forces in Spain through the prism of knowledge of the situations in Germany and

---

[13] The law anticipated that the government would be able to modify the military regions by decree because it was intent on reducing them, at least the Army's, but the intention was to do this as some Captain-Generals entered the reserve, in order to minimize tensions that might arise as a result of this reduction. The number of peninsular military regions was reduced from nine to six, basically by combining adjacent regions, as can be seen in Ministry of Defence 1986: 111f.

[14] The Minister in his speech to the Senate affirmed: 'I insist yet again that the solution is in no way original, because it is simply an adaptation of solutions adopted by many countries, by practically every country in Europe'. Cortes Generales, 1984: 520.

France in particular.[15] Felipe Agüero has pointed out the similarity between the prerogatives of the Spanish minister and those of his German counterpart who 'directs, controls and administers the Bundeswehr'. It is hardly surprising, given the background in Spain, that the preferred model had been conceived after the Second World War precisely to make it crystal clear that the German armed forces were subordinate to democratic government.

Strengthening the Ministry of Defence

The Royal Decree 135/1984, promulgated on 25 January, was conceived in parallel and as a necessary complement to the LODNOM 84. If the law proposed an increase in the remits of government, and in particular, of the president and minister of defence, the Royal Decree aimed to equip the government with an instrument to enable it to exercise these remits, namely a powerful ministry of defence on a par with those in neighbouring countries. The Royal Decree also complemented the law reducing military autonomy, since it integrated the armed forces within the structure of the ministry.

In this way the two dispositions, together with a determined implementation of their spirit and letter, resolved the problem of the watertight divisions set up between the forces and the political-administrative spheres. It has been pointed out repeatedly that this permeability is necessary for democratic control of the armed forces, but they must function effectively. The appearance of new missions for the Spanish armed forces, especially in the international arena, clearly required coordinated action across the whole department. Conversely, control from the legislature both of the civilian minister and the other civilian figures of authority within the department is easier than direct parliamentary control of military command. Consequently, by increasing its role in giving a lead in defence, the legislature's ability to control the executive increases in this field.

The decree structured the ministry in three important areas, the first led by the JEMAD was strictly military; the second, of an economic

---

[15] The defence ministers of Germany, Manfred Werner, and of France, Charles Hernu, had a special advisory brief for the new situation in Spain, and in the first six months of the Socialist government there were visits between both countries in both directions.

nature, was led by a secretary of state and the third, involving personnel and organizational issues, was in the hands of an under-secretary, while the Civil Guard became directly dependent on the minister, in its military role, and CESID, the intelligence services. This decree raised the status of under-secretary for defence to secretary of state, which gave him pre-eminence over the chiefs of staff who were assimilated at under-secretary level. It is opportune to begin to coordinate and control the armed forces in the area of economic issues, budget, purchases and research, for two main reasons. Firstly, they are less delicate issues than those involving personnel, which the military consider – rightly in part – as falling into their area of autonomy. Secondly, they are issues where the department may be more effective in the short term, and that is why these changes are more easily accepted.

The reform process is viewed critically, above all in relation to two aspects that require detailed attention, in the work *Hablan los militares* by Miguel Platón, the interest of which derives from the fact it was written in collaboration with various military figures who held posts of responsibility and high rank in this phase. First, he claims:

> [T]he organisation of the ministry in general, and of the central office in particular, suffered from a basic confusion: it confused the political, the military and the administrative, and did not demarcate distinct areas of competency. The most blatant example was to attach the Armies of Land, Sea and Air to the minister in a strange decision that meant the Minister of Defence was seen as the 'minister of the Armed Forces'.[16]

Second, the view is that 'the most disturbing decision was to establish a functional dependency of the Director-Generals and deputy-Director-Generals in military headquarters, on their equivalents in the Central Office, thus inverting the logical relations between administrative bodies and the Armed Forces, and breaking the line of hierarchy that is the inalienable *sine qua non* of every military organization'.[17]

In terms of the integration of the armed forces within the structure of the ministry, it is hardly necessary to underline the fact that this is an essential measure if the aim is to incorporate them into the administration of state and no longer consider them as an institution in dialogue with the other higher reaches of state. Functional dependency is emphatically the way to gradually reduce and eliminate reserve domains

---

[16] Platón 2001: 490.   [17] Platón 2001: 490.

created in previous eras. This measure had already been heralded in the speech introducing the LODNOM 84 to the Senate.[18] It was included in the Royal Decree on the restructuring of the ministry. The formula used was to add to the attributes of each Department (Dirección General)[19] a section establishing that the relevant bodies in the departments of each of the three armies had to report to the Ministry's Central Office when preparing and developing their own policies and coordinating their implementation. This part of the decree was difficult to put into practice such was the resistance from the respective military headquarters. Consequently it was reformulated in the new 1987 decree on the reorganization of the ministry, adding the following sentence to the description of the remits of each department within the ministry: 'the relevant bodies in the aforementioned areas (those covered by each department of the three Armies and autonomous Bodies) will report to the Ministry of Defence's Central Office'. The Royal Decree 1207/1989 of 6 October establishing the basic structure of the armed forces reinforced even further this wish to create relations of functional dependency with a series of additional dispositions that point up one by one the way each body within the respective headquarters is functionally dependent on the central body. The decree also detailed the responsibilities of the departments within the ministry in terms of this dependency, from the issue of instructions and circulars of a general nature to the coordination of the activities of the bodies within each army, ensuring its own instructions are followed and setting up working committees with these bodies to report to them. Constant scrutiny to ensure these measures were implemented and the introduction of civilians into the executive management of Central Office were the necessary preconditions to guarantee that functional dependency was increasingly respected.

---

[18] The speech to the Senate on 22 December 1983 said: 'the decrees developing this Organic Law will gradually organize the Ministry of Defence and introduce criteria of functional dependency between the Departments for Personnel, Matériel, Infrastructures or Economic Affairs within the Ministry and the respective departments in the three armies', Cortes Generales 1984: 521.

[19] The Royal Decree changed the nomenclatures from Secretarías Generales to Direcciónes Generales. The word 'Secretaría' was chosen in the decree creating the ministry in order to distinguish it from other departments within the administration.

The two features mentioned as defects in the work written by various generals and admirals and Miguel Platón are precisely those that are crucial in the process of normalizing government relations with the armed forces. They were at once powerful levers on behalf of civil supremacy and a clear message to the military about the will of government to follow this through. I also think that they are two steps that have to be taken at some time or another in any process of democratic consolidation in relation to the armed forces.

However, the creation of a powerful ministry on a par with those in consolidated democracies is not simply a matter of legal reform or decree passing. Action is required in day-to-day business that often calls for great tenacity. That is why it is so important that the mandate of civilian ministers of defence is stable and long lasting. In the case of Spain, the first step was to give the ministry its own building, since in the transition the two civilian ministries occupied offices in two of the three military headquarters, and that was incompatible with the necessary structure of a ministry. The fact that the Ministry of Culture was located in the building that housed the former regime's Ministry for Information and Tourism, and did not need such vast office space – an area of some 60,000 square metres – meant that Defence could move there. This typically Francoist building with its large front courtyard for military ceremonies and parades meant it was ideal for this new use.

Apart from a new building, it was necessary to adopt several measures to ensure that the new department could function as such. Five are particularly significant. First, the Ministerial Order 18/1985 allowed senior officials in the ministry, whether they belonged to central office or the respective military headquarters, to request reports and data from each other, exchange information and deal with matters, even though they enjoyed no organic dependency. This order was necessary to enable Director-Generals to communicate directly with those in command in the military headquarters, since the military as such were very reluctant to accept they had to report to officials on whom they did not depend organically. These difficulties were even mentioned in the Report from the Ministry to the Legislature.[20] The Ministerial Order had to specify that Director-Generals could give 'instructions of a functional nature relating to the preparation and drawing up of their

---

[20] Ministry of Defence 1986: 70.

respective policies, as well as to the coordination of implementation' to comparable bodies within each branch of the armed forces.

Secondly, there was the matter of who would decide which military personnel should be assigned to Central Office, since that had been previously decided by the norms governing criteria for transfer within the three forces. It was now necessary to ensure there were similar criteria for the transfer of officers to Central Office and for those being moved to military headquarters to guarantee that all the posts in the ministry were filled. This issue led to real difficulties because the armed forces were reluctant to 'lend' staff to a Central Office they immediately decided was over-staffed. That meant the regulation had to be changed again in 1986 in an example of the many modifications that have to be introduced gradually in the period of consolidation.[21]

Thirdly, there was the creation of the Official Bulletin of the Ministry of Defence that replaced the official bulletins of the three branches of the armed forces. This innovation was another example of the fact that in 1977 the remits of the three ministries previous to the creation of the Ministry of Defence had been transferred to the respective military headquarters, rather than moving their responsibilities to the new department. Now the minister controlled the publication of its own decisions as well as those taken by the different military headquarters.

Fourthly, in line with the previous measures, every opportunity had to be grasped when setting up the new ministry to coordinate activities and to increase the 'critical mass' of its Central Office. Such actions can be quite diverse and must always be linked to the concrete situation in each country. As an example in the case of Spain, one could mention the setting up of the Department for Infrastructures, the Headquarters for Defence Telecommunications, the Centre for Defence Publications or various mechanisms for coordinating computer services established in the Ministry's Technical General Secretariat. Another example, related to service abroad, was making the military attachés dependent on Central Office, whichever armed force they belonged to, at a stroke suppressing unnecessary duplication in terms of representation and increasing the number of countries covered. All these measures tend to reinforce the Ministry as the sorting-house for the employment of the

---

[21] The first Ministerial Order is 69/1984 of 26 November. The second is the OM 78/ 1986 of 13 September, changed on 2 October in the same way.

armed forces and to direct the three branches of the armed forces towards the operational tasks that corresponded to them.

Last but not least, the policy of increasing the number of civilians in the ministry's staffing quota and in its executive bodies must be signalled as one of the most effective ways to consolidate the ministry. It must be remembered that the order creating the ministry stated that generals should fill leadership positions and that in February 1981 the minister, Rodríguez Sahagún, was the only civilian in post in the department. In the wake of the 1984 decree a gradual policy was implemented of bringing civilians into the ministry so that in that same year, two of the seven Director-Generals and four of the twenty-nine deputy Director-Generals were civilians. In 1987, three of the six Director-Generals were civilians and the ministry had nine civilian deputy-heads out of a total of thirty-five. By 1989 there were more civilian directors than military (five out of nine), while 34 per cent of deputy Director-Generals were civilian. Subsequently these percentages have changed in line with the policies of successive governments, but the presence of civilians in senior posts in the ministry has been established as something that is perfectly normal.[22]

The process of strengthening the ministry must also derive from increasing effectiveness and from the way it acts to help the armed forces in the new situation in the country. This can be exemplified in two areas: the increase in the forces' international links and arbitration between the different interests of the three forces. It was clearly necessary to have a civilian minister and a ministry equivalent to its counterparts to make the most of the potential for modernization that membership of NATO brought. The same was true of bilateral relations with the United States and European countries and, later on, of the growing number of international missions for the armed forces.

Conversely, arbitration in the crucial decisions that impacted on the three armies was, and still is, necessary. As was noted, the 1980 Organic Law granted the JUJEM the capacity to propose the Joint Strategic Plan, but in fact the JUJEM never managed to approve such a plan because of the differences that divided the Chiefs of Staff. Consequently it made complete sense for these powers to fall to the civilian minister, who by definition belonged to no specific area of the forces, as the only way to

---

[22] See Iglesias 2001: 80–1.

reach decisions on these matters. To execute these tasks the minister requires a properly functioning department.

Reforming the military system of justice

The chapter on the transition analysed the 1980 partial reform of the Military Penal Code that mainly focused on preventing military courts from trying civilians, but which already signalled two paths to follow: the separation of military command and the judiciary and the integration of military justice within a single judicial system. The stability of the government formed after the October 1982 elections allowed it to tackle the complex process of fulfilling the mandate from the Constitution that in article 117 required a unified judiciary and the restriction of military courts to 'strictly military area and states of emergency'. The measures to be enforced were not very different from those applied by Manuel Azaña in the Republic of 1931 and although it would clearly have been a big mistake at the time to invoke any parallels with what he did, it was true that very shortly after its creation, the Second Republic abolished the 1906 law on jurisdiction, stripped the military command of any judiciary powers and dissolved the Supreme Council for War and the Navy, and transferred its functions to the High Court.[23] The 1931 Constitution also suppressed the military Courts of Honour, while the 1978 Constitution had banned them only 'in the area of civil administration and professional organisations'. Consequently, they had to be abolished in the reform of the military justice system undertaken in the period of consolidation.

As will be seen, the basic lines of the reforms carried out between 1985 and 1989 are not very different to those implemented in 1931. In 1980, the main concern of government and parliament was to restrict military courts to the area of the military and thus prevent military courts from intervening in civilian life. On the other hand, from 1983, the central concern focused on the abolition of the military justice system as a power-centre independent of a single unified judiciary. This was in response to the lenient sentences given to the leaders of the 1981 coup, which were then stiffened by the Supreme Court, and to the attempts made by the Supreme Court of Military Justice to amnesty those then sentenced.

---

[23] See Cotino 2002: 425.

The first decision within the reform process was to break the previous Penal Code into four different laws: the penal code as such, a quite separate law enforcing military discipline, a law on military legal procedures, one reorganizing military jurisdiction and one that centred on personnel and territorial organization. Additionally there was law 14/ 1985 that modified the Common Penal Code in order to include crimes now excluded from military jurisdiction that must now pass through the ordinary courts – in particular the crime of military rebellion. The decision was taken to split the reform into several laws because it facilitated the task of the commission structuring the reform in that it could then concentrate on each stage in turn once general guidelines had been established. It also gave the minister and his colleagues more control over the text and facilitated dialogue between the minister of defence, the minister of justice and the Congress and Senate as well as debates in these chambers. All reforms in the institutional field of the military have a huge political content, and the minister must lead and manage them at every point. To that end, he should have a thorough knowledge of the subject, and must not hand over any part of the reform 'to experts' but rather shape it constantly following a body of knowledge that comes from management of the entire reform process. He must also display a command of detail that is often what most clearly communicates to the military the guidelines for change emanating from the democratic state.

The Ministerial Final Year Report sets out clearly the aims of the reform, some of which have already been mentioned:

- To limit the exercise of military jurisdiction to the strictly military area, as prescribed in the Constitution.
- To structure the system of military justice into the civil system, thus applying the constitutional principle of a unitary system of jurisdiction.
- To speed up the administration of justice by clarifying and simplifying the way it operates.

As a step to meet the first aim it was decided that the area covered by the military courts would be limited to the crimes defined in the Military Penal Code. In other words the criteria of place (military premises) or person (a professional or conscript soldier) were no longer valid and only the kinds of crime included in the new code were relevant. The military justice system is almost irresistibly inclined to bias when the following two conditions exist: when its scope is defined in relation to the individual, that is when any kind of crime committed by the military is being judged; and secondly when the lines between military command and judiciary are blurred, and the actions of the military are no longer subject to the single source of judicial power acceptable in a democracy. The reform put a stop to both situations and to the idea that the military code is a law which takes precedence over the Common Penal Code.[24] In other words, a big effort was made to make it clear that the code was not applied to military simply because they were that, but to particular acts within the field of defence. Military justice was not a distinct, discrete preserve of the military, but was applicable to some of their acts as an area within a single legal system. For this reason military justice does not have its own ruling body and falls within the remit of the General Council for Judicial Power.[25]

The integration of military justice into the ordinary system was achieved through the creation of a Military Issues Tribunal at the High Court to which all the powers of the Supreme Council for Military Justice were transferred. The first article of the Organic Law 4/1987, on the remit and organization of the military justice system, rules that it is part of the judicial power of the state. Moreover, the Military Justice Code is conceived as a special law that relates to the general system established by the Common Penal Code. The goal of clarifying and streamlining the administration of military justice was pursued through the simplification of procedures in the laws related to organization and courts. This task was given to military judicial bodies and a single military judiciary was created to replace those in place that differed for each branch of the armed forces. The ground was thus prepared for the unification of the three separate legal bodies of military jurists into a single unit, which then became dependent on the Central Office of the Ministry of Defence like other unified bodies.

The separating out of military command from the judiciary also meant that the captain generals lost their powers in terms of approving sentences given by military courts held within the remit of their command, and this was accompanied by the separation of the penal code and disciplinary law regulating the military's capacity to give out sanctions to maintain discipline in units and bodies under their command. In this way it was made clear that military command had no judicial

---

[24] For these issues, see Suárez Pertierra 2004.   [25] See Mozo 1995.

function, but only an ability to issue sanctions that was in turn regulated and subject to legal control, since the sanctions they decided were open to appeal and fell within the remit of the general legal system. To that end, a new legal procedure appeared on Spanish horizons: the military appeals administrative procedure.

Throughout the process of reform, special attention was paid to the guarantees for those tried or disciplined with sanctions, and to legal oversight of the application of disciplinary measures: all sanctions that could have a degrading content were withdrawn, such as, for example, sending individuals to disciplinary units or giving them menial tasks. This was a way of implementing the criterion that all tasks are equally worthy and cannot be considered as sanctions. The whole reform process was also used to establish new criteria more in keeping with a democratic society. Articles 102 and 138 of the Military Penal Code concerning insubordination and abuse of authority are good examples of this as they recommended the same punishment for both.

The death penalty is another example of a solution achieved over time. Article 15 of the Spanish Constitution abolished the death penalty 'except for the dispositions in military penal laws for times of war'. When the new Military Penal Code was drawn up, it included this rider about times of war but always as an alternative to prison sentences, so that no court was obliged to impose the death penalty because it was the only sentence available. Years later, in 1995, the death penalty was removed entirely from the Military Penal Code.[26]

Deciding defence and military policy

Before embarking on an analysis of this process, I must point out I do not use the expression 'military policy' here in the broad sense as the government's complete envelope of actions and measures in relation to the armed forces, but in the more limited sense as contained in the 1980 Organic Law. Article 4.2 of the latter defines military policy as 'an essential component of defence policy, determining the organisation, training and fulfilment of military potential, fundamentally constituted by the Army, Navy and Air Force, taking into account the nation's possibilities in terms of defence'. In the rest of the book I use the

[26] By Organic Law 11/1995, 27 November.

expression in its broader meaning, thus placing reform of the armed forces substantially at the heart of military policy.

With the LODNOM 84 and the Royal Decree on the organization of the Ministry of Defence, the government had shown its determination to decide and implement defence and military policy. That is why legislative reform granted the president and minister clear remits and endowed them with a powerful weapon, the Ministry of Defence, if these new dispositions prospered.

To implement this proposal, a new round of drafting of defence policy began that would be immediately and vigorously developed following the government's lead and the guidelines on national defence signed by the president. This invoked one of the distinguishing features of a period of consolidation: it is no longer a question of the military not interfering in politics, but of the government deciding and implementing the appropriate policy in the military ambit. First of all the General Plan for National Defence was put in place, with the National Defence Directive signed by the president on 10 July 1984, and approved by the Council of Ministers on 31 July 1985. Soon after the referendum on continuing membership of NATO and fresh elections, the president signed a new directive on 29 October 1986 that initiated a new round of planning. The General Defence Plan involves all ministries and is divided into three phases. The first is the planning phase, when goals and general lines of action are agreed and articulated through the Joint Strategic Plan. The second is the programming phase, when the programmes for the respective ministries are drawn up. The third relates to budgeting and the inclusion of respective allocations in the state budget.

Military planning was set out in Directive 17/87 signed by the minister, who decides military planning, the statements setting it out and the procedures for development and revision. The process was articulated in two cycles: one was biennial in order to formulate the Joint Strategic Plan and the other annual in order to revise the five-year plans derived from the latter. This was all designed to match NATO planning procedures and meet defence planning requirements set by the Atlantic Alliance.

The implementation of these planning procedures allowed the minister, JEMAD and military headquarters to revisit policy in a way that was determined and driven by government. This move had two goals in mind: one aimed to reduce the domestic missions of the armed forces, and the other to connect military policy with the new international policy being developed.

The major change to ensure the first objective involved abandoning the concept of 'internal defence'– a corollary of the Francoist goal of fighting the enemy within – as a mission for the forces. They were to be concerned entirely with questions of external defence or collaboration with allied armies. Later on there would be international peace missions, almost always under the flag of the United Nations. This process could not be enacted overnight, but the aims of national defence approved by the president's directive of July 1984 signal this change of philosophy, despite some remaining throwbacks to the past.

The objectives defined in July 1984 were as follows:

- Defence of the constitutional order guaranteeing the unity, sovereignty and independence of Spain and its territorial integrity.
- Protection of the population of Spain against the risk of direct attacks against their lives in situations of war, catastrophe or public disaster.
- Making the greatest contribution possible to maintaining peace between nations and the security and defence of the Western world to which Spain belongs.
- Development of an appropriate force of deterrence against foreseeable threats, as well as effective control of the Straits of Gibraltar and approaches to them.

These objectives no longer mentioned the defence of Ceuta and Melilla that had been the previous strategic priority for the three armies. Effective control of the Straits of Gibraltar implemented the decision to reduce NATO interest in the British base in Gibraltar as much as was possible. Later on, in the autumn of 1986 and after the NATO referendum, these four objectives were reformulated with greater clarity and concision to reduce them to three:

- To contribute to the maintenance of peace between nations and to the security and defence of the Western world to which Spain belongs, especially in relation to the nation's immediate strategic concerns.
- To develop an effective military capacity to deter foreseeable threats.
- To develop an effective civil defence system able to act in any situation.

The 1990 National Defence Directive preserved the three previous objectives in almost identical wording and added five significant strategic goals:

1. To guarantee the sovereignty and independence of Spain, by defending territorial integrity and constitutional order.
2. To achieve an appropriate deterrent capacity in order to allay foreseeable risks, and if this fails, an ability to react and deal with them.
3. To achieve a military capability that allows Spain to meet its commitments in international agreements to which it is signatory.
4. To guarantee control in the Area of National Security and over traffic linking its areas under its sovereignty.
5. To contribute within the framework of the Atlantic Alliance to ensure defence and control of the Straits of Gibraltar and approaches to them.

Two years later the new directive responded to the new situation at the end of the Cold War, eliminated the word 'deterrent' and included contributing to the creation of peaceful relations between countries:

- To guarantee the sovereignty and independence of Spain.
- To protect the lives of the population and vital interests of the nation.
- To contribute to collective defence and security with our allies, as laid down in the international commitments underwritten by Spain.
- To collaborate in the strengthening of peaceful relations between nations particularly in our immediate geographical environment.

A comparison of the different wordings of these objectives illustrates the evolution over a period, the first marker being the abandoning of the objectives of internal defence and Ceuta and Melilla as priorities. A second is the elimination of the guaranteeing the unity of Spain as an objective and also the abandoning of the idea of a deterrent capacity isolated from our allies in terms of foreseeable threats, thereby introducing the notion of collective defence. The basic idea was quite simple: for the Spanish armed forces, and in particular the army, to look outwards rather than inwards, and to achieve a change in perspective from considering their essential role to be that of preserving internal order, to that of defending the country as a member of a broader alliance. A third marker was the abandoning of deterrence as an objective and the incorporation of tasks that can contribute towards peace.

This change in outlook served to guide the reduction in manpower in the forces, above all in the Army, a reduction we will analyse on the axis of professional measures. The Army was substantially cut back from twenty-four to fifteen brigades through the removal of the so-called defence of the territory brigades that were operational within Spain and which reflected the previous mission of maintaining control of the country. At the same time, a policy of closing barracks situated in city centres – another example of the model from the previous period – was begun and attempts were made to locate these brigades in places where they had space to carry out manoeuvres.

In the field of international relations, the change in philosophy was marked by the so-called Decalogue: a list of ten points to establish a consensus on foreign policy and security that the president put forward in the debate on the state of the nation in October 1984. The first four elements in the Decalogue were included in the question formulated in the referendum about membership of NATO held on 12 March 1986. Briefly the ten points proposed the following:

1. That Spain should stay in the Atlantic Alliance.
2. That it should not join NATO's integrated military structure.
3. The ban on installing, storing or bringing nuclear arms into the territory of Spain should be continued.
4. A new bilateral agreement reducing US military presence in Spain.
5. The ratifying of the Treaty Banning Nuclear Tests, not excluding the signing of the Treaty on the Non-Proliferation of Nuclear Arms.
6. Participation in the Western European Union.
7. To continue demanding the sovereignty of Gibraltar.
8. The maintaining of an active presence in the European Conference of Disarmament and in the United Nations.
9. To continue developing bilateral agreements in terms of defence cooperation with other European countries.
10. The inclusion of the Joint Strategic Plan as an element in the dialogue to achieve a consensus in the area of defence policy.

The idea was to resolve the difficult situation in which the government had to hold the referendum it was pledged to and, at the same time, keep Spain in the Atlantic Alliance. The points constituted a message sent out to the parties, starting with the Socialist Party itself, in order to over- come the difficulties involved in what was a necessary policy turn towards NATO. Conversely, they were a clear set of principles to articulate a defence and security policy for Spain, necessary both to structure the defence and military policies that were being drafted and to show to the military that their field of activity must be integrated into something much broader. After the referendum, which brought a difficult and reduced victory for the 'yes' vote – though it was still a great triumph for the government – a period opened when the points in the Decalogue began to be implemented culminating in entry into WEU, a new bilateral agreement with the United States and an agreement on how to continue membership of NATO. These accords were all signed in quick succession: 14 November, entry into the WEU; 1 December the new agreement with the United States and 1 and 8 December the agreements with the Defence Planning Committee and the Atlantic Council on General Guidelines for the development of Coordination Agreements that would express concretely Spain's contribution to the Alliance in that period. This shows how the negotiations were all interrelated and how it would have been almost impossible to finalize one accord if the path to agreement had not been opened up in others. The three agreements required imagination and careful preparation by the different bodies in the Ministry of Defence in collaboration with the Ministry of Foreign Affairs. This finally led to the creation in the Ministry of Foreign Affairs of a Security and Disarmament Office to study and oversee these questions, another sign that the need for civilian experts in defence matters had been recognized. These all brought materials and ideas that helped draft defence and military policy and the phased introduction of defence policy. They all also required concrete actions: the Air Force took charge of the Air Base in Torrejón, and various maritime security operations were carried out in the Mediterranean or during the Gulf War coordinated by the WEU.

However, there is no doubt that it was the agreement reached with NATO that required most imagination and cooperation with the Ministry of Foreign Affairs. The General Guidelines listed six important missions that all need specific agreements of coordination in order to prosper. These were as follow:

- The defence of Spanish territory.
- Air defence and the control of Spanish airspace.
- The control of the Straits of Gibraltar and approaches thereto.
- Naval and air operations in the Eastern Atlantic.
- Naval and air operations in the Western Mediterranean.
- The use of Spanish territory as an area of transit, support and rearguard logistics for the Alliance.

It is easy to see that all these missions opened up new fields of work and planning for the three branches of the armed forces and, although the manner of Spain's membership of NATO was seen only as an ingenious, if provisional, solution that would be sooner or later ironed out, all these factors were a good guide to the professional work that had to be undertaken at that point. The NATO missions were almost entirely framed within what we could call Spain's area of strategic interest (a concept much in vogue at the time, particularly with the Navy, was the Balearics–Straits of Gibraltar–Canary Islands Axis). We had to wait for the fall of the Berlin Wall and the situation after the end of the Cold War before the armed forces could begin to carry out missions in scenarios far from areas considered to be of strategic interest.

All these activities strengthened the government's leadership in the development of defence and military policy and showed the vital need for close alignment between government international policy and the Ministry of Foreign Affairs. They highlighted the need to incorporate members of the diplomatic corps into the Ministry of Defence, and shaped the decision to link the Defence Policy Office directly to the minister, as was already the case in other European countries, in order to manage department policy on all these fronts.

Reform on the professional change axis

I pointed out in chapter 4 that this reform involves a very heterogeneous set of measures that are difficult to implement because they relate to areas in which the military like to concentrate their efforts to try to keep internal control of the profession and sustain a reserve domain exempt from external control. This is why I have argued it is best to take the first steps to reduce military autonomy in the period of democratic consolidation in budgets and economic matters or in the supply of armaments and equipment.

The overall process of reform on this axis involves a package of policies to do with staffing, modernizing policies and, evidently, in terms of the relationship between the armed forces and society, increasing the military's openness to social change and to mainstream principles and values. These are policies that have to be phased in carefully and the military require time to assimilate them. In many cases the majority of the military see them as necessary or, at least, as inevitable as, for example, the reduction in personnel or the rejuvenating of leadership cadres. However, it is very difficult for the military command to enforce these measures. If they do so, there is a considerable risk that their actions will be seen as betrayals, particularly in fields so closely linked to the military's sense of itself as an institution. They have to be led by civilians, and with due caution at that, once there is sufficient grasp of the issues at stake and proper control of the level of conflicts within the military body.

As reflected in previous chapters, the goals behind the measures to be applied on the professional axis are two-fold: first, to encourage the armed forces to see themselves as more occupational and less institutional. Secondly, to establish the loyalty of the armed forces to the democratic system in order to make the question of control of the military one of managing civilian–military relations and not one that affects the functioning or survival of the system.

In terms of the first goal, it should be emphasized that changes in the international situation, the way conflict now occurs (limited wars, peace operations, etc.) or threats arising from terrorism, justify the move towards an occupational army or towards positions we could say are à la Janowitz.[27] In the case of Spain, General Diez Alegría had advocated more than thirty years ago armies that combined institutional and occupational features.[28]

In terms of the second, what Diego López Garrido had described in the early days of this period of consolidation is at stake: 'it is not enough for the armed forces to be formally under the government's hierarchical control; the armed forces must be materially, ideologically and sociologically in agreement with the constitutional principles of democracy'.[29]

We will now analyse how these policies can be linked to this axis following the headings set out in chapter 4.

Reducing the size of the armed forces and reorganizing their territories

The reduction in the three forces was not uniform because it was principally the Army that was hugely over-manned. It was decided to do this through legislation because this seemed the best way to give most

---

[27] On this point, see Sarkesian 1984.
[28] 'there must be room in the military spirit, for high level administrative and technical expertise, without that diminishing the old heroic attitudes'. See Diez Alegría 1972: 80.
[29] López Garrido 1983: 963.

weight to the decision to establish set numbers for staffing levels and because the Army did not have levels decided by law. The draft law in relation to the Army was sent to parliament in the spring of 1984 and was passed on 1 December. The laws fixing staffing levels in the other two forces were easier to draw up, since there were precedents and the Cortes approved this legislation in February 1986. The reductions were most significant in the higher ranks, because that was where the Army had most excess. The across-the-board reduction was 13 per cent of the total of the armed forces and 15 per cent of the Army, but if we exclude petty-officers where there was quite rightly almost no reduction, the number of officers diminished by 23 per cent and within that, there were 37 per cent fewer colonels and more than 42 per cent fewer generals. It was a law introduced to reduce the number of officers in terms of the staffing for 1991 and a six-year period was given to reach the new staffing level. It responded to a general feeling, one shared by the armed forces themselves, that the number of officers was excessive and that this was incompatible with proper professionalism and effectiveness. Numbers of rank-and-file troops were also cut by reducing effective military service to twelve months. Later on, the new international situation and further cuts in the length of military service or lack of budget, led to reductions that were cuts in the number of soldiers rather than officers, reductions that became even more marked when conscription was abolished and an entirely professional army was established. In 1993, when the so-called '2000 Model for the Forces' was approved, a set staffing level of 42,978 was fixed for officers and the military command across the armed forces, a third less than in 1984 and a total number of troops (professionals and replacements) of 130,272 soldiers, less than half the number of 305,500 soldiers in 1984.

The best, and almost only, way to implement this number of reductions in the officer class is to create incentives for a sufficient number to leave the service voluntarily. An exceptional provisional measure was introduced in Spain with the creation of a 'transitory reserve' where officers were paid to the age of 65 and promotion was still possible. The formula worked quite efficiently, particularly in the first years it operated, which was when it most helped cut the excess numbers of commanders and generals. The 1986–89 Ministry of Defence Report gives data to September 1989 that coincides almost exactly with the consolidation period we are now studying. In these years a total of 6,185 commanders and officers and 4,109 petty officers entered the transitory reserve, figures that surpass the 8,282 excess between the reality of the armed forces in 1984 and the new staffing levels legislated for 1991.

An essential instrument to control army size in the mid-term was the policy determining matriculations in the military academies, which had been controlled by each army up to that point. The law in relation to the state budget for 1986 was used to establish the fact that it is the Minister of Defence who yearly informs the government of the required intake in the military academies. After this remit was created there was a policy of prudent but sustained reductions and the intake in the academies for army officers and petty officers was gradually reduced from 962 in 1983 to 560 in 1989. The intake into the Naval Academy was reduced more gently from 84 to 58 over the same period and into the Air-Force Academy from 96 to 67. As far as troops were concerned, the new decree regulating military service also established it was the government's task to decide on the annual intake into the ranks.

These processes of reduction in manpower were accompanied by important changes in the operational structure and territorial organization of the armed forces. In terms of army reorganization the brigade was chosen rather than the division (that usually comprises three brigades), because it was the unit most suited to the new missions that seemed likely to occur and also the most controllable in terms of cost effectiveness. All nine defence of the territory brigades that operated in Spain were suppressed, with the exception of one that became the motorized brigade, because they were responsible for missions that were now non-existent: at a stroke the Army went from twenty-four to sixteen brigades. The further decision was taken to close teaching centres for recruits that also had land for carrying out manoeuvres and were far from city centres. Brigades were located in those with the best space and installations so they in turn could leave their urban barracks.

The Army's number of military regions – called Captaincy-Generals – was also reduced from nine to six on the Peninsula. That opened the way for the subsequent elimination of the captain general as a figure of authority in the country, as well as provincial military governments, a legacy from an era when the army performed missions to maintain internal order. This is a measure that eliminated prerogatives and the military's ability to intervene in civilian life, and it is appropriate for the institutional reforms axis, but is also another example of the need to interrelate actions across the three axes when the sequence for implementing reform measures is decided.

In less than ten years the Army developed the so-called Plan 'Meta' that included the measures I have mentioned, followed by the Plan 'Reto' then followed by the Plan 'Norte' that fell outside the consolidation period of the reform. The military complained, rightly, of the speed of change and also that the decrease in the number of soldiers did not lead to any apparent improvement in the arming of the units. These were years of great changes on the international scene, and consequently in the conception of the missions suited to the armed forces. Although nobody had a precise vision of the future, it seemed clear that the traditional heavy weaponry the armed forces wanted would not be the most appropriate for the new situations that were on the horizon. There was also the need to reduce the budget and the fact that many of the measures to reduce personnel that saved costs in the medium and long term, did not do so in the short term, and even led to increased expenditure (the transitory reserve, for example).

Measures impacting on the military profession: staffing policies

This is an essential set of measures that must be included on the axis now under consideration, in terms of transforming the professional profile. The case of Spain shows that these are the most difficult to conceptualize and implement and the hardest for the military to accept and assimilate. Precisely for this reason the systematizing of all these measures, the Law regulating Status of Military Personnel, was not passed until July 1989, at the end of the period we are studying.

This law had two main purposes. The first was to streamline the structures (units and career lines) in the military profession by trying to unify and remove distinctions that had lost all meaning. The development of the armed forces in previous years, without any external mechanism to oversee their effectiveness had produced, as already noted, three ministerial departments that practically prevented any kind of joint action. At the same time, bodies and career paths were being created in complete isolation within each force. When the reform was begun there were 207 such bodies across the three branches of the armed forces. The streamlining and, as inasmuch as is possible, unifying of these compartments is a complex task that is difficult to implement since the military are attached to their traditions and display a notable resistance to changes that imply the disappearance of organs that already exist. A good example in Spain is that the biggest resistance to any area being shut down related to the suppression of the Unit for War-Wounded, which belonged to another era and had no reason to exist in the new circumstances.

Secondly, the law aimed to establish a general norm for career development in the military from entry to retirement based on a series of selection systems and not exclusively on length of service as a criterion for promotion. The novelty here was the partial introduction of appointment criteria in promotions to lieutenant colonel and colonel and their equivalents in the Navy. This system was called a selection procedure. In this way, a military career path, when this law was applied, would have three mechanisms for promotion, seniority, appointment and selection.

Before the law was passed, steps had already been taken to prepare the way for its reform: the unifying of the control units in the three forces into a single body, law 9/1985 10 April, the application to the military of the dispositions in law 30/1984 on the reform of the civil service, and bringing retirement age down to 65 from the 70 in place at the time.

Apart from regulating the mechanics for promotion, the law also regulated posts to be filled and established clear demarcations. On the one hand, the Council of Ministers appoints the posts of lieutenant general and divisional general following proposals from the minister of defence. On the other, the minister decides those posts not subject to competitive examination, and those that depend on seniority and competition depend on the chiefs of general staff and, in their case, on the under-secretary. Immediately, the posts not subject to examination became the responsibility of the chiefs of staff and the under-secretary, except for a series of posts such as colonel or ship's captain that the minister reserved for himself because of the importance of the leadership involved or the nature of the post, in educational centres, for example.

Military education

Although this belongs entirely to personnel policy, it is extremely important and therefore the reform of military education should be reviewed separately. If the military consider personnel policy to be their own preserve, this feeling is even stronger in relation to the education of the military. Consequently, the pace of reform and modernization must be cautious, backed by very clear, uncontroversial objectives, and determined in each step it takes following thorough research and careful implementation. In Spain the first step in this phase was the creation of the sub-department of Education, which provided the ministry with an organ responsible for studying the situation and proposing ongoing policy in this field. In the 1987 decree organizing the ministry, this sub-department became a fully fledged department and its rise in status facilitated dialogue and coordination of educational procedures across the three branches of the armed forces.

Initially it was thought a single law would best regulate this issue. However, a few months into the period it became clear that it was not a good idea to wait until there was a law to initiate the process of reform because there were urgent and necessary changes to be made. It was finally decided to include military education in a section of the law regulating the status of professional military personnel. On the other hand, the process of gradual, measured changes allowed a sufficient body of knowledge to be established in order to prepare the law. Civilian experts in the field of military education are hard to find. The creation of mechanisms based on sufficient knowledge to drive reform is also a difficult business. A prudent, relatively safe way to act is to observe the results from measures being applied before taking further decisions, and to correct whatever does not work in practice before preparing subsequent measures from a greater knowledge base.

The first dispositions to be implemented were the Royal Decree 2078/1985 that standardized entry requirements to the military academies, and introduced changes that clearly showed the direction to be followed, a simple ministerial directive (OM 66/1985) aimed at regulating the profile of the teaching staff. The Royal Decree that fixed the entry requirements aimed to make them the same for the three forces and equivalent to those for university entrance. From then on, it was necessary to have passed university entrance tests in order to enter the military academies. New subjects were also introduced into the curricula for the military profession such as constitutional law and the geography and history of Spain, complementing subjects that were already studied such as mathematics, physics and chemistry and languages. One innovation that seemed strange at first was the permission given to aspiring military to enter the competitive examinations for the three forces so these now had legally to be organized on different dates.

The role of teaching staff was the other issue that was tackled in this first set of measures. It was relatively easy to see that teaching posts were neither highly valued nor well paid. That meant they were often filled by military who were not particularly well educated and who, moreover, took refuge in these posts for prolonged periods of time. The Ministerial Order, as was mentioned, detailed the nature of the teaching posts, the means to recruit them and the economic means assigned. However, the most far-reaching impact of this order was the regulation that fixed the maximum time a teacher could remain in post in a military academy at six years. This led to a 70 per cent renewal of the teaching staff in the Military Academy in Zaragoza within two years, to give an example of how effective the measure was. The renewal of teaching staff was a necessary precondition for any process of reform of military education. Felipe Agüero notes in his book on the reform: 'the three chiefs of staff communicated their fierce opposition to the minister'.[30] This was understandable as it was the first time that civilians had taken decisions that impacted on the nature of military education.

Once the referendum on continued NATO membership and fresh elections had been held, it was possible to tackle the overall organization of military education, drawing on the body of experience from the implementation of previous measures. A proper diagnosis of the state of military education could be made: it was an autonomous, self-sufficient system, that is, sealed off from the general system of state education.[31] The network of centres was too large, all depending on a boarding system and an almost exclusively military teaching staff. Recruitment procedures entrenched the boundaries existing between the three armies. One of the biggest problems was that the academies taught values that were increasingly distant from those shared by the majority of society and that continued to be entirely Francoist on the pretext that these were military, patriotic values. However, this aspect was tackled without too much fuss. This all signalled the basic lines of the reform to be carried out: the devising of an all-round educational curriculum, open to other disciplines and integrated into the educational system. The explicit aims of the reform process could hardly be controversial:

[30] Agüero 1995a: 325.
[31] I am following Suárez Pertierra's description here 1988: 19ff.

- To adapt the structure of military education to the general organization of the educational system, integrating it into the latter as far as
  possible.
- To reduce and rationalize military teaching centres in terms of resources,
  teaching methods and internal organization.
- To facilitate joint action by the three forces.
- To establish an appropriate curriculum for the new circumstances
  and improve conditions for all teaching staff.

Following these guidelines that had already been drawn up by the first
government, the reform in the second period began with the creation of
the Education Department that had the remit 'to prepare, plan and
develop policy for military education, as well to oversee and lead
its implementation'. The article on the department lists its extensive
powers to allow it to become the engine of the planned modernization
that included features such as proposing models for the system of
education, approval of curricula and text books, the creation, coordination and closure of teaching centres, the drawing up of the regimes for
staff and students, norms for teaching methods and establishing equivalent evaluation and control procedures.

These items were set out to prepare the way for norms to be included
in the 1989 Law Regulating Requirements for Professional Military
Personnel and to control and direct implementation of what had been
agreed up to then. While the process of coordinated entry into the three
academies was begun in 1987, from 1988 the entry tests for advanced
military education were conducted in a uniform way, with a single
board for the three forces coordinated by the Education Department.

The 1989 law, as mentioned, also regulated military education under
its fourth heading and encompassed every aspect of military education.
It coordinated education at basic, middle and advanced levels, regulated
the different centres and entry to military education, allowing the
government to determine the annual quota of places and the qualifications required to enter at each level. It also regulated the procedures for
internal promotion so military at one level could accede to the next level
after two years of effective service. It regulated the curricula, the requirements for the student body prescribing, among other things, its adaptation to the 1985 Law on Disciplinary Procedures, and the teaching staff
in the centres. The 1989 law also cleared the way to establishing agreements with universities and other centres in the educational system in

order to provide specific courses, at the same time as supplying civilian teachers in the areas of human, technical and physical training. When the law was implemented, some centres were closed down and new ones of a general nature were created such as the Joint Language School. New curricula were approved for all academies and new rules were drawn up for domestic arrangements which allowed students to be non-resident, as some of the many steps to facilitate translating into reality what was established in law in the Official Bulletin of State.

With the 1989 law the government was proposing and parliament was approving a global vision of how it wanted to organize military education and how it wanted it to function. The legislation and its implementation showed that the area of education could not be a reserve domain of the armed forces. What I described as the sixth level in my analysis of the phased control of the military in chapter 3 was finally being tackled. As I have emphasized, it is not a straightforward question or one to be carried out in a rush, since, in the best of cases, it will take time for the military to assimilate the changes. We find anecdotal confirmation of that in Miguel Platón's book that we have already quoted from. Referring to education, it says 'such astonishing extremes were reached as the secretary of state giving approval to the curricula in the academies, including military instruction, and even approving the content of subject programmes'.[32] Firmness of will and ability in regulating this area, even in the fine detail, must be shown because this is where a position of military autonomy can become entrenched. Such an attitude demonstrates moreover that government and legislature are completely committed to such an essential principle as bringing the values cultivated in military academies into line with those shared by most of society. It is a government's duty to show the military what kind of armed forces it wants. The most practical of the many ways do to this is to pass laws that have the overall support of the diverse political forces, and to follow them through with tenacious policies that the executive applies cautiously.

Bringing women into the armed forces

Ten years after the Constitution was approved, the principle of gender equality that it established still had not been implemented in the armed

---

[32] Platón 2001: 517.

forces. Although at that time the preparatory work on the law to be passed in 1989 was quite advanced, a decision was taken not to procrastinate further on the issue of bringing women into the armed forces, not so much because there was a strong demand from society for this reform, as to avoid adding the problems of adjustment to this measure to those of adjustment to the other professional reforms in the pipeline. The formula of the decree-law was chosen (1/1988 22 February), developed by a ministerial order the day after, in order to enable women to respond to the call that would go out that same year from the different forces, though not from the academies which trained the officers responsible for arms in the three forces.

The incorporation of women was structured drawing on experiences in other countries, establishing that a woman can aspire to any job and has guaranteed progression in equal conditions to men. When the regulations were drawn up, restrictions present in part or across the board in some European armies were rejected. Concretely, the setting of quotas for the maximum presence of women in the bodies of each army was rejected; the establishing of different career paths for females was also avoided and no ceiling was created for women on any of these career paths.[33]

Seventeen women joined in the first year and eighteen in the next, particularly in general bodies like health, or comptroller units. The following year the government allowed access to armed bodies and although there were requests to enter these, women were only admitted to general units. Teaching centres were adapted to the new situation more easily than was expected and, although the process of incorporation was slow, it soon became clear these problems were not caused by the incorporated women's lack of preparation or ability, but by the inertia and mindset generated by the previous situation that excluded women. Proof of this is the fact that at the present time Spain has one of the highest percentages of women in its armed forces compared to other forces in Europe, close on 10 per cent, although it should be recognized that the percentage is greater at rank-and-file level than in the officer class, and that the percentage of women in armed bodies is still very small.[34] A clearly discriminatory factor persisted in this period that prevented a clear-cut focus being given to the process of incorporation. Women were excluded from compulsory military service in a way that

[33] See Martín Pérez 1995: 601–2.   [34] In this respect see Cotino 2002: 491.

was as anti-constitutional as was their exclusion from the officer cadres and this was not resolved until rank-and-file soldiers were fully professionalized ten years later.

In the case of Spain, a clearly *machista* vision of the military had been cultivated: it was believed that hallmark virtues such as courage, strength or even comradeship were male and not female virtues. Consequently, this legislation sent out a fresh, powerful message about the will of the government to change the profile of the military. The lack of volunteers to become professional soldiers made it clear it was necessary to open up the armed forces to women, since no country could afford to exclude half of its workforce from its armed forces.

Military service

No dictatorial or authoritarian regimes have professional armies. That is why in periods of transition the problem is always posed of how to adapt the conscript military force to the new situation. The reform of compulsory military service usually comes as a very strong demand from society and affords a very special opportunity to communicate to the military the criteria of democratic government in terms of the treatment of the ordinary soldier and respect for his rights.

In Spain military service was regulated by a 1968 law. The new regulations, ready at the beginning of 1984 in tandem with Law 48/1984 of 26 December regulating the question of conscientious objectors at a moment when the chiefs of staff had been replaced, were urgently needed. The most relevant features of the law aimed to communicate a different conception of military service and were as follows:

- Centralizing all recruitment in the ministry, under the leadership of the minister and the recently created Personnel Department.
- The reduction of service in the ranks to twelve months in each branch of the forces.
- Call-up at the age of nineteen.
- The regionalization of military service to facilitate military service in the conscript's region.
- The opening up of a path to the professionalizing of the soldier class through the creation of a special kind of volunteer.

It was necessary to transfer the work of recruitment from the forces to the ministry in order to establish a new relationship with conscripted citizens. Provincial recruitment offices of the ministry were set up to this end. Both the reduction in length of service and bringing forward the age of conscription by a year were measures Spanish society was demanding forcefully and which had to be addressed. Regionalization was an opposite policy to the one that had been in force from 1975 that banned soldiers from military service in their own region. It was introduced gradually at the beginning, with 25 per cent regionalization in 1985. In 1986 it was 30 per cent, in 1987, 60 per cent and in 1989, 100 per cent in the Balearic and Canary Islands, Ceuta and Melilla and 70 per cent in the rest of the national territory. If it was impossible to do military service in one's own region, the rule now was it should be done in an adjacent region. The opportunity to become professional began with the creation of a form of volunteer post that was called 'special' in order to counterpoint it to normal volunteering that lasted sixteen months but where recruits called to the ranks listed in order of preference the units where they wished to do it. Special volunteer service could be extended for up to three years and was paid. This formula did not attract the desired numbers: in 1989, only 4,249 of the 13,781 places offered across the armed forces were filled. A series of changes from 1987 led to better results so that the percentage of professionals in the soldier class kept increasing until compulsory military service was ended.

As with all aspects of military reform, what is difficult is not to legislate but to implement the letter and spirit of the new laws. As far as conscription was concerned, it required firm, sustained action that was driven from the centre and encompassed rather diverse measures, from improving soldiers' food, gradually applying regionalization, improving accommodation and developing an anti-accident programme, to an anti-drugs in the barracks programme and an assertive attitude in the fight against the bullying of new recruits. The first step in overcoming these problems was the creation of mechanisms to get up-to-date accurate information and make military command conscious of the extent of each problem and the need to confront it head on. One measure the military hierarchy opposed but which was very simple and exemplified the new concept of conscription, was Ministerial Order 34/1987 that allowed soldiers and sailors to go in and out of their barracks dressed in civilian clothes.

All in all, the nature of the law supposed, at the time, a significant change in the concept of service to society precisely in an area the military considered to be its own in terms of how it was described and managed. The government was demonstrating through the text of its new law that conscription could not be a military reserve domain but was an issue that concerned the whole of society and that should be carried out according to criteria decided by elected government.

Measures to change the living conditions of the military

The measure that probably has most impact is housing policy because of its repercussions on the quality of life of the military and on the working of the system of postings and its contribution to the isolation of the military from the rest of society. In the middle of 1985, the number of military houses in Spain was almost 42,000, while the total number of officers and petty officers in service was over 66,000. In addition, much of the housing was occupied by retired military or widows of military. The number of houses under construction was 1,777. It was impossible to envisage a programme to provide all the accommodation required, insofar as much of the accommodation built to facilitate postings to particular units ended up being occupied by military who no longer held those posts or were no longer on active service. Consequently guidelines were needed for a new, realistic housing policy in line with the operational needs of the armed forces.

As with changes to the military justice system, housing policy aimed to counter the idea of housing as a privilege that went with being a soldier. Housing was linked to a posting, was described as 'logistical housing' and was strictly regulated so it was only occupied by personnel posted to a specific unit. The rest of the housing that was not registered as logistical following the reduction in the number of units or changes in deployment across national territory would be offered in the first instance to widows and retired soldiers who were improperly occupying housing designated for logistic purposes. Parallel to these developments, a social action programme was implemented to facilitate access to housing on the free market for any member of the military community. To ensure these guidelines were followed, the departments for military housing that existed in each branch of the forces became the responsibility of the Personnel Department.

The existence of the Infrastructure Department was a great help in carrying out these policies. Land that was no longer useful for the activities of the armed forces (almost 1,500 million square metres in

1988) was transferred to this department, which proceeded to sell it and invest the income in new buildings, land for military manoeuvres or the improvement of existing plant. It also helped to focus on the new criteria, breaking with the traditional practice of holding on to the property of the armed forces independently of whether it served any defence purpose. Before the period of consolidation ended, military barracks in several cities had already been transformed into university buildings, and even into an autonomous parliament building.

Other measures to change the profession: peace missions

Although we have pointed out how the reforming policies included on this axis are quite heterogeneous, that does not mean they cannot be applied in a structured way. Within the envelope of actions suggested here to change the profession, we would highlight cooperation with the United Nations, organizations like NATO or the Western European Union or directly, as was the case with interventions in countries in Central America, El Salvador and Nicaragua, carried out after the period under analysis. Cooperation with the UN opened up a path to change and enrich the profession that was different to the potential for change created by membership of the Atlantic Alliance or the WEU. The latter represented a professional challenge and a reference point in terms of modernization and policy reorientation, but all still for defence – and war – interpreted in the traditional meaning of the word and very much linked to the Cold War situation that still persisted. The actual missions of the armed forces were not extended, although Spain's incorporation into these bodies was a necessary stimulus to encourage them to work with greater technical and operational expertise. Conversely, the UN peace missions implied new roles for the Spanish armed forces. They began in this period at a moderate pace, but the way was opened for Spain to become one of the countries that would contribute most to this kind of exercise in relation to its resources. It also brought greater legitimacy to the Spanish armed forces in terms of public opinion, to the extent that the Spanish see this kind of mission as more than justifying the existence of armed forces in the country, as is the case in Canada, Sweden or Argentina.

The first mission under the United Nations flag in this period was the UN Angola Verification Mission, created in 1988 by the Security Council to supervise the withdrawal of Cuban troops from Angola.

The mission lasted until the end of 1991 and nineteen army officers were involved. Another contribution was made in 1989 that was shorter but more substantial. Framed by UNTAG, the Group for the Namibian transition, it involved the use of eight transport planes and up to 150 military. This ensured that the UN's air transport needs in the Namibian independence process were covered: the transport of personnel and necessary supplies, the evacuation of the sick and wounded and the carrying out of reconnaissance operations on the frontier with Angola.

Later there would be missions in Central America, Mozambique, former Yugoslavia, and Haiti. In this way, a new role was gradually taken on that strengthened the external element in the missions of the Spanish armed forces. However, simultaneously the Berlin Wall had fallen, the Cold War had come to an end and another stage was opened up, heralding a new period of change for the armed forces of Spain, a country now integrated into international bodies and institutions that provide joint responses to the challenges from the new world situation.

Conflict with the military in the period of consolidation

In the period of consolidation that opened with the 1982 elections, some factors that had caused tension and conflict in the previous period still survived, including the creation of a plural Spain and ETA terrorism.

The creation of a less centralized state began in the first years of the government formed after the October 1982 elections, under the rubric of the possibility of 'coffee for everyone', the expression coined by Adolfo Suárez to describe the extension of the status of the three autonomous regions created by the Second Republic to the seventeen that make up the entire territory. This development ended the privilege represented by limiting autonomy to certain regions and hence reduced the opposition to such a process. Combined with the strength of the government backed by a healthy majority, it also helped mitigate the anxieties of the military in relation to the federalizing structure the democratic state was establishing. Proof of this is that only one of the declarations by leading officers in the period between 1982 and 1989 requiring reprimands touched on this issue.

ETA terrorism cruelly vented its anger on the military in the years of consolidation: between January 1983 and December 1990 it murdered thirty-three military and seventy-six civil guards. The first victim was pharmacy captain Alberto Martín Barrios who was not the victim of a terrorist bomb, but was kidnapped and assassinated a few days after. The deceased included retired petty officers, generals and vice-admirals, one being Admiral Fausto Escrigas, who held the post of Director-General of Defence Policy. ETA attacked the Ministry with anti-tank missiles, though there were no fatalities. Nonetheless, terrorism was losing strength as a factor bolstering military discontent.

Quite predictably, as the process of military reform progressed and new measures no longer focused on preventing the military from intervening in political life, but on reducing its space for autonomy, these new measures now became the area provoking pretexts for possible conflict with the military. Reforms and actions on the institutional axis must take care to avoid allowing a reserve domain in relation to the government and this process in itself provokes considerable discontent among the military. Consequently, if the factors generating conflict in this period are more professional or organizational, it stands to reason that the ways to avoid conflict will also be found in these areas. The strength of the government is always a decisive factor but I would say that in this phase membership of international bodies can be even more decisive than the development of democratic consolidation itself. The pace and order of reforms on the professional axis are also influential factors, both in avoiding conflicts and resolving new ones. It is a mistake, for example, to attempt to reform military education without the backing of a ministry experienced in leading the activities of the armed forces. It would also be a mistake to decree that the forces should be opened up to women if the ministry is unable to control entry to military academies and teaching centres.

Nonetheless, there were incidents or public statements from some leading officers that meant disciplinary measures had to be taken, particularly in the early years of consolidation. Agüero describes several cases: the Captain General of Valladolid, September 1983, the Vice-Admiral of the Naval Academy, July 1984, the Captain General of Zaragoza, October 1984, the military governor of León, January 1985, a general posted to the Civil Guard, October 1986, the military governors of Guipúzcoa and of Zaragoza, June and October 1987.[35] In some cases, the motive was the attempt to minimize the significance of the attempted coup in 1981 or to heap praise on the protagonists, in others, there were internal problems that were always accompanied by

[35] See Agüero 1995a: 351.

praise of General Franco or criticism of the model of autonomous regions. In every case the individual involved was dismissed from post because of the impact the incident had made in the public sphere. From 1987, the frequency of such public interventions fell considerably and almost disappeared.

One of the points of friction with military command, especially with the army, was the decision to allow the former UMD members to re-enter the forces, individuals who had nearly all been given eight-year prison sentences by a court-martial in March 1976 when they were all allowed to benefit from the November 1975 amnesty granted when Don Juan Carlos was proclaimed king, and also from the subsequent Amnesty Law put forward by Adolfo Suárez. However, they were not allowed to return to their military careers and when parliament tried to remedy this in 1980, determined opposition from the military obliged the UCD to retreat from such a move. It then became a problem that had to be resolved, not only for reasons of justice, but also to make it clear that the military could not block a decision sought by the majority of the legislature. On the other hand, it was not possible to reintegrate the UMD members, since ten years after breaking off their military careers, reinsertion constituted a real problem for the individuals concerned.

The moment chosen was autumn 1986, after the referendum on joining NATO and new elections that confirmed the Socialist Party majority. It was an opportune moment to change the membership of the Joint Chiefs of Staff and it was decided to pass the draft law just prior to appointing the new chiefs of staff, so they were not implicated in the decision. The law was passed by parliament on 24 December of that year.

Along a very different route, the removal from service of those sentenced by a military court, this time those behind the 23 February coup attempt, was also the issue prompting the last conflict with the Supreme Council for Military Justice. The reform of the Common Penal Code had transferred the crime of rebellion under the military code to the general code so that if there were any new cases, these would have to be tried by ordinary civilian courts. In July 1987, the law on the competencies and organization of military jurisdiction had been promulgated and this closed down the Supreme Council as a step to placing military justice under the aegis of the Supreme Court, even though this law would not enter the statute books till May 1988. Just a few months before it was about to disappear, the Supreme Council tried to revise the

23 February verdicts to allow those sentenced to return to the forces after they had seen out their sentences. On this occasion, it was necessary to make some appointments so that the final outcome continued to exclude the officers involved in the coup from active service.[36] This is a good example of the type of conflict that has to be managed in the period of consolidation.

In relation to policies that can help reduce conflict, we should again mention the need for the phased introduction of reforms with a carefully considered sequencing of the measures being implemented, within the framework of a satisfactory development of the general process of democratic transition. Generally, a reform should not be begun, let alone announced, if the means do not exist to direct and manage it and above all guarantee its implementation. Laws that are not implemented, a frequent reality in Latin America, are the worst enemies of the process of consolidation. The order in which the measures are proposed is also a crucial way to avoid or reduce conflict. In chapter 3, the levels in the gradual reduction of what Stepan called military prerogatives were noted. Actions at one particular level should not be started if those corresponding to the previous level have not been successfully implemented.

Secondly, there were also measures in the area of personnel policy that in Spain during this period undoubtedly contributed to reducing the potential conflict that any reform process brought. Law 20/1984 15 June on pay in the armed forces figures among these. It sought to find a formula to bring the pay of the military up to a level with those in the rest of the state administration. A salary system was put in place that was similar to the one enjoyed by civil servants, putting a brigade general on the same footing as level 30 and a sergeant on level 13, to give two extreme examples (under this system divisional generals earned 10 per cent more than brigade generals and lieutenant generals 20 per cent more). Thus the salary increase for lieutenant generals was in the order of 33 per cent, and for sergeants it was 15.5 per cent, reflecting the fact that in comparison with the civil service, high-ranking officers were the worst paid. The law represented a considerable increase in salary and a simplification of the scales that had previously existed.

---

[36] There is a description of these events, although from a perspective favourable to the decision that was avoided in Platón 2001: 628–30.

Another example of personnel policy created to accompany the reform process and soften some of its blows was the creation of the so-called 'transitory reserve' already described in this chapter. Its generous conditions meant that the reduction in the number of officers was met by the quantity volunteering for this reserve. Another policy move in the same direction was to improve the services provided by the ISFAS, the institute created by General Gutiérrez Mellado to endow the armed forces with an efficient, global system of social and health insurance.

Thirdly, one must emphasize the importance of international connections, membership of the Atlantic Alliance and UN missions as instruments that furnished the armed forces with tasks, reasons to exist and tangible goals. The outcome from these situations was not so much their contribution to resolving existing conflicts as the demonstration of how relations between the armed forces and governments in already consolidated democracies work and also the call for an intense level of activity that was often quite a novelty. These factors perceptibly reduce the potential for the creation of a climate of conflict.

Additionally, an aspect must be mentioned that belongs to this period and relates to the government's attitude. The government must clearly demonstrate that it is determined to direct both defence and military policies. This stance poses the familiar problem of the necessary education of civilians in defence and security matters in order for them to be able to execute this task. This is one of the reasons that these issues are tackled in the period of consolidation and that the reform is protracted. In any case, it is vital the government (and parliament) show a growing interest and knowledge in this field and that this should be visible in the eyes of the military. It may seem paradoxical, but when the government can move from a position of asserting political and organizational control over the military to one where it progressively demands the armed forces be more effective, it is laying the foundation for overcoming the conflicts that come with transition and entering what we could call the normal situation (that definitely exists) in democratic countries.

In Spain, a very powerful factor existed that has been referred to repeatedly and which is unlikely to exist in processes in other countries. I am referring to the attitude of King Juan Carlos, who had earlier used the occasion of his annual speech to the armed forces to formulate strong calls for discipline and in this period demanded support for the reforms. This was what he did, for example, in his New Year speech in

January 1984, only a few days before the publication of the 1984 reforming law discussed in this chapter. He referred to it in these terms:

Such reorganizations as are about to be carried through, represent the overcoming of criteria that are now antiquated or that experience has shown can be improved upon. And it is necessary to collaborate in these reforms wholeheartedly, because the modernization of the armed forces is only one facet of what the nation itself requires in other areas. I am confident that the new measures being taken; the changes being introduced in the organisation that has existed until now; the regulations to be promulgated in the future and that the Minister of Defence has announced will lead to the creation of Armed Forces that are increasingly effective and prepared for the goals they have to pursue and that are happy with their useful role in the defence of peace.[37]

Finally, some mention must be made of an instrument that can play a very powerful role in the furthering of reform and the detection and management of the conflicts involved, but that can also become one of the greatest obstacles to reform: in other words, the military intelligence services. In Spain, at the same time as the Ministry of Defence was created in July 1977, the Central Military Intelligence Service was also created (CESID) under the aegis of the ministry, although duty-bound to give priority to the needs of the Joint Chiefs of Staff. A simple change of director, the appointment of Colonel Emilio Alonso Manglano led to a root-and-branch shake-up after the February 1981 coup. In the decree organizing the ministry in January 1985 that was linked to the reform of the LODNOM, CESID remained organically dependent on the Ministry of Defence although it was stated that it was functionally dependent on the president.

The first point to make about the intelligence services is that they must be placed under civil control as soon as possible and linked to the minister. Civilians can be gradually brought into these services at a later stage, but it is vital they become a tool of the civilian minister and not of the military. In this way a channel of information on the armed forces is set up that goes to the minister and not in the opposite direction informing the military command about government activities.

This was an essential task, particularly while the risk of reaction was still present. However, during the whole reform process, and not only in

---

[37] He repeated this position in later speeches. The king's speeches on the occasion of the military new year can be read at www.casareal.es/smrey/Discursos-ides-idweb.html.

the period of the trial of those involved in 23 February, the Director of CESID provided information about the situation within the three branches of the armed forces that was essential in terms of taking decisions linked to the normal running of the department, such as promotion policy or the selection of appropriate personnel for the different tasks within the ministry. For these reasons, dependency on the minister, and especially, loyalty to him, are vital requirements if conflict levels in the period of the consolidation of military reform are to be kept under control.

7 | Controlling the armed forces in the stage of democratic persistence: the debate in the United States over the last ten years

In chapter 3 we examined the phased reduction of levels of military autonomy and provided a summary description of democratic control of the armed forces. This issue was also briefly reviewed at the end of chapter 4 and we suggested that the radical changes over recent years in the missions undertaken by the armed forces can severely test control of the military even in a consolidated democracy. The fact that the Executive defines military policy does not meant that conflicts and tensions with the military do not exist or that it is easy to define the area of autonomy as circumstances change. On the one hand, as we shall see, it is always necessary to keep a careful eye on the influence the military try to bring to bear on the Executive, especially on the information they supply when decisions have to be taken, including ones related to foreign policy. On the other, in almost all democracies, but above all in the United States, the demarcation of what are 'military issues' or 'civil issues' has generated a large number of the conflicts between governments and the military. This is not surprising because it has direct implications for the scope for military autonomy and becomes embroiled in the debate about imprecise delineations of what is civil and what is military, to the extent that weighty arguments have been forwarded to defend the thesis that this distinction is losing all meaning.[1]

For all the above reasons, a review of the debate provoked by this question in the United States in the 1990s might be a good route into considering how to tackle the problem of controlling the military in the stage of consolidated democracy.

This debate about control of the military was partly sparked by an increase in conflicts between government and military and partly by an

[1] Feaver 1999: 219.

202

evident lack of any theoretical discussion of the issue. The overarching cause was the new situation created by the end of the Cold War that sharply impacted on relations between civil society and the military in the United States. The debate responds quite clearly to events, causes and situations that are part of US realities. What is more, the discussion came to an abrupt end when military force became the key instrument of US foreign policy after the terrorist attack of 11 September 2001, and it could thus never explore all possible issues. Nonetheless, I think that the different positions and contributions in the debate can lead to conclusions in terms of military policy and to interesting reflections which can be applied in other countries, whether in consolidated democracies or countries in transition to democracy.

In a book that develops his previous thinking, Michael C. Desch (1999) describes a total of sixty-five conflicts between the presidents of US governments and military high command in the period from 1938 to 1997. According to his analysis, the president's views pre-vailed in the thirty-three conflicts that took place before 1950. From 1950 to 1989, out of the thirty conflicts or differences of criteria, the military prevailed in one, the maintaining of the doctrine of protracted nuclear war, and forced a compromise position in another, the with-drawal of American forces from Korea. However, between 1989 and 1997, Desch reports there were twelve issues where there was a difference of opinion and military criteria prevailed in seven and the president's in just four and there was one compromise solution, related to restrictions on women in the armed forces.[2]

Russell F. Weigley was already in 1993 engaging with a perspective that other academics would categorize as 'The Crisis School' with an article that concluded with a warning: 'The principle of civil control of the military in the United States faces an uncertain future'.[3] Kohn and Luttwak expressed similar conclusions.[4] These three writers agree in their assessment of various attitudes expressed by the chair of the Joint Chiefs of Staff, General Colin Powell, as indicating a weakening of civil control over military affairs, together with percep-tible tensions between the government of President Clinton and military command in terms of internal matters (the acceptance of homosexual soldiers) or external matters (the Powell Doctrine on

---

[2] See Desch 1999:135–9.   [3] Weigley 1993: 58.
[4] Kohn 1994 and Luttwak 1994.

interventions internationally). Peter Feaver has called this period 'post-Cold War friction in US civil–military relations'.[5]

Mainly conducted in the academic field in the pages of the *Armed Forces and Society* journal, this debate has taken place against the backcloth of the pioneering positions of Huntington and Janowitz. We should now analyse the contributions of both these authors before analysing the recent debate.

Two pioneering approaches: Huntington and Janowitz

As is well known, Huntington believed that the military profession, that he defines as the 'administration of violence', is incompatible with the civil values derived from liberalism. Consequently, in order to be effective, the army must isolate itself from civil society, and cultivate its own values and ethical codes. The necessary subordination to civil power derives from the fact that this is an essential feature of military professionalism.[6] Following this line of argument, Huntington developed the concept of '*objective civilian control*' that he considered to be characteristic of industrial democracies and that in his 1995 formulation implies:

1. A high level of military professionalism and recognition by the military of the limits to their professional competencies;
2. Effective subordination of the military to a civilian political leadership that takes the basic foreign and military policy decisions;
3. Recognition and acceptance by that leadership of an area of professional competence and autonomy for the military;
4. As a result, military interference in politics and political interference in the military sphere are minimized.[7]

Huntington coined an opposite concept that he dubbed '*subjective civilian control*' that would be direct in nature, would try to maximize civil power, although it cannot do this in a generalized way because

---

[5] Feaver 2003: 284.
[6] Huntington 1957: 71: 'Politics is beyond the scope of military competence and the participation of military officers in politics undermines their professionalism, curtailing their professional competence, dividing the profession against itself, and substituting extraneous values for professional values. The military must remain neutral politically'.
[7] Huntington 1995: 9–10.

of the conflicts of interests between different civilian groups. In Huntington's own words: 'Subjective civilian control achieves its end by civilianizing the military, making them the mirror of the state. Objective civilian control achieves its end by militarizing the military, making them the tool of the state.'[8]

As Huntington underlined: 'The essence of objective civilian control is the recognition of autonomous military professionalism; the essence of subjective civilian control is the denial of an independent military sphere.'[9] Subsequently, the key element in the debate has been this definition of professionalism and the link the author takes for granted between professionalism and subordination to civil power. To say that the problem between civilians and the military is resolved if the latter are good professionals since military professionalism assumes the acceptance of civil supremacy is to engage in a circular argument that is more akin to wishful thinking than a description of reality, particularly in countries that have suffered from military dictatorships and cannot be considered to be consolidated democracies. In another classic work S. E. Finer emphasizes that the acceptance of the principle of civil supremacy was not part of the concept of military professionalism. After listing the reasons that foster conflict with civil authorities because of the very nature of the military profession, Finer states: 'Professionalism is not, therefore, what Huntington says it is – the sole or even the principal force inhibiting the military's desire to intervene. To inhibit such a desire the military must also have absorbed the principle of the supremacy of the civil power. For this is not part of the definition of 'professionalism'. It is a separate and distinct matter.'[10] J. Samuel Fitch is very clear on this question: 'in the Latin American context, higher levels of military professionalism have historically resulted in more institutionalized military intervention in politics and high levels of military autonomy'.[11]

Feaver has pointed out that Huntington's proposal is more a definition than a relation of cause and effect. He sums this up in list of four hypotheses:

- Hypothesis 1: models of civil control vary with changes in domestic ideology, in legal institutions and external threats.

---

[8] Huntington 1957: 83.   [9] Huntington 1957: 83.
[10] Finer 1976: 24.   [11] See Fitch 1998: 3.

- Hypothesis 2: A liberal society (like that in the United States) will not produce sufficient military power to survive in the Cold War.
- Hypothesis 3: A professional soldier will become less professional the more autonomy in military matters is undermined.
- Hypothesis 4: A professional soldier will always remain subordinate to civil authority.

For Feaver, these hypotheses are either not verifiable or have never been tested by comparison with reality. Consequently, he has suggested a new typology which distinguishes between *delegative control*, practically the same as Huntington's objective control and that implies 'granting the military the necessary autonomy to decide the operations in which they are especially expert' and *assertive control* that embraces the simultaneous existence of civil interference and military professionalism and in which four conditions are met: 1) civil and military institutions are different, 2) the military are not involved in domestic politics, 3) civilians do not accept the traditional division of labour with the military and, consequently, are implicated in military operations and 4) a high level of conflict exists between civilians and military.[12]

Eliot Cohen has shown how the theory of objective control does not at all describe either what has happened or what can happen and that success in the biggest armed conflicts has been accompanied by intense subjective control that rejects the separation of the military or strategic field from the political: 'The most successful cases of wartime leadership in a democratic state – Lincoln's stewardship of the Union cause in the American Civil War, Winston Churchill's conduct of British affairs during World War II, or David Ben Gurion's skilful handling of Israeli war policy during the country's struggle for existence – reveal nothing about the rigid separations dictated by the 'normal' theory of civil–military relations.'[13]

In fact, Huntington's theory is no help whatsoever in guiding civil control in processes of democratic transition and it does not tell us what to do when the concept that the military have of their own profession does not include acceptance of civil supremacy. Arthur D. Larson

---

[12] Feaver 1995: 123 and 1996a: 163. In a previous work, see Feaver 1992: 7, he defines the concept as direct civilian supervision over the military, particularly over military operations.
[13] Cohen 2002: 229–30.

described it as static, in the sense that by defending the military's isolation from the values and influences of society it leaves no space for interaction with the evolution in the society to which the armed forces belong.[14] What then are the factors that should determine the evolution of the profession? It is ridiculous to postulate that these can only come from within the military.

The problem of control of the military is posed above all when they are not committed to democratic values or simply do not share the same values and basic beliefs as the society to which they belong. Hence the sterility of Huntington's theory, since, in the best of cases, it is only valid for situations in which the military embrace democracy and the necessity of civil supremacy. In all other situations, military autonomy is a dangerous threat to democracy and the policy to be followed must be one that brings the military close to the values of civil society, as Morris Janowitz implicitly suggested.

For his part, Huntington did explicitly attest to the ideological character of his formulation: 'The real problem was the ideological one, the American attitude of mind which sought to impose liberal solutions in military affairs as well as in civil life. This tendency constituted the gravest domestic threat to American military security.'[15] This attitude is clearly reflected in the last paragraph of the book: 'Yet today America can learn more from West Point than West Point from America. Upon the soldiers, the defenders of order, rests a heavy responsibility. The greatest service they can render is to remain true to themselves, to serve with silence and courage in the military way. If they abjure the military spirit, they destroy themselves and the nation ultimately.'[16] Given this explicit ideological content, it is difficult today to understand the broad academic acceptance sustained by Huntington's theory, although the quality of his pioneering study goes some way to explaining it.

Morris Janowitz's focus in studying the military profession is practically the opposite, although it is clear that he did not develop his research as a response to Huntington's positions. Janowitz starts out with the declaration that 'the use of force in international relations has been so altered that it seems appropriate to speak of constabulary forces, rather than of military forces'.[17] Consequently, he focuses on

---

[14] Larson 1974: 67. [15] Huntington 1957: 457.
[16] Huntington 1957: 466. [17] Janowitz 1960: 418.

the development of the military profession and its orientation towards actions of a police character that he defines in the following way: 'The military institution changes into a police force when it is always ready to act, agrees to use minimal force and looks for viable international relations rather than victory, all arising from the fact that it has adopted a protective military stance.'[18] Janowitz considers that this orientation 'would enable (the military profession) to perform its national security duties, and provide it with a new rationale for civilian leadership'.[19]

For Janowitz, the profound changes experienced by the armed forces, especially after the Second World War, are the result of social changes that have exercised a huge influence over the military profession. This influence is not just restricted to giving new missions to the armed forces, but has led to a transformation in the way they are organized and even in the values that are appropriate to the institution. Finally, they imply a process of moving closer to the structures and norms of civil society, or to use his words 'the interpenetration of military institutions and civil society'.[20] He describes the impact of these changes on the military profession with what he calls five basic hypotheses.

The first is the *changing organization of authority* that represents a 'shift from authoritarian domination to greater reliance on manipulation, persuasion and group consensus'.[21] This implies a shift from an insistence on rigid discipline to the combination of empowerment, motivation and initiative.

The second is the *narrowing skill differential between military and civilian elites*, since 'the new tasks for the military require that the professional officer develop more and more of the skills and orientations common to civilian administrators and civilian leaders',[22] including organizational, negotiating and even public relations skills.

The third is the *shift in officer recruitment*, from a relatively high social status base to a broader base more representative of the population.

The fourth refers to the *significance of career patterns*, in the sense that if conventional career paths, competently followed, lead to the highest levels within the military profession, professionals with

---

[18] Janowitz 1990: 80.   [19] Janowitz 1960: ix.   [20] Janowitz 1990: 55.
[21] Janowitz 1960: 8.   [22] Janowitz 1960: 9.

unconventional track records make up the core of the elite that requires political acumen and original insights.

The fifth hypothesis relates to *trends in political indoctrination*. After affirming that the military establishment has grown to constitute a vast managerial enterprise with increased important political responsibilities, Janowitz considers that 'there has been a strain on traditional military self-images and concepts of honour' and also that 'the new indoctrination seems to be designed to supply the military professional with opinions on many political, social, and economic subjects, opinions which he feels obliged to form as a result of his new role, and to which he was expected to be indifferent in the past'.[23]

The result of these changes is that professional military have switched from having the traditional profile of heroic warriors to a function we could describe as being one of managers and administrators, which makes the profession more and more like the big non-military bureaucratic institutions and implies that the army is civilizing itself.[24] Janowitz does not suggest removing distinctive military features, but a new blend or balance of elements that define the profession: 'Skill changes in the military profession have narrowed the difference between military and civilian occupations. The professional soldier must develop more and more skills and orientations common to civilian administrators. Yet, the effectiveness of the military establishment depends on maintaining a proper balance between military technologist, heroic leaders, and military managers'.[25]

Janowitz gives a vivid description of the importance of these changes in the life of an American professional soldier:

The transformation has been spectacular for career officers who have remained on active service since the end of the Second World War. Above all, there have been changes to the military justice system that have exposed broad expanses of military life to scrutiny by civil courts. The redefining of the workday in barracks and adjustment of work activities to an eight-to-five timetable, thus reducing the nature of the military community as an

---

[23] Janowitz 1960: 12–13.

[24] See in this respect the summary in Harris-Jenkins and Moskos 1984: 52. Janowitz 1990: 46, expresses it in this way: 'There is no doubt that a notable feature of the army is the tremendous increase experienced in the ratio of personnel and resources devoted to technical, logistical and administrative issues that, in effect, create an organization the connection of which to military life is fairly remote.'

[25] Janowitz 1960: 424.

all-encompassing institution, have been hugely important. The army has prioritized a particular approach to training for leadership and management and in procedures to reduce authoritarianism and arbitrariness. Special courses have been introduced on human and race relations and deviant behaviour. A sizeable minority of officers and petty-officers are convinced these changes have been excessive and represent an undue leaning towards the civilian.[26]

In this context Janowitz deals with civil control, the necessity of which he defends throughout the work: 'recognition of the specialized attributes of the military profession will provide a realistic basis for maintaining civilian political supremacy without destroying required professional autonomy'.[27]

Fourteen years after the publication of his work Morris Janowitz analysed the impact on his hypotheses of the elimination of conscription and the creation of armies that are entirely salaried and made up of volunteers. He concluded by pointing out that factors have arisen that check the tendency towards greater and greater convergence and understanding between the military and civilian sectors of society. In the period reviewed by Janowitz (1974) it was difficult to separate the impact of the Vietnam War from that of the ending of obligatory military service, which led him to draw more drastic conclusions than might be drawn today. Very recently Charles Moskos, for example, has maintained that the phenomenon of the transformation of the military profession is continuing and that in what he deems to be the post-modern situation after the end of the Cold War the perspectives in the military profession continue to become more like civilian ones and the interpenetration of civilian and military spheres continues apace both structurally and culturally.[28]

Arthur D. Larson wrote one of the first and more lucid comparative analyses of the positions of Huntington and Janowitz published in 1974 and, consequently, with sufficient hindsight to deal with the problem of civil–military relations created by the Vietnam War.[29] Larson's starting point is that both authors agree that the military profession possesses particular features that contribute to its

---

[26] Janowitz 1990: 51.   [27] Janowitz 1960: 15–16.
[28] Moskos 2000: 2. Note how he uses exactly the same expression 'interpenetration' coined by Janowitz 1990: 55.
[29] Larson 1974.

effectiveness and also to its obedience to civil authorities. Larson defends, however, the thesis that the military profession cannot be considered a profession in the same sense as law or medicine, since it lacks one of their essential characteristics: autonomy or professional self-government.

From this base Larson develops two conceptions of professionalism. First, *pragmatic professionalism*, the result of reconciling the military profession with the tradition of civil supremacy, shaped by the needs of society, fitted to what it requires and tolerates, and fostering professionalism as a means of guaranteeing effectiveness in its missions. This concept is probably linked to Morris Janowitz's positions. Secondly, *radical professionalism*, closer to Huntington's, where professionalism is bound to military values and ideals and to the evaluation the military themselves make about their effectiveness and, consequently, does not seem linked to the social and political realities of society in the broad sense.

He also differentiates himself from Huntington when he studies the military context using the concepts of external and internal control created to analyse bureaucracies. They are simpler concepts and more readily applied to other professions, although they introduce an element of confusion by giving a different meaning to the adjectives 'objective' and 'subjective'. *External control* is that which is imposed by judicial, executive and legislative powers or by interest groups. *Internal control* is based on the values and norms assumed by the people who make up a particular bureaucracy, and their sense of what is right and feasible. *Internal control*, in its turn, can be objective internal control, based on scientific, technical and professional values and norms, or *subjective internal control*, which is based on social, moral and political values.

Larson was perfectly aware of the unsuitability of Huntington's concepts and position on the practical terrain of controlling the military. His conclusion could not be clearer: 'only the pragmatic professionalism suggested by Janowitz provides a proper basis for objective control without damaging subjective control'.[30] It is also interesting how he rejects Charles Moskos's compromise when he suggests accepting 'military pluralism' according to which the army is not situated homogeneously at a single point between traditional and civilianized

---

[30] Larson 1974: 69.

poles. Such pluralism would in fact rather disrupt that homogeneity, with technical, health, logistic or administrative sectors that bring them closer to the civilized pole and the armed or combat sectors that are closer to the traditional pole. Larson argues the need to avoid a plural military profession, by bringing it closer globally to its new missions and consequent civilianizing.[31]

The recent debate on controlling the military

Although Janowitz devotes a large part of his book to the analysis of armies as a pressure group and the controls that civil authorities can use, he does not provide many theoretical insights as to how to secure control of the military at an institutional level.[32]

On the other hand, as I have already pointed out, several contributions have been published in the last ten years on the issue of civil control of the armed forces that focus on the American context. The first of these were largely normative in character and critiqued positions held by American military chiefs that were understood to oppose the necessary subordination to civil power. Some theoretical contributions would appear later on that tried to explain the development of civilian–military relations.

The article by the historian Russell F. Weigley is outstanding among the first reactions to General Colin Powell's publication of a position paper[33] that in Weigley's opinion was an attack on the principle that civilians decide policy and the military carry it out. Above all, Weigley criticises Powell's attitude that was hostile to military intervention in Bosnia and was based on the argument that 'the military can be better employed to achieve a decisive victory'.[34] Weigley, in his turn, states that Powell's opinions were more political than professional and that 'Bosnia can reasonably be considered to be the type of situation in which limited rather than unlimited military force is preferable.'[35] Weigley points to three factors to explain the evident deterioration in civilian–military relations once the Cold War was over:

---

[31] See Moskos 1985. This article was published for the first time in 1972.
[32] See Feaver 1996a: 165.
[33] Namely the article 'Why Generals Get Nervous' published in the *New York Times* 8 October 1992.
[34] Powell 1992: 40.   [35] Weigley 1993: 29.

1. The Vietnam War and its 'poisonous effect' on civilian–military relations.
2. The Goldwater–Nichols law that boosted the figure of the Chairman of the Joint Chiefs of Staff.
3. The fact that civil supremacy is based on a concept of military professionalism that was born in the nineteenth century and cannot easily be adapted to the present circumstances of the United States as a super power.

Richard H. Kohn was also arguing already in 1994 'it was under Colin Powell's tenure that civilian control eroded most since the rise of the military establishment in the 1940s and 1950s'.[36] Kohn could add to the article denounced by Weigley the one Powell published a few weeks later in the *Foreign Affairs* journal.[37] In the final part of his own article, Kohn outlines a definition of civil control of the military that he developed three years later in a new study, in which the statement stands out that 'civilian control is a not a *fact*, but a *process*' and that 'The *real problem* of civilian control is the relative weight or influence of the military in the decisions that government makes, not only military policy and war, but in foreign, defence, economic, and social policy.'[38]

One of the first theoretical contributions in the field was Rebecca L. Schiff's *theory of concordance*. This writer criticizes what she calls current theory or institutional separation, that is, Huntington's, first of all because she considers it is linked to American history and culture. In the second place, because of its excessive emphasis on the institutional, scorning cultural factors, the values and vision that ordinary citizens have of military missions as well as the one the military themselves have. As an alternative Schiff proposes the theory of concordance, the central argument of which runs as follows: 'if the military, the political elites and the society achieve concordance on four indicators, then domestic intervention is less probable'.[39] The four indicators on which there should be agreement are the social composition of the officer class, the process for reaching political decisions, the method for recruiting soldiers and what Schiff calls

---

[36] Kohn 1994: 9.   [37] See Powell 1992: 32.
[38] See Kohn 1994: 16.   [39] Schiff 1995: 12.

military style and defines as the external manifestations of the military and the mental attitudes that go with them.[40]

The *theory of concordance* represents not just a reaffirmation of what Janowitz had called 'interpenetration', but a call to foment the latter: 'In contrast to the prevailing theory, which emphasizes the separation of civil and military institutions, concordance encourages cooperation and involvement among the military, the political institutions, and the society at large. In other words, concordance does not assume that separate civil and military spheres are required to prevent domestic military intervention. Rather, it may be avoided if the military cooperates with the political elites and the citizenry.'[41]

Schiff's contribution invites three comments in terms of the aims of our analysis. First, it is a proposal based on subjective control and the dissolving of the boundaries between the civil and the military, and in this sense, although it is not that different from what Huntington called forty years ago the political–military fusionist theory, it reopens the door to the only real concept of control, what Huntington saw as subjective.[42]

Secondly, she introduces a third agency, the citizenry, to the analysis, and thus enriches the view of the problem by allowing the study of democratic civilian–military relations to go beyond the duality of armed forces–government analysis. Alfred Stepan had already suggested distinguishing three arenas or scenarios for the polity in order to study the process of democratization: civil society, political society and the state.[43] They do not concur entirely with Schiff's formulation but they are in agreement with her when they point to the need to bring society into the analysis of civilian–military relations. Stepan forwards arguments we could call negative and positive. In the first category: 'It is an obvious point but one that bears repeating: the capacity of the military as a complex institution to develop a

---

[40] Schiff 1995: 15.   [41] Schiff 1995: 12.

[42] Huntington considered that fusionist theory expressed itself in two ways. The first was the demand that military leaders incorporated political, economic and social factors into their thinking. The second was the demand that military leaders took on responsibilities that were not of a military character. See Huntington 1957: 351–3 and also Wells 1996: 271.

[43] Stepan 1988: 3–4. In a later work, together with Juan Linz, he extends the number of arenas to five, in terms of a consolidated democracy. See Linz and Stepan 1996: 7–15.

consensus for intervention is greatly aided to the extent that civil society "knocks on the doors" of the barracks'.[44] In the second: 'increasing effective control of the military and intelligence systems requires an effort by civil and political society to empower themselves to increase their own capacity for control'.[45]

If we bring the citizenry into the model, as well as extending the scope of the analysis, we simultaneously introduce a normative criterion, since an accommodation of the popular will to the views of the armed forces is unthinkable in a democracy, for any adaptation that takes place must go, in any case, in the other direction. A corollary of that would be a shift in values and attitudes in what Schiff calls military style to those that society wants its military to have. And that is exactly the opposite of what Huntington proposed in *The Soldier and the State*. This point has to be emphasized, since the normalization of civilian–military relations in a democracy requires the values assumed by the citizenry and professional military to converge to an extent, although they will never be identical, and that might not even be desirable. Anything else reinforces the military's feeling of isolation or autonomy and, with that, their desire to impose the ideas of the collective, see themselves as guardians of values that are losing substance as society evolves and even to assume they are called upon to restore their centrality. Robert Dahl has also referred to this question in his reflections on the conditions necessary to create polyarchy or democracy: 'the chances for polyarchy today are directly dependent on the strength of certain beliefs not only among civilian but among all ranks of the military'.[46]

In any case, the bringing of society into the argument is a necessity if we place ourselves in the context of processes of transition or democratic consolidation. The level of social support for the elected government, to give just one example, is a crucial factor in determining the potential for government control over the military, a control that in the first stages of the transition simply means the reduction of the scope the military enjoys to intervene in politics.

Thirdly, it is worth underlining that the aim of Schiff's suggestion is to prevent the interventions of the military or suggest policies that make them less likely. It is then a less wide-ranging concept than

---

[44] Stepan 1988: 128.   [45] Stepan 1988: 144.
[46] Dahl 1971: 50, quoted by Stepan 1988: 111.

control of the military that implies a level of command and leadership from the civil to the military sphere.

Finally, one must point to the risk inherent in this kind of approach that over-values the institutional character of the armed forces. When they are seen as an agency with its own dynamic of social and political relations with civil society or the state, features are being emphasized that should rather be watered down over time in order to establish the right democratic relationship between armies and institutions. In a democracy the armed forces are not an institution that dialogues with the state or political or civil society: they should be a branch of the state administration with specific missions and organization, but entirely embedded there.

Undoubtedly, one academic who has most contributed to this debate is Peter D. Feaver, who had already dealt with the issue of civil control in relation to nuclear arms.[47] President Clinton's difficulties with the armed forces led him to write a first article in which he reviews the positions of Huntington and Janowitz and concludes that there is a need for a new theory of civil control over the military. In his opinion, this theory must respond to the challenge to society in civilian–military relations, that is to reconcile the need for armed forces that are powerful enough to carry out the missions society requests of them with armed forces that only do what the civil authorities ask them to do. In other words, there is a contradiction between the need to be protected *by* the armed forces and the need to be protected *from* the armed forces. Feaver approaches this question as a special case of the general problem of political agency: 'how do you ensure that your agent is doing your will, especially when your agent has guns and so may enjoy more coercive power then you do?'[48]

He does not define an alternative theory, but suggests some points that one should include. The first is that the theory must start out from a clear distinction between civilian and military spheres. That allows him to critique R. Schiff's contribution, by pointing out that the theoretical separation of spheres does not prevent there being a convergence in practice. The second point is the fact that theory should explain the factors that shape the way civilians exercise control over the military. The third, a direct fruit of his previous analysis of Huntington's positions, is that theory must go beyond the concept

---

[47] Feaver 1992.   [48] Feaver 1996a: 149.

of professionalism as the key element in the explanation. Here he quotes Abrahamsson, who, like Finer, has expressed a view that professionalism does not guarantee subordination to civil society. For Abrahamsson the military institution internalizes certain conservative, nationalist values that predispose it to resist when they diverge from civilian values.[49] Feaver's position is very clear on this: 'however, the hypothesis that professionalism equals subordination has not held'.[50] His last point is methodological in character: the theory should be worked out deductively before being tested out in the light of historical data.

In the same year Feaver published another work that was a first attempt to concretize the theory he himself had put forward, using microeconomic analysis from agency theory as his critical tool.[51]

Two years later Feaver went a step further by applying game theory to his outline of a possible theory of agency in his contribution to the proceedings of the *Armed Forces and Society* symposium published in 1998. His perspective attempts to complement the traditional one that he sees as centred on the analysis of how exogenous factors, which may be potential threats or society's values, influence civilian–military relations. Feaver attempts to tackle what he calls the microfoundations of the relationship, namely, an examination of the logic of the civilian–military relationship in itself. He moves from there to apply game theory to a study of the range of possibilities according to whether civilian control exists or not, whether there is obedience or disobedience, whether or not the latter is detected when it arises, and whether it is then punished. He combines these situations with what he calls endogenous factors, which are the cost of civilian control, particularly when it is 'intrusive', and the risk of punishment or penalization for the military if there is insubordination or disobedience. All that leads him to conclude that the theory of agency encompasses Huntington's, in the special circumstances when there is military obedience and civil control is not intrusive. Similarly, the crisis after the end of the Cold War would be a case of military insubordination under intrusive civil control.[52]

Recently Feaver has rearranged and revamped his studies on civilian control of the military into a single book.[53] His analysis allows one to

---

[49] Abrahamsson 1972: 17.   [50] Feaver 1996a: 163.
[51] Feaver 1996b.   [52] Feaver 2003: 284–5.   [53] Feaver 2003.

introduce the influence of exogenous factors into the model for controlling the military through their impact on the endogenous factors already present. The reduction in external threats can, for example, decrease the level of punishment the civil authorities are likely to impose if orders are not obeyed, or at least the perception the military have in that regard. Similarly, other exogenous elements may be introduced, for example, an increase in the powers of the Chair of Joint Chiefs of Staff or the so-called lack of expertise of President Clinton and his team in military matters. All these factors have had their impact on the cost of civil control, on expectations in terms of punishment for disobedience and on the widening of the gap between what civilians demand of the military and what the military want to deliver. His conclusion is that the so-called crisis of civilian control is characterized by the flourishing of 'intrusive' attitudes of civilian control and an increase in military disobedience.[54]

However, the fact is that this conclusion is asymmetrical and ambiguous in the sense that even though military insubordination can be measured objectively, the same is not true of the notion of intrusive civilian control that seems to carry negative connotations in relation to civilian control that is non-intrusive. We must remember that in his previous article Feaver coined a new term, that of *assertive control*, bringing together civilian interference and military professionalism, without clarifying the difference between the two. Feaver himself states the control of the military is the area where the conflict between civilians and the military is concentrated: 'Whereas traditional explanations would highlight resource issues (size of budget, force structure, and so on), my model would expect the most contentious issues to be those having to do with the monitoring connection itself (operational control questions, constraints on the kinds of force to be used) because they represent a renegotiation of the basic terms of relationship.'[55]

But it is the political civil powers that must decide what is appropriate space for military autonomy at a particular moment in time and the use of the adjective 'intrusive' seems to derive more from a defence of military corporate positions than from an academic analysis of the facts. On the other hand, the American experience (and that in many other countries) tells us that the problem of civilian–military relations

[54] Feaver 1998a: 408–20.   [55] Feaver 1998b: 418.

is not rooted in possible acts of disobedience that, moreover, can or cannot be detected. The increase in conflict levels in the United States after the Cold War came about when the military collective publicly began to defend its corporate positions with its chiefs, acting as a pressure group – as Janowitz had already noted[56] – and leaning on part of the legislature in order to resist change and orders that are contrary to its plans as a collective. Feaver has to use the attitude of the American armed forces to allowing homosexuals to join their ranks (as previously in relation to the entry of persons of colour or women) as an example of intrusive control for it to fit with his conclusions. Nor does the other example analysed by Feaver, related to army activity in Bosnia, fit a model that tries to explain decisions in terms of the cost of control or the cost of disobedience. There was clearly negotiation between civil power and the military over the scope for the latter's autonomy, as reflected by Feaver himself: 'Bosnia only became "doable" because President Clinton gave the military a "silver bullet" – permissive rules of engagement in the conduct of operations – which guaranteed considerably more autonomy over operations than they enjoyed in Somalia.'[57] The tools of utilitarian analysis and rational choice theory give at best only partial explanations in situations where the main issue at stake is the scope for autonomy or the power of a social formation like the army.

In spite of the level of formal argument we are once more faced by analyses that are very linked to American realities and even a particular political conjuncture in this country. They also take for granted civilian–military relations that in no way question civil supremacy and the authority of elected politicians. The theory of agency, as is evident, cannot be applied to situations in which the military do not accept that their power is delegated and do not consequently recognize the power of the civil authorities. In countries like Peru, or Guatemala, or even Colombia, we might ask whose agents the military are considered to be.[58]

---

[56] In Janowitz's preface 1960: vii: 'But to believe that the military are not an effective pressure group on the organs of government is to commit a political error.'
[57] Feaver 1998b: 418–19.
[58] Feaver himself 1998b: 421, says as much: 'In some countries, notably Latin America, until very recently, the question "of whom is the military an agent?" is unsettled.'

In addition, Feaver's contribution has another limitation in its dual civilian–military focus that is precisely trying to refute Rebecca Schiff's theory of concordance that we have already examined. It seems impossible to consider civilian–military relations as only a dialogue between the military and the government without touching on society as such, and its values, ideas and political positions. The author is aware of this limitation, since in his latest book he affirms that the citizen is the final political player on which the government depends.[59]

These are also studies that have little to say on the terrain of practical politics, which requires reflections on the relative usefulness of tools for controlling the military and the pace and order of the measures to take in reinforcing civilian control over the armed forces. For these reasons this kind of analysis does not help in processes in which democracy is being consolidated and civilian–military relations cannot be considered to be normalized and stable. Nor does it help to formulate suggestions as to how the process of control should be carried out, although this is one of the goals Feaver had set himself. The fact is that the analysis of control of the military cannot be disassociated from the analysis of relationships between civilians and the military and the way these develop and relate to the democratic functioning of the political system.

Feaver begins his paper by stating 'the alleged crisis is best explained by grounding it in a general theory of civil–military relations rather than in an *ad hoc* exegesis of recent events'.[60] Cori Dauber follows a radically different path in his contribution published in the same issue. From the perspective of a devotee of studies of argumentation or rhetoric, he focuses on the analysis of a single event, the Weinberger Doctrine, to try to explain the crisis in relations between civilians and the military over the last ten years. Cori Dauber engages with the issue of how to assess different arguments or positions on a similar topic and describes three spheres into which students of theories of argumentation divide standards in order to make their evaluations: the first is personal or individual, the second is technical, and the third is public. Dauber believes the American military have managed to impose a technical standard in the evaluation of attitudes to military

---

[59] He also suggests he will complicate his theory in the future by considering at least two players, the government and the legislature, Feaver 2003: 294.

[60] Feaver 1998b: 407.

interventions abroad: 'the crisis in civil–military affairs stems from the fact that technical standards for argument evaluation are today widely believed more appropriate than public ones for determining military policy'.[61]

Dauber describes the Weinberger Doctrine as proposing the use of maximum force on few occasions in order to win, and rejects the phased use of force (as in the Vietnam War) and when reasonable support from parliament or the citizenry is forthcoming or expected. She believes that the doctrine contains two implicit ideas about military interventions: the first, that they should not cost American lives and second, that they should finish in swift, total victory. Her conclusion is that insisting on these conditions to decide on a military operation allows the military to control the debate since they have a monopoly on such relevant information as the cost or length of a mission. Dauber also states that according to the Weinberger Doctrine it is almost impossible to approve humanitarian operations and, finally, that the implicit parameters mix justification of the intervention (that is, an end) with the definitions of military success (that is, the means). The Doctrine does not bear out Feaver's assertion in his 1996 article: 'The military quantifies the risk, the civilian judges it. Regardless of how superior the military view of a situation may be, the civilian view trumps it.'[62] The quantifying of the risk determines the civilian view, limits alternatives and biases choice.

A summary of the Weinberger Doctrine must include the six points from his 1984 speech on 'The Uses of Military Power':

1. The United States should not commit forces to combat overseas unless the particular engagement or occasion is deemed vital to our national interest or that of our allies.
2. If we decide it is necessary to put combat troops into a given situation, we should do so wholeheartedly, and with the clear intention of winning.
3. If we do decide to commit forces to combat overseas, we should have clearly defined political and military objectives.
4. The relationship between our objectives and the forces we have committed – their size, composition and disposition – must be continually reassessed and adjusted if necessary.

[61] Dauber 1998: 438.   [62] Feaver 1996a: 154.

5. Before the United States commits combat forces abroad, there must be some reasonable assurance we will have the support of the American people and their elected representatives in Congress.

6. The commitment of US forces to combat should be a last resort.

This doctrine is now usually called Weinberger–Powell Doctrine because in his time as Chair of the Joint Chiefs of Staffs, Colin Powell added one more to the six points listed by Weinberger when he was Secretary of Defence: the use of overwhelming force when the military is sent into battle.[63]

This summary of the Weinberger–Powell Doctrine allows us to evaluate Cori Dauber's arguments. In their interventions abroad over the last twenty years, from Lebanon to Bosnia and the wars unleashed by President George Bush after the terrorist attack of 11 September 2001, the American military have intervened decisively influenced by most of these points, the fifth included. It is also a fact that this is a reaction to failure in the Vietnam War, consistent with deeply rooted views within the American military body. First, its resistance to accepting any evolution to a policing role as called for by Janowitz: 'The military establishment becomes a constabulary force when it is continuously prepared to act, committed to the minimum use of force, and seeks viable international relations, rather than victory, because it has incorporated a protective military posture'[64]. In fact, the Weinberger–Powell Doctrine is an attempt to direct the use of military force in a direction that is totally opposed to the one foreseen by Janowitz. Secondly, it defends an area for autonomous decision making by the military. In a seminal study of civilian–military relations and the decision-making processes in relation to the use of force, Richard Betts indicated that top of the list of points that American officers defend and value as their own are 'autonomy in their internal organization and their operations and the principle of tactical autonomy', that is, the right to command

---

[63] See the description in Johnson 1996: 6–8.

[64] Janowitz 1960: 418. Kaldor 1999: 128–9, quotes the term 'minimum necessary force' from the new British peacekeeping manual as a notion opposed to that of the use of overwhelming force: 'the measured application of violence or coercion, sufficient only to achieve a specific end, demonstrably reasonable, proportionate and appropriate; and confined in effect to the specific and legitimate target intended'.

their forces in military operations without civilian interference.[65] As we have seen, the control and restricting of operational autonomy is an essential aspect of the new concept of *assertive control* as suggested by Feaver.

Consequently, one cannot really evaluate the phenomenon of the growing military influence on decision-making processes in American foreign policy by analysing it as an example of disobeying given orders (Feaver) or as excessive control of the technical parameters of the debate about decision making (Dauber). It is rather the defence of a military doctrine that refuses to shift despite the huge changes on the international stage. This doctrine is defended more properly when the defence is led by a civilian minister, as was the case with Weinberger. Later on Powell did so directly, by publishing his positions before the new president took up office, in an attitude that would have been quite unacceptable in Europe given the views on military subordination held in the majority of democracies there.[66] This doctrine has been defended – and in great measure imposed – by using to the full the American military's potential as a pressure group, in that it has had the support of most of the Republican Party and a very considerable slice of public and media opinion.

To sum up rather too succinctly but very clearly: the world changed in the 1990s, American military doctrine did not, and adjustment took place through a worsening in civilian–military relations. Inasmuch as the American civil authorities accept or adopt that military doctrine, the crisis in civilian–military relations is reduced or resolved. This happened in the first months of George Bush's presidency. Two examples suffice. In the first place, the definition of foreign policy that privileges the defence of the national interest, as formulated by Condoleeza Rice in a well-known article published shortly before she was appointed, is perfectly consistent with military

---

[65] Betts 1991: 5–12, quoted by Bland 1999: 12.

[66] In the first part of his article in *Foreign Affairs*, Powell 1992: 32 declared: 'As chairman of the Joint Chiefs of Staff of the US armed forces, I share the responsibility for America's security. I share it with the president and commander in chief, with the secretary of defence and with the magnificent men and women – volunteers all – of America's armed forces.' Sharing responsibilities is an expression that is too far removed from the obedience and submission necessary in the chain of military command.

policy that is hostile to international humanitarian operations.[67] Secondly, the so-called anti-missile shield is a project that is consistent with the supposition that the enemy continues to be other states (that are now labelled 'rogue states'), assumptions very characteristic of American military doctrine.

The attacks of 11 September 2001 have made it possible to give body to and implement a new foreign policy led by the conviction that it is possible to create a new international order based on America's huge military superiority. This also implies a new period in civilian–military relations that is quite different from the one that sparked off the debate we are analysing. Once the military operations were effectively and swiftly completed in the strict sense, both the chaotic situation in Afghanistan and the insurgency and internal war in Iraq have shown the errors in such a perspective. Ironically, the American armed forces in both of these countries have had to take on tasks that fit with Janowitz's police force vision that the Weinberger–Powell Doctrine tried so hard to fight.

To return to the debate from the 1990s, I have already mentioned the way that support from part of the legislature was used to defend the American forces' corporate positions. This is the factor chosen by Deborah D. Avant to explain the crisis situation existing in civilian–military relations in this period, although it had already been analysed by Huntington[68] and used by others who participated in the debate.[69] Her diagnosis is that 'the conservatism of the US military makes sense as a response to the lack of consensus among the civilian leadership in the United States about the importance of low-level threats'. For her the solution to this problem is 'to generate civilian consensus'.[70]

Avant also has recourse to agency theory to find support for her views. When the principal, that is civil, institutions are divided between the president and the legislature, control becomes somewhat

---

[67] Rice 2001 ends her article on a comparison of 'the firm ground of national interest' with the 'interests of an illusory international community'.

[68] Huntington examined the impact of the separation of powers on control of the military: 'The separation of powers is a perpetual invitation, if not an irresistible force, drawing military leaders into political conflict. Consequently, it has been a major hindrance to the development of military professionalism and civilian control in the United States.' See Huntington 1957: 177.

[69] Kohn 1994: 7 states 'the military raised the conflict between Congress and the President to the category of an art in order to achieve their own ends'.

[70] Avant 1997: 90.

more complicated. That situation arises, in the first place, because the existence of different electoral structures for the president and for congress encourages disagreement between them about policy goals and 'when Congress wants the military to do one thing and the President another, the military is likely to align with the civilian preferences closest to its own'.[71] Secondly, the situation can arise where there is agreement about political goals, but not on the mechanisms that should be used to control the military. Electoral costs are one of the main causes of rivalry between these two principles: 'when civilian institutions unify power over control of the military in one branch of government, civilians can exercise *ex post* checks to punish military indiscretions relatively free from electoral costs'.[72] After examining decision-making processes and interventions in Somalia, Haiti and Bosnia, Avant concludes 'the "out-of-control" claims [the title of a pioneering article by Kohn] may be overstated, but it is clear that military advice in these crises has generally reflected a reluctance to intervene in low-level conflicts, and this reluctance has often frustrated at least a portion of the civilian leadership'.[73]

Explanations focusing on even more concrete factors in the network of institutional relations between civilians and the military have also been published. Gibson and Snider, for example, consider 'that the recent increase of military influence in the national security decision-making realm has been caused by qualitative changes over time in the experience levels of key senior civilian and military officials and as a consequence of the structural changes brought on by the Goldwater–Nichols Act of 1986 which have accelerated these learning experiences among some of the most talented and aspiring younger officers'.[74] These kinds of institutional explanations – rather than theories – help one to understand concrete factors that naturally influence events, and they suggest ideas to shape decisions that can help right the situation. From this perspective, Gibson and Snider, like Deborah Avant, consider the importance of the differences between the president and the legislature, as can be seen in part of their conclusions: 'In fact, with Congress and the President split over post-Cold War strategic vision, new and relatively inexperienced political appointees working in the DOD, and a

---

[71] Avant 1997: 56–7.   [72] Avant 1997: 56.
[73] Avant 1997: 87.   [74] Gibson and Snider 1997: 3.

military adept at political–military affairs, one wonders why the civil–military tensions aren't worse'.[75]

A third contribution, by Michael Desch, was published in volume 48 of *Armed Forces and Society*, which has a different focus to the two previous ones, attempting as it does to build a structural theory of civilian–military relations. One of Janowitz's aims, as already indicated, was to analyse the impact of changes in military missions on the mechanisms for civilian control. Desch had already argued that civilian control was more feasible when the forces were focused abroad rather than being employed on domestic missions.[76] In his new contribution he states that military thinking with a foreign focus is a necessary prerequisite for civilian control over the military. He believes that the independent variable is each country's perception of existing threats, and he develops a table that combines external and domestic threats with – low or high – intensity in each and concludes that the worst scenario, in terms of civilian control, occurs when a high domestic threat coincides with a low external threat, namely the situation in most Latin American countries in the 1970s or the present one in Colombia. Conversely, the most favourable situation for civilian control of the armed forces occurs when a low domestic threat combines with a high external threat. In this situation, it is more than likely there will be civilian leaders with expertise in the military field who are familiar with security issues. In the other two cases, when a low domestic threat comes together with low external threat or when the threat is high on both counts, theory anticipates problems in controlling the military and suggests resorting to military doctrine as the determining factor.

According to Desch, this doctrine can impact on civilian control in three ways. First, because it shapes or moulds the structure of military organizations. Secondly, because of its effect on what we might call the culture of military organization, understood as a set of assumptions and ideas that determine how the body adapts to society and manages internal matters. Thirdly, because doctrine is a central factor in creating divergences between civilians and the military in terms of the use of force and actions abroad. Desch quotes what he calls the Powell Doctrine as an example of crucial influence in a situation where threats at home and abroad are considered to be low.

---

[75] Gibson and Snider 1997: 47.   [76] Desch 1996.

He believes that the Powell Doctrine undermines the degree of control over the military, particularly because it has given a much bigger role to the military in the processes of deciding foreign policy. This fact concurs with his theory: 'This weakening of civilian control of the US military is the result of a less challenging international environment.'[77]

Subsequently Desch published a book on this question where he extends the application of his theory to situations[78] as diverse as his own country, and those in Japan or Latin America. He reaches conclusions that are a refinement of the conclusions in his previous article, and he sums them up in four points:

1. The field of civil–military relations is an extremely broad and multi-faceted issue, from the prevention of coups to the creation of effective national policies. However, the most important issue of civil–military relations in developed democracies is civilian control: can civilian leaders reliably get the military to obey when civilian and military preferences diverge?
2. Excessive influence by the military on national policy jeopardizes successful conduct of a war.
3. Lack of civilian control is bad for the country, but it is also bad for the military itself.
4. War, or at least challenging external threats, can, under certain conditions, enhance civilian control of the military and thereby strengthen democracy.[79]

The book ends with some thoughts on the effects of globalization, which he perceives as debilitating, and on the impact of the Revolution in Military Affairs (RMA), which he sees as strengthening control. But after 11 September, in Desch's opinion, a new situation was created which will be very different, although it has yet to consolidate, and in which he anticipates big changes in the missions entrusted to the armed forces and also an increase in the variety of their roles.

Desch's perspective can be applied to realities in the countries of Latin America, though it is weakened by his inability to shake off the concepts of subjective and objective control. Although he quotes Huntington in an article in which he asserts 'Domestic war demands

[77] Desch 1998: 398.   [78] Desch 1999.   [79] Desch 1999: 114–15.

subjective control',[80] we have seen how the use of this distinction makes it impossible to draw clear conclusions. In this connection, Desch also advises the need to look at military doctrine: 'Civilian leaders in southern Latin America should pay close attention to the military doctrines adopted by their armed forces.'[81] It is difficult to find a single country in the area where this advice is put into practice.

Pion-Berlin and Arceneaux adopt a similar focus to Desch in a later article. Their starting point is the view that civilian control exists when Felipe Agüero's definition of civil supremacy is met. For Agüero, civil supremacy, a situation that obtains in consolidated democracies, exists when the democratically elected government succeeds in 'carrying out general policy without any interference from the military, defining the goals and general organization of national defence, formulating and implementing defence policy and overseeing the application of military policy'.[82] When considering the relationship between different missions and control of the armed forces they state: 'operations and missions that call for the armed forces to apply those skills that are distinctively military in nature enhance civilian control'.[83] In a manner similar to Desch they combine domestic and external missions with those that are restrictive or expansive. Restrictive missions are those that only require the use of military skills and capacities. Expansive ones are those that require in addition that the military call on organizational, administrative or analytical skills that come from the civilian camp. Expectations from relating these missions to the potential for control indicate that, at first sight, internal, expansive missions would be more likely to undermine civilian control, whereas those that are external and restrictive would facilitate it. According to these writers, reality is much more complex and does not allow clear parameters establishing a relation between civilian control and different types of mission. Civil supremacy is not sustained by sending the forces on external missions, but for other reasons, including memories of failure and the experience of government by military regimes now replaced by ones of a democratic nature.

The contributions published in *Armed Forces and Society* led to a brief debate joined by historian Andrew J. Bacevich and sociologist

---

[80] Desch 1998: 393.   [81] Desch 1999: 121.
[82] See Agüero 1995a: 126. The definition is more precise in Agüero 1995b: 47.
[83] Pion-Berlin and Arceneaux 2000: 416.

James Burk. In essence both deny that civilian–military relations in the United States are experiencing moments of crisis. To defend his position, according to which nothing now happening is new, Bacevich gives a cogent description of conflicts produced from the First World War to the end of the Cold War.[84] Burk also disputes the common denominator of the three contributions, namely that something is wrong with civilian control over the military in the United States, asserting that two common factors led them to draw wrong conclusions. The first, as previously discussed, focuses attention on relations between the two groups, civilian political elites and military elites. The second factor merits a comment here. Burk states that the issue of whether civilians or military prevail when disagreements over policy exist is important for democracy and it must be taken a step further. For Burk it is not important who wins the policy debate, but to know how the resolution and implementation of policy affects the country's capacity for self-government. In other words: 'we need to push theory further to say how the strength of civilian control is related to effective civil–military relations'.[85] Feaver at least cannot be accused of not taking this into account, because he starts his 1996 article with the problem of balancing control and effectiveness. However, it is also useful to emphasize the dangers in any approach that attempts to contrast democratic principles with the effectiveness of results. In order to defend the division of powers theorized by Montesquieu, we must not wait on practical results, or an increase in the wellbeing of the citizenry in order to approve the principles for a democratically elected government. I mean that any scope there is for military autonomy must be what guarantees that the elected government leads all policy in a country, including military policy. This is the basis on which the government must try to build relations with the military that are effective for the pursuit of the security goals the country has set itself. However, when democracy is at stake, the fulfilling of its principles is a priority in terms of criteria of effectiveness.

We shall now examine the theory of Douglas Bland as part of this sequence of theories on control of the military that we are studying. He calls it the theory of *shared responsibility*. This approach rests on two assumptions: the military cannot legitimately act by themselves and control of the military is a dynamic process influenced by

---

[84] Bacevich 1998: 448–9.   [85] Burk 1998: 461–2.

changes in ideas, values, personalities and other circumstances.[86] He goes on to list four problems in civil–military relations: military control by force; guaranteeing that the military act in a disciplined way; democratic control of the government that in turn controls the military so they are not used for party ends; and, finally, 'the relationship between minister and expert' or the problems of controlling a group when one has no professional knowledge of how it works. According to Bland, there are no definitive solutions to the four problems: the military must be involved in the effort to ensure they are managed satisfactorily. The paradox exists then that civilian control depends partly on military command. This idea is confirmed by experience in many countries, including Spain.[87] It is also self-evident for anyone familiar with military problems in political transitions, but it is a feature not taken on board by established theories.[88]

Bland refines Feaver's application of agency theory:

While some might regard officers as mere agents of the civil authority, officers tend to see themselves in some circumstances as professionals exercising command in their own right, according to military values and standards and thus apart from civilian control. This attitude may be mitigated by other concepts in some liberal democracies, but the idea that 'command' is sacrosanct is a defining belief in officer corps in many states and, therefore, agency theory might be limited to civil–military relationships in special circumstances.[89]

---

[86] Bland 1999: 10.

[87] The phase when General Gutiérrez Mellado was Minister of Defence was essential for the success of military reform in Spain. Though it is difficult to find other cases of such commitment to democracy, examples can be found in other countries like Uruguay and General Medina in the first presidency of Sanguinetti.

[88] Bland (1999: 14) says this: 'It is easy to conceive and accept that the military shares responsibility with civilian leaders for, say, finding national defence strategy. However, to suggest that the military also shares responsibility for controlling the armed forces in the interest of civil control challenges intuition and current theory.'

[89] Bland 1999: 14. Bland also provides an example of autonomy in decision making of the American armed forces that would probably not be acceptable in the view of European democracies: 'At the top of any list of issues that American offices value and defend as their own is "autonomy over internal organization and operations" and the "principle of tactical autonomy". Many officers in other countries would like to construct similar professional boundaries against civilian control' (p. 12).

On the other hand, he shares Feaver's view that it is useful to separate theory of control of the military and the concept of the military as a profession: 'Shared responsibility theory states that national regimes of civil–military relations shape how civilians exercise control over the military, and thus releases civil–military relations theory from the grip of indefinable "professionalism" placing it in the hand of a verifiable paradigm.'[90]

As with previous contributions, Bland's seems to be applicable in cases of consolidated democracies in which the possibility of military intervention in politics and the principle of civilian supremacy are not at stake:

When civil–military relations are thought of as a struggle for power between irreconcilable adversaries, then civil control becomes defined as dominance over and the restraint of a potentially dangerous opponent. On the other hand, when civil–military relations are conceived as exchanges between 'friendly adversaries' where each party is confident about how the other will react in most situations, then civil control may be defined as aiming and guiding the military toward socially acceptable goals. Rather than civilian control, the more accurate and descriptive term is civilian direction of the military.[91]

These are clearly assumptions that one finds in consolidated democracies.

Richard Kohn's contribution instead looks to analyse the mechanisms for controlling the military in a democratic regime and does so with a much more wary attitude towards the behaviour of the military than Bland: 'The military is, by necessity, among the least democratic institutions in human experience; martial customs and procedures clash by nature with individual freedom and civil liberty, the highest values in democratic societies.'[92]

Kohn defines four premises for civilian control. The first is governability in itself, the combination of elements that characterize the workings of democracy, as, for example, the rule of law, electoral procedures, etc. In this context, military missions must be established by the state and not by the military, and Kohn advises that they should be limited as much as possible to external defence. The second is the principle that the military must be subordinated to the structure of government and not simply to the figure of the president of the nation.

---

[90] Bland 1999: 21.   [91] Bland 1999: 18–19.   [92] Kohn 1997: 141.

The third element that reinforces civilian control is the existence of powers that counterbalance the power of the military. Kohn lists two: other armed bodies like the police and the knowledge that illegal acts will be punished through law. Finally, Kohn points to a fourth: 'The essential assumption behind civilian supremacy is the abstinence by the military from intervention in political life.'[93] This is more like a prerequisite for democracy itself than a feature of civilian control, although it coincides with the theory of shared responsibility inasmuch as it implicates the military in the process of civilian control.

He goes on to list three necessary elements for civilian control to exist. The first is a clearly defined chain of command, with the head of government at the top. The second is the guarantee that the beginning and end of any war intervention is in civilian hands. The third is the existence of a military policy, namely, that the government decides the size, form, organization, weapons and operational procedures of the military apparatus. From this point, Kohn argues that control should be rooted in the Ministry of Defence and the minister should be a civilian. These are interesting suggestions that, in this case, seem more relevant to scenarios that exist in the countries of Latin America than for a consolidated democracy like the United States. Kohn also supports a position that has been developing in recent contributions and which is worth holding on to. This amounts to seeing civilian control not as a state to be reached but as a process that must be worked at day in, day out, tenaciously.

Some conclusions from this debate

As previously mentioned, the debate was abruptly broken off when George Bush decided to use military power as the principal instrument of his foreign policy after 11 September, although it will be resumed when it inevitably becomes time to correct this policy. In the same year, 2001, the important set of contributions edited by Feaver and Kohn was published, but events prevented it from becoming a key incentive to continue the debate. It is essentially a set of sociological analyses, based on a broad survey of the differences in culture and values between American military and civil society. The editors conclude that if there is indeed a big distance separating the views of

[93] Kohn 1997: 145.

military officers and civilian elites, it becomes less so when the views of the military are compared to those held by the American public in general. Nevertheless, considerable differences exist: the military are more religious than the rest of the population, reject more emphatically international policing missions and are less tolerant than public opinion in terms of the losses these bring, are very largely opposed to untrammelled integration of gays and lesbians into the armed forces against the views of the US elites and public, and have moved to a position where the vast majority also belong to the Republican Party.[94]

However, one feature among those detected in the conclusions drawn by Feaver and Kohn that is very relevant for our analysis is the resistance of American officers to accepting that their role, in relation to the decisions taken by politicians, is advisory. These authors assert that the military think that their superiors must insist on taking the lead in reaching decisions they think appropriate for the use of force, and resist wrong decisions or even resign if they are in disagreement with them. This reflects an attitude consistent with the principles we saw in the Weinberger–Powell Doctrine and that may be the source of a large percentage of the conflicts and tensions between government and the military in a consolidated democracy.[95]

This debate ground to a sudden halt in 2001. A collective feeling that there is a big foreign threat hides or reduces the cultural gap that exists between the military and the rest of the citizenry. And the collective feeling of being at war, nurtured by the Bush administration after 11 September, prevented a debate as we have analysed it from proceeding. Nonetheless, one can say that the debate has not only acted to draw attention to this question among the experts in civilian–military relations, but has also served to introduce new concepts, perspectives and analytical tools, all of which allow us to have today a much richer view of the complexity of the relations between the armed forces and civil society. The concept itself of civilian control has been the object of scrutiny and, on the basis of the situation discerned over the last ten years, there now exist alternative positions and robust critiques of the conceptual apparatus created by Samuel Huntington.

Although their contributions are much richer than the details we will now mention, we must recognize the merits of Feaver and

---

[94] See Feaver and Kohn 2001: 460–1. [95] Feaver and Kohn 2001: 465–8.

Kohn who detected a new situation and began a serious debate. Apart from striving to incorporate new analytical tools, Feaver managed to see the impasse created by linking the concept of military professionalism to the subordination of the armed forces to civil power. Rebecca Schiff opened the way to broadening out the civilian–military duality by introducing society or the citizenry as a third element. Desch brings in a pragmatic definition of civilian control when he states that the best test is who prevails when civilian preferences differ from the military's. It was Kohn who saw that civilian control is not a single act but a process.

The participants in this debate, including Huntington, agree on one point. They do not limit the definition of control to the prevention of coups d'état. Huntington wrote that 'the activities of the Praetorian Guard offer few useful lessons for civilian control: the problem in the modern state is not armed revolt but the relation of the expert to the politician'.[96] Forty years later, Feaver insisted, 'A theory that focuses only on coups will miss much of what is interesting about American civil–military relations.'[97] Huntington's statement requires two amendments. The first, that the expression 'modern state' should be replaced by 'consolidated democracy'. The second, that in a consolidated democracy the range of problems that arise in the relations between civilians and military cannot be reduced to the relation of experts to politicians. Though this aspect must be borne in mind, the difficulties arising in civilian–military relations must centre on the tendency of all bureaucratic groupings to defend and extend their area of autonomy. This tendency is particularly marked in terms of the definition of the profession, and organizational and operational aspects of the armed forces. But Huntington could not consider these features to be essential parts of the problem, since for him they constituted its solution.

The debate has reinforced recognition of the importance of military doctrine and its adjustment to changes in reality and decisions taken by governments. Many researchers have attributed the causes of recent conflicts to the Weinberger–Powell Doctrine (and also to the Goldwater–Nichols law). Desch also agrees that it is necessary to look to doctrine to find explanations for the conflicts between military and civilians, although only in certain situations when perceptions

---

[96] Huntington 1957: 20.   [97] Feaver 1996a: 157.

exist of domestic and foreign threats. The impact of doctrine has been studied as the factor framing political decisions, but few have analysed the adaptation of military doctrine to the new situation opened up by the end of the Cold War. The Weinberger–Powell Doctrine is a response to the tremendous impact the Vietnam War had on the American military. Powell's own writings are clear testimony to that. It was vital to prevent a repetition of two factors that, according to the military, caused that disaster, namely, the concept of restricted war and civilian interference in military operations. Any foreign observer will be surprised by the extent to which the idea that President Johnson's interventions were the cause of the defeat in Vietnam has become embedded in American military thinking. Although his intervention was decisive in terms of the intensity, extent and timing of the bombing of North Vietnam (because of the possible international repercussions of the conflict), it is hard to maintain that the wrong strategy in South Vietnamese territory was the result of civilian control over the American military. In this respect, Eliot A. Cohen has remarked: 'Lyndon Johnson and Robert McNamara failed as war leaders not so much because they micromanaged the war, but because they failed to manage it properly.'[98] Cohen goes further in a later work: 'More than one author has suggested that the Vietnam failure stemmed at least in part from the stubborn resistance of American officers to adapting their conception of professionalism to the war before them. And American bafflement when facing unconventional opponents like Somalia's Muhammad Farah Aideed reflects, in part, the American military's reluctance to walk away from an essentially conventional conception of what it is to be "a professional".'[99] Afghanistan and Iraq can today be added to the examples given by Cohen.

Neither limited war nor civilian interference are mentioned among the points in the Weinberger Doctrine, but both are ruled out by the requirement that force should only be used when the vital interests of the United States are at stake or that it has to be used with the clear intention of delivering a military victory. Also point five, that prescribes the support of the American people and its representatives, influences the nature of the interventions to be decided, since, as Dauber and Avant have emphasized, a consensus exists in America (probably

---

[98] See Cohen 2001: 453.   [99] Cohen 2002: 243.

strengthened after the intervention in Somalia) that vetoes risking American lives in operations not considered to be vital to American interests, as is normally the case with peace-making operations. The example of Bosnia was proof enough of this.[100] When Powell added the prerequisite about the use of overwhelming force, he was shielding himself not only in respect of the limited use of force, but also from civilian interference in operations.

As David E. Johnson has pointed out, the American military use all their professional skills and knowledge to ensure that defence policy guarantees they are not involved in operations that have the same restrictions they think existed in Vietnam and Somalia. 'These institutional imperatives are grounded in a belief that only military professionals are competent to make decisions about the deployment of the armed forces and that they must exercise operational control during any military commitment.'[101] These are longstanding positions. In his 1957 book Huntington quotes from a 1936 publication of the Command and General Staff School that says 'politics and strategy are radically and fundamentally things apart. Strategy begins where politics ends'.[102] This is a position opposed to the one defended by Clausewitz. When Clausewitz defended the idea that war is the continuation of politics by other means he defended, at the same time, the permanent subordination of military strategy to politics. In the case of the United States, and closely linked to prevailing military doctrine, there is broad support for the position that believes that war happens because of a failure of politics and that, in these circumstances, its management must be left to the military, and the politicians' role is to announce when the war is over. Cohen has shown that that has not happened in any of the examples of major warfare in which the Unites States has been involved.[103] In 'Supreme Command' he rejects the traditional concept of military professionalism based on creating an autonomous area of military science in respect of political goals. He quotes Winston Churchill to that end: 'The distinction between politics and strategy diminishes as the point of view is raised. At the summit true politics and strategy are one.'[104] With the dramatic change in the nature of bellicose conflicts and the

---

[100] See Dauber 1998: 443 and also Avant 1997: 84–5.
[101] Johnson 1996: 62.   [102] See Huntington 1957: 308.
[103] See Cohen 2001: 454f.   [104] Cohen 2002: 242.

practical disappearance of wars between states, the view that defends an area of military autonomy in respect of politics can no longer be put into practice.[105] In fact, we must believe that one of the reasons why the American military are reluctant to join in peace operations is because these require permanent political control in order to be successful.[106]

However, these positions are not just held by the military. A large part of Congress, particularly its Republican members, shares them, as well as a high percentage of American citizens.[107] Consequently, although there was an evident mismatch between American military doctrine and the needs of the new situation created at the end of the Cold War, there were no related changes in military doctrine in the first months of George Bush's presidency or after the terrorist attack on the twin towers in New York. The wars in Afghanistan and Iraq are clear examples of decisions that are extreme interpretations of the points contained in the Weinberger–Powell Doctrine, rather than a questioning of them.

This debate is closely linked to different political conceptions and therefore we should not be surprised if ideology appears continually, even in these reflections. We should not be shocked either if the normative focus prevails, since the final aim of the debate must be to suggest measures and actions to guarantee civilian control over the military in a range of circumstances.

---

[105] Kaldor's 1999 book contains a good description of these changes.

[106] Although for almost as long as they have existed the US armed forces have carried out this kind of operation that American military language labels 'non-traditional'.

[107] For the differences in thought and values between civilians and military in the United States the articles contained in the first part of Feaver and Kohn's work repay study.

8 | Conclusions

I signalled in my introduction to this book that the focus would be normative, both because of my own experience and because I think it is necessary to sustain a discussion on military policy that can inform particular contexts. It is like this because it is the field where I can best contribute, given my own experience, and because I think there should be a constant debate on military policy even though the armed forces have now adapted entirely to the democratic system. The debate on military policy is moreover a good way to discuss each country's role in an increasingly globalized world. Consequently, rather than drawing out the thread guiding the development of the analysis, I intend to review briefly the features I think most important in the series of normative conclusions I have reached in the preceding chapters. I shall divide them into those referring to reforms necessary in a process of transition and, secondly, those related to civilian control of the military in a process of transition and a situation of consolidated democracy.

On reforming the military

In terms of the process of reform, we must first take into account the fact that military reforms do not belong to a hermetically sealed compartment that can be isolated from the overall process of transition. Success in the other partial regimes of the transition process is essential if failure is to be avoided in the military field. If progress is not made in the general process of democratization, the armed forces cannot be democratized, and even in processes of democratization where firm advances are made, evolution in the area of controlling the military may be slow and protracted. Control of the military requires greater institutional substance than the mere existence of free elections. The corollary of all this is that in order to complete a successful reform of the military it is very important to assess the range and limits of the measures to be implemented in the context of the possibilities allowed by the general process.

238

Secondly, before undertaking a process of reform, particularly if it is somewhat challenging, one must be sure that the previous necessary prerequisites are in place in order to proceed. These include most importantly a consensus between democratic forces that must translate into maximum support from the legislature for the changes planned. An agreement between political parties that they will not seek the armed forces' support for their respective stances is also a necessary prerequisite for the start of reforms, because an army that is being courted is an army that is difficult to reform. Also, it is very helpful to have a large majority from the ballot box if the reforms are ambitious or a protracted process is likely. Once the necessary initial conditions obtain, before starting or even announcing the reform, reasonable guarantees must exist that there is a real possibility the reform can be mapped out and implemented, namely that the process can be managed to a successful outcome.

Thirdly, it is good to be aware that the process of democratization will be a long one if it includes what we called the processes of transition and consolidation. The transition to democracy may take place in a short period, but that is not the case with the process of consolidation that is usually much longer than analysts anticipate because, among other reasons, changes in mentality require extended periods of time. When we shift from general overviews to analyses of a partial regime like the regime of the relations between society and the armed forces, the length of the processes of transition is inevitably longer. We cannot conclude that consolidation has come to an end when the military are no longer a threat in terms of possible coups d'état. Fitting the armed forces into a democratic system means that the government must determine and apply security policy and military policy, as well as embed the armed forces into the administration of the state as just one more branch of the latter and not as an institution that dialogues with the other powers in the state.

As the process of military reform is extended, it must be envisioned as a gradual process. Military reform cannot be undertaken rapidly and that is why careful attention must be paid to the speed at which various measures are applied, and to the order in which they must be implemented. Mistakes in this area can lead to an increase in conflict with the military or, worse still, to measures or dispositions not being carried out.

In terms of the gradual nature or pace of change it is vital for every step taken to head in the right direction. However, in the first phases of military reform it is not necessary to think of definitive solutions, among other reasons because the process will in each case contain a necessary element of 'trial and error', in order to test out the effectiveness – and consequences – of each step or action. As an example of gradualism in the case of Spain we can mention the gradual establishing of the Ministry of Defence between 1977 and 1989 or the two steps set out in the Law of National Defence of 1980 and 1984. In other words, speed cannot be a goal, in particular in the stage of consolidation, in which it is more effective to establish a marker for behaviour and patiently nourish that than to attempt to rush change. Consequently, civilian defence ministers must have mandates that are as extended as possible. The short-lived nature of ministerial posts, so frequent in many countries in Latin America, is the biggest obstacle to processes of military reform, which require tenacity in imposing change rather than wisdom in drawing up grand plans for reform.

As well as adopting a gradualist approach, reformers must take care over the sequencing of the implementation of different aspects of the reform. In general, the process requires more advances on the axis of legislative or institutional reforms than on the professional profile axis. Experience in Spain shows that reforms must begin in the area of economic control, thus helping to impose some economic order on the armed forces and in the planning of their activities. Civilians are more expert in this field and their intervention can bring positive results in the short term. Manpower issues and questions of doctrine and education must be left to later, except in partial aspects that can lead to reductions in conflict, such as improvements in pay or arrangements for retirement.

During the process it is important to strike the right balance in the progress made across the three axes, namely, for legal or institutional reforms, changes to the profession and doctrine and control of conflict levels. It is not possible to make advances along a single axis and the process must be planned bearing in mind the potential for change on the axis where advances are less likely and the general factors conditioning the length of the process.

Later on I will emphasize that civilian control is a process requiring dynamic input from the government. That is even truer in a period of military reform. The government must take the initiative both in the order of measures to be taken and in their pace or speed. It must also take the initiative in allocating missions, organizational matters and the other components of defence and military policy. If that is necessary in situations of consolidated democracy, it is vital in the state of transition and consolidation of military reform.

In fact, all processes of military reform that have been successful have had an endogenous character. A world context clearly favourable to processes of democratization, the joining of international bodies and extraction of support from specific countries can no doubt be extremely helpful factors. However, if the reform process is to create a new situation of stability, the engine must be domestic government and institutions. External support and similar developments elsewhere are to be welcomed but these factors cannot replace the domestic forces that have to conceive and execute reform.

Clarity and simplicity must be the aim in changes to legislation. The autonomy of the military has not come about, in the majority of cases, with the support of favourable legislation. For autonomy to prosper, it only requires ambiguous laws in the pertinent areas. Ambiguity or possible different interpretations always favour bodies with corporate defence strategies and never the interests of the citizenry. On the other hand, in processes of reform, the changes that are being proposed cannot easily be justified by reference to existing legislation. Consequently, it is often useful to seek justification in comparative law or practices in other countries. In the case of Spain, it was not easy to put forward some of the legal reforms as a development of the Constitution. In such circumstances, it may be more effective to say they are simply down to pure commonsense.

In every reform of the military the greatest difficulties do not derive from the drafting or approval of laws. They arise when efforts are made to enforce these laws, when they have to be applied in spirit and letter. And that demands persistence rather than strength. Hence the need to keep ministers of defence in post for as long as possible. It must also be recognized that many concrete measures and non-legislative actions can be more effective in achieving the proposed changes than the laws themselves.

The vital basic instrument for civil control is the ministry of defence. This is so much the case that the best way to measure the extent the government of a particular country is in control of its armed forces is to gauge the degree to which its ministry of defence has developed and takes decisions. In the consolidation phase the latter must have the ability to plan, to lead in terms of manpower and to draw up and control budgets, often incorporating help from the forces themselves.

Gradual involvement of civilians is necessary for the department to work effectively. In most cases the strengthening of the ministry of defence is seen by the armed forces as a process of dispossessing them of attributes they thought their own. This is why the process must be pursued in stages and must not be continued if the decision-making powers anticipated in previous phases have not really been transferred.

A civilian minister must head the Defence Department. Experience has shown that military ministers have in some cases been able to make key contributions to the initial phases of a transition, but the minister has to be civilian if the government wishes to make it crystal clear that it decides and leads defence policy, that is, if it wants to stabilize a situation of democratic consolidation. To that end, in most cases, the process of military reform is also a process of reinforcing the minister's power of command over the armed forces. At this point, we must remember the generalized tendency of the armed forces to want to base their dependency on the head of state or president, thus reducing the role of the minister, because that is a way to increase their potential for autonomy. The support of the rest of the Executive for the minister is vital and must include a refusal to engage in any contact that is not known to the minister. If fissures exist in the Executive the military will undoubtedly take advantage of them to maintain or strengthen its autonomy. The connecting link between government and the armed forces and, to a large extent, between them and society, is the defence minister and neither the president nor the head of state can replace him in this task that requires total dedication.

Both the civilian minister and the whole of government must be aware that power is the key factor in civilian–military relations. That is why it must be gradually made clear that the minister occupies a position of power over the armed forces. His mission is to lead and 'command', and in this sense the military must perceive that the minister and the president of the government of the nation are totally united behind this line of command. It is then preferable, as happens in the majority of consolidated democracies, that the title given to the highest post in each force is not Commander-in-Chief but Chief of Staff. On the other hand, the minister must find a way to listen to the armed forces and get to know their opinions and the views of their leaders, without implying for one moment that they can think that the minister 'is negotiating' a particular issue. Decisions must be taken after receiving information and advice from the military, but must never be agreed or reached with them.

As I pointed out in chapter 6, all the reforms in the legislative or institutional fields, as well as those we have included on the professional axis, have a high political content, and the minister has to be conscious of this and manage these aspects personally. He can under no circumstance delegate them to specialists or members of his department in posts that have no political content. The involvement of the minister is the best way to communicate to the military the involvement of the whole government.

In the process of military reform special attention has to be paid to the collective bodies that exist within the armed forces, such as the Joint Chiefs of Staff or the Higher Councils in each force or even the National Defence Councils or Committees. Progress must be made towards line management by individual commanders, a situation in which these collective bodies can advise but not decide. Decision-making powers must reside in the government and, from it, in the chain of command responsible for implementing its actions. Collective bodies with decision-making powers turn into instruments for defending corporate or sector interests in some cases and, in others, into a way to avoid responsibilities.

Joint action by the three armies, which has been an operational necessity for years, is very helpful in processes of military reform. This is an absolutely necessary transformation that means the armed forces must make many changes in the way they act and, above all, it justifies the existence of the ministry and the leadership and control remit that it has. On the other hand, it empowers the role of civilians since they have an obvious advantage in coordinating tasks in that they do not belong to any of the three branches of the armed forces that can have different positions on many issues.

Control of military intelligence services is a factor that is essential in most processes of reform of the armed forces. Armed forces that have endowed themselves with intelligence and espionage mechanisms focused on their domestic scene, a situation that is quite usual in Latin America and the Balkans, inevitably tend to intervene in the internal affairs of their country and believe they are an institution that must not only defend but also keep a vigilant eye on their country.

The reform of a military justice system is one of the most delicate areas in the whole process of adapting the structures and attributes of the armed forces to a democratic framework. In some cases, though in very few, it has been possible to carry out a thorough reform in the period of transition. The military justice system usually tries to maintain itself as an instrument to give immunity or at least a degree of protection to the domestic use of force, not forgetting those countries in which it serves or has served to avoid, entirely or partially, responsibilities in relation to crimes committed in the era of military dictatorship. The armed forces are sorely tempted to use their system of justice as a source of privilege, even in consolidated democracies, as can be seen from the way the American military justice system has acted in relation to crimes committed by that country in the Iraq war. It is necessary to give this issue priority and take gradual steps that benefit from a broad political consensus and support of the judiciary.

A single unitary judiciary is a deeply rooted democratic concept that can be considered to be indispensable if a democracy is going to function. In that sense, the reform of military justice is a project that is undertaken not only in order to end the immunity the military grants itself as a body or to punish previous crimes, it is undertaken above all to strengthen the judicial system and democracy in a particular country. Thus, the move to a unitary judiciary has an important immediate consequence in the process of democratizing the armed forces: it gets rid of an autonomous power centre that has been used to making its own rules and ordering itself, even ideologically, in opposition to the wishes of the duly constituted government.

On controlling the armed forces

In relation to civilian control of the armed forces once the process of reform has been consolidated, that is in the phase of consolidated democracy, I would like to propose some ideas that illustrate the need to keep focusing on the goal of control of the armed forces, always taking into account that problems will arise, although these will be different from ones that occurred in previous stages.

The first thing a government has to bear in mind, particularly given the preponderance of the so-called 'objective control' approach begun by Samuel Huntington, is that the degree of civilian control at a given moment in time is not measured by the professionalism of its armed forces, but by observing who takes decisions in the field of military policy and by checking whether these decisions are carried out. The process of decision making and the level of implementation by the military are the two areas where we can measure the civilian control of governments over their armed forces.

Civilian control of the armed forces is a much broader task than is suggested by the literal meaning of the words and cannot be reduced to scrutinizing and containing the military in their proper area of activity. It is necessary to proceed with the normalizing of relations between civilians and military in a democratic context and to direct and encourage the military to act on behalf of their country by controlling their effectiveness. At the present time, moreover, they must adapt to new missions that become vital for many different reasons. These include the change in the nature of conflicts themselves and the interdependence generated by the process of globalization that has made peace missions a widespread activity, since the security of countries is today affected or threatened by conflicts that arise far from their frontiers. Consequently, the bodies drawing up defence policy must be closely linked to the minister, who in turn must ensure close collaboration with the ministry of foreign affairs, since the missions of the armed forces are gradually becoming an instrument for implementing each country's foreign policy. Cooperation between these two ministries to develop a consistent security policy is an increasingly important element in the control of the armed forces in consolidated democracies.

As I have repeatedly pointed out, establishing civilian control of the armed forces is a process and is not a state that once attained releases the civilian authorities from having to continue acting. Such a process has to adjust to the development of civilian–military relations as a democratic regime begins to work properly. It must also be modified as society, the international context and military profession themselves change. Even in situations of consolidated democracy, civilian leaders must be constantly managing the military, as can be seen from the development of civilian–military relations in the United States in the 1990s. Civil control of the military is not a set of measures and techniques oriented to prevent a coup d'état. That would be to restrict this broad concept to a specific, extreme situation in civilian–military relations.

Civilian control is not an issue that is restricted to government and the armed forces. Society is involved. Democratic normalization of civilian–military relations requires agreement on the three fronts in which each agency (society, government and the military) has a comfortable relation with the other two and shares a sufficient level of confidence in terms of their future actions. Relations between society and its government are crucial to deciding the government's potential for controlling the military. Finally, we can also say that relations between the three agencies are normalized in a democratic sense when the armed forces have an area of autonomy that is decided by government, and when this space is consistent with the role society wants its armed forces to perform. To that end the government has to spell out to the armed forces how it wants them to act. It is all to the good if this is done through laws that have been passed with a broad consensus. The executive's task then is to concentrate on carrying out these laws prudently and painstakingly until they become a fully assimilated practice.

In the course of enacting these changes, the government and parliament must show an interest in problems of security and in the military, and they must build up a body of knowledge in the field. When the government has sufficient knowledge to move on from politically and organizationally controlling the armed forces to demanding that the latter should be more effective and to being able to define their missions, then it is preparing the terrain to abandon the conflicts that come with transition and the period of reform to enter what I have called the phase of minimal conflict level (it certainly exists) that comes with consolidated democracy.

The biggest problem posed by some suggestions in defence of military autonomy does not come so much from the fact that they suggest the armed forces should have a margin of autonomy as from their wish to isolate the forces from civil society in order to preserve martial values even when values in society are developing in another direction. If there is a great difference in values between society and the military, this is a source of instability in a democratic system and can lead to the forces themselves being ineffective: it will be difficult for them to carry out the multi-tasked missions that society demands of its armies if they do not share the same values.

Civilian control must involve the military themselves as much as is possible. Self-regulation is not a sufficient guarantee, and cannot replace civilian control inasmuch as this implies giving decisions on military policy entirely over to the civil authorities. Nonetheless, loyalty to the established democratic power is a key element in the control of the armed forces in consolidated democracies.

Control must be modified as the traditional mission of external defence is broadened out to include others of a domestic nature or international peacekeeping roles. Actions to help in situations of natural catastrophe or collaboration in the struggle against drug-trafficking, to give just two examples of present-day tasks, demand important changes in the models for how the armed forces should act and in the ways civilian control is sustained over them.

Bibliography

Abrahamsson, Bengt (1972) *Military Professionalization and Political Power.* Beverley Hills, California: Sage.

Agüero, Felipe (1992) 'The Military and the Limits to Democratization in South America', in Mainwaring, Scott, O'Donnell, Guillermo and Valenzuela, J. Samuel (eds.) (1992).

(1995a) *Militares, civiles y democracia. La España postfranquista en perspectiva comparada.* Madrid: Alianza Editorial.

(1995b) 'Democratic Consolidation and the Military in Southern Europe and South America', in Gunther, Richard, Diamandouros, P. Nikiforos and Puhle, Hans-Jürgen. (eds.) (1995).

(1998) 'Legacies of Transitions: Institutionalism, the Military and Democracy in South America'. *Mershon International Studies Review.* Vol. 42, No. 2, November.

Aguilar Olivencia, Mariano (1999) *El Ejército Español durante el Franquismo. Un juicio desde dentro.* Madrid: Akal.

Alonso, Sonia and Maravall, José María (2001) 'Democratizations in the European Periphery'. *Estudio/Working Paper. Fundación Juan March.* No. 169, October.

Alonso Baquer, Miguel (1996) 'La Función Política de las Fuerzas Armadas en el Último Tercio del Régimen del General Franco', in De La Torre Gómez, Hipólito (ed.) (1996).

Alpert, Michael (1982) *La reforma militar de Azaña.* Madrid: Siglo Veintiuno de España Editores.

Aracil, Rafael and Segura, Antoni (eds.) (2002) *Memòria de la Transició a Espanya i Catalunya.* Barcelona: Edicions de la Universitat de Barcelona.

Armesto Sánchez, Julio, Becerra, María Luisa, García, Manuel and Pérez Guillén, José A. (coords.) (1992) *La Transición Española.* Córdoba: Diputación Provincial de Córdoba.

Avant, Deborah D. (1997) 'Are the Reluctant Warriors Out of Control?' *Security Studies.* Vol. 6, No. 2: 51–90.

Bacevich, Andrew J. (1998) 'Absent History: A Comment on Dauber, Desch, and Feaver'. *Armed Forces & Society.* Vol. 24, No. 3: 447–54.

Ballbé, Manuel (1983) *Orden Público y Militarismo en la España Constitucional (1812- 1983)*. Madrid: Alianza.

Bañón, Rafael and Barker, Thomas M. (eds.) (1988) *Armed Forces and Society in Spain: Past and Present*. New York: Columbia University Press.

Bañón, Rafael and Olmeda, José Antonio (eds.) (1985) *La Institución Militar en el Estado Contemporáneo*. Madrid: Alianza Editorial.

Betts, Richard (1991) *Soldiers, Statesmen, and Cold War Crisis*. New York: Columbia University Press.

Blanco Valdés, Roberto L. (1988) *La Ordenación Constitucional de la Defensa*. Madrid: Tecnos.

Bland, Douglas L. (1999) 'A Unified Theory of Civil–Military Relations'. *Armed Forces & Society*. Vol. 26, No. 1: 7–26.

Bruneau, Thomas C. (2005) 'Civil–Military Relations in Latin America: The Hedgehog and the Fox Revisited'. *Revista Fuerzas Armadas y Sociedad*. Vol. 19, No. 1: 111–31.

Bruneau, Thomas C. and Goetze, Richard B. (2006) 'Ministries of Defence and Democratic Control', in Bruneau, Thomas C. and Tollefson, Scott D. (2006).

Bruneau, Thomas C. and Tollefson, Scott D. (2006) *Who Guards the Guardians and How*. Austin: University of Texas Press.

Burchill, Scott *et al.* (2001) *Theories of International Relations*. New York: Palgrave.

Burk, James (1998) 'The Logic of Crisis and Civil–Military Relations Theory: A Comment on Desch, Feaver, and Dauber'. *Armed Forces & Society*. Vol. 24, No. 3: 455–62.

Busquets, Julio (1984) *El Militar de Carrera en España*. Barcelona: Ariel.
 (1991) 'La Legislación Militar en la Transición Española'. *Revista de las Cortes Generales*. No. 22: 153–82.
 (1996) 'Las Fuerzas Armadas en la Transición Española', in De La Torre Gómez, Hipólito (ed.) (1996).
 (1999) *Militares y Demócratas. Memorias de un Fundador de la UMD y Diputado Socialista*. Barcelona: Plaza & Janés.

Caciagli, Mario (1986) *Elecciones y partidos en la transición española*. Madrid: Centro de Investigaciones Sociológicas.

Carothers, Thomas (2002) 'The End of the Transition Paradigm'. *Journal of Democracy*. Vol. 13, No.1: 5–21.

Cohen, Eliot A. (2001) 'The Unequal Dialogue: the Theory and Reality of Civil–Military Relations and the Use of Force', in Feaver, Peter D. and Kohn, Richard H. (eds.) (2001).
 (2002) *Supreme Command: Soldiers, Statesmen and Leadership in Wartime*. New York: The Free Press.

Colomer, Josep M. (1991) 'Transitions by Agreement: Modeling the Spanish Way'. *The American Political Science Review*. Vol. 85, No. 4.

(1998) *La transición a la democracia: el modelo español*. Barcelona: Editorial Anagrama.

(2000) *Strategic Transitions: Game Theory and Democratization*. Baltimore: The Johns Hopkins University Press.

Cortes Generales (1980) *Constitución Española. Trabajos Parlamentarios*. Madrid.

(1984) *Defensa Nacional. Trabajos Parlamentarios*. Madrid.

Cotarelo, Ramón (1992) *Transición Política y Consolidación Democrática (1975–1986)*. Madrid: CIS.

Cotino Hueso, Lorenzo (2002) *El Modelo Constitucional de Fuerzas Armadas*. Madrid: Instituto Nacional de Administración Pública.

Cottey, Andrew, Edmunds, Timothy and Forster, Anthony (2002) 'The Second Generation Problematic: Rethinking Democracy and Civil–Military Relations'. *Armed Forces and Society*. Vol. 29, No. 1: 31–56.

Dahl, Robert A. (1971) *Polyarchy: Participation and Opposition*. New Haven and London: Yale University Press.

(1989) *Democracy and its Critics*. New Haven and London: Yale University Press.

Dauber, Cori (1998) 'The Practice of Argument: Reading the Condition of Civil–Military Relations'. *Armed Forces & Society*. Vol. 24, No. 3: 435–46.

De La Torre Gómez, Hipólito (ed.) (1996) *Fuerzas Armadas y Poder Político en el Siglo XX de Portugal y España*. Mérida: UNED.

Desch, Michael C. (1996) 'Threat Environment and Military Missions', in Diamond, Larry J. and Plattner, Marc F. (eds.) (1996).

(1998) 'Soldiers, States, and Structures: The End of the Cold War and Weakening U.S. Civilian Control'. *Armed Forces & Society*. Vol. 24, No.3: 389–406.

(1999) *Civilian Control of the Military*. Baltimore: The Johns Hopkins University Press.

Di Palma, Giuseppe (1988) 'La consolidación democrática: una visión minimalista'. *Revista Española de Investigaciones Sociológicas*. No. 42: 67–92.

(1990) *To Craft Democracies: An Essay on Democratic Transitions'*. Berkeley: University of California Press.

Diamond, Larry (1996) 'Democracy in Latin America: Degrees, Illusions and Directions for Consolidation', in Farer, Tom (ed.) (1996).

(1998) 'Political Culture and Democratic Consolidation'. *Working Paper del Centro de Estudios Avanzados en Ciencias Sociales*. Instituto Juan March de Estudios e Investigaciones, No. 118.

(1999) *Developing Democracy: Toward Consolidation*. Baltimore: The Johns Hopkins University Press.

Diamond, Larry and Platter, Marc F. (eds.) (1996) *Civil–Military Relations and Democracy*. Baltimore: The Johns Hopkins University Press.

Díez Alegría, Manuel (1972) *Ejército y sociedad. Un Enfoque Actual del Problema de los Ejércitos*. Madrid: Alianza.

    (1975) 'El Cambio en el Gobierno de la Defensa Nacional'. *Anales de la Real Academia de Ciencias Morales y Políticas*. No. 52, anexo: 3–31.

    (1979) 'La Defensa en el Proceso Constitucional'. *Anales de la Real Academia de Ciencias Morales y Políticas*. No. 56: 159–82.

Domínguez-Berrueta De Juan, Miguel *et al.* (1997) *Constitución, Policía y Fuerzas Armadas*. Madrid: Marcial Pons.

Encarnación, Omar G. (2000) 'Beyond Transitions. The Politic of Democratic Consolidation'. *Comparative Politics*. Vol. 32, No. 4, July: 479–99.

Farer, Tom (ed.) (1996) *Beyond Sovereignty, Collectively Defending Democracy in the Americas*. Baltimore: The Johns Hopkins University Press.

Feaver, Peter D. (1992) *Guarding the Guardian: Civilian Control of Nuclear Weapons in the United States*. Ithaca: Cornell University Press.

    (1995) 'Civil–Military Conflict and the Use of Force', in Snider, Don M. and Carlton-Carew, Miranda A. (eds.) (1995).

    (1996a) 'The Civil–Military Problematique: Huntington, Janowitz, and the Question of Civilian Control'. *Armed Forces & Society*. Vol. 23: 149–78.

    (1996b) 'Delegation, Monitoring, and Civilian Control of the Military: Agency Theory and American Civil–Military Relations'. *Project on U.S. Post Cold War Civil–Military Relations*. John M. Olin Institute for Strategic Studies. Harvard University. Working Paper No. 4.

    (1998a) 'Modeling Civil–Military Relations: A Reply to Burk and Bacevich'. *Armed Forces & Society*. Vol. 24, No. 4: 595–602.

    (1998b) 'Crisis as Shirking: an Agency Theory Explanation of the Souring of American Civil–Military Relations'. *Armed Forces & Society*. Vol. 24, No. 3: 407–34.

    (1999) 'Civil–Military Relations'. *Annual Review of Political Science*. Vol. 2: 211–41.

    (2003) *Armed Servants: Agency, Oversight and Civil–Military Relations*. Cambridge: Harvard University Press.

Feaver, Peter D. and Kohn, Richard H. (eds.) (2001). *Soldiers and Civilians: The Civil–Military Gap and American National Security*. Cambridge Mass.: MIT Press.

Fernández, Carlos (1982) *Los Militares en la Transición Política*. Barcelona: Argos Vegara.

Fernández Campo, Sabino (2003) *Escritos Morales y Políticos*. Oviedo: Nobel.

Fernández López, Javier (1998) *El Rey y los Militares. Los Militares en el Cambio de Régimen Político en España (1969–1982)*. Madrid: Trotta.

Fernández Segado, Francisco (1996) 'La Posición Constitucional de las Fuerzas Armadas'. *Revista Española de Derecho Militar*. No. 67: 13–71.

Ferrer Seguera, Julio (1985) *La Academia General Militar. Apuntes para su historia*. Barcelona: Plaza & Janés.

Finer, Samuel E. (1976) *The Man on Horseback: The Role of the Military in Politics*. Harmondsworth, Middlesex: Penguin Books.

Fitch, J. Samuel (1998) *The Armed Forces and Democracy in Latin America*. Baltimore: The Johns Hopkins University Press.

  (2001) 'Military Attitudes Toward Democracy in Latin America: How do we Know if Anything has Changed?', in Pion-Berlin, David, (ed.) (2001).

Flórez Estrada, Álvaro (1958) 'Constitución Política de la Nación Española por lo tocante a la Parte Militar'. *Obras Completas*. Madrid: Atlas.

Franco Salgado-Araujo, Francisco (1976) *Mis Conversaciones Privadas con Franco*. Barcelona: Planeta.

Geddes, Barbara (1999) 'What do we Know about Democratization after Twenty Years'. *Annual Reviews of Political Science*: 115–44.

Gibson, Christopher P. and Snider, Don M. (1997) 'Explaining Post-Cold War Civil–Military Relations: A New Institutionalist Approach'. *Project on U.S. Post Cold-War Civil–Military Relations*. John M. Olin Institute for Strategic Studies. Harvard University. Working Paper No. 8.

González García, Manuel (1977) 'Las Fuerzas Armadas: Pariente Pobre del Régimen de Franco', in Preston, Paul (1977).

Graham, Robert (1984) *Spain: Change of a Nation*. London: Michael Joseph Ltd.

Grotius, Hugo (2005) [1625] *The Rights of War and Peace*. Indianapolis: Liberty Fund.

Güney, Aylin and Karatekelioglu, Petek (2005) 'Turkey's EU Candidacy and Civil–Military Relations: Challenges and Prospects'. *Armed Forces and Society*. Vol. 31, No. 3: 439–62.

Gunther, Richard, Diamandouros, P. Nikiforos and Puhle, Hans-Jürgen, (eds.) (1995). *The Politics of Democratic Consolidation*. Baltimore: The Johns Hopkins University Press.

Gutiérrez Mellado, Manuel (1981) *Al Servicio de la Corona. Palabras de un Militar*. Madrid: Ibérico Europea de Ediciones.

  (1992) 'Las Fuerzas Armadas', in Armesto Sànchez, Julio, Becerra, María Luisa, García, Manuel and Pérez Guillén, José A. (coords.) (1992).

Harris-Jenkins, Gwyn and Moskos, Charles (1984) *Fuerzas Armadas y Sociedad*, Madrid: Alianza Universidad.

Herrero de Miñón, Miguel (1993) *Memorias de Estío*. Madrid: Temas de Hoy.

Howard, Michael (1959) *Soldiers and Governments*. Bloomington: Indiana University Press.

Huntington, Samuel P. (1957) *The Soldier and the State: The Theory and Politics of Civil–Military Relations*. Cambridge/London: The Belknap Press of Harvard University Press.

   (1968) *Political Order in Changing Societies*. New Haven: Yale University Press.

   (1991) *The Third Wave: Democratization in the Late Twentieth Century*. Norman: University of Oklahoma Press.

   (1995) 'Reforming Civil–Military Relations'. *Journal of Democracy*. Vol. 6, No. 4: 9–16.

Iglesias Gutiérrez, Jaime (2001) *Creación y Fortalecimiento del Ministerio de Defensa*. Trabajo de Investigación. Universidad de Santiago de Compostela.

Janowitz, Morris (1960) *The Professional Soldier*. New York and London: The Free Press and Collier-Macmillan Limited.

   (1990) *El Soldado Profesional*. Madrid: Ministerio de Defensa, Secretaría General Técnica. First edition in 1960 under the title *The Professional Soldier* by The Free Press. The preface which appears in the Spanish edition comes from the edition of 1974.

Johnson, David E. (1996) 'Wielding The Terrible Swift Sword: The American Military Paradigm and Civil–Military Relations'. *Project on U.S. Post Cold-War Civil–Military Relations*. John M. Olin Institute for Strategic Studies. Harvard University. Working Paper No. 7.

Johnson, Douglas and Metz, Steven (1995) 'American Civil–Military Relations: a Review of the Recent Literature', in Snider, Don M. and Carlton-Carew, Miranda A. (eds.) (1995).

Juliá, Santos, Pradera, Javier and Prieto, Joaquín (eds.) (1996). *Memorias de la Transición*. Madrid: Taurus.

Kaldor, Mary (1999) *New & Old Wars: Organized Violence in a Global Era*. Cambridge: Polity Press.

Karl, Terry Lynn (1990) 'Dilemmas of Democratization in Latin America'. *Comparative Politics*. Vol. 23, No. 1: 1–21.

Kohn, Richard H. (1994) 'Out of Control: The Crisis in Civil–Military Relations'. *National Interest*. Spring: 3–17.

   (1997). 'How Democracies Control the Military'. *Journal of Democracy*. Vol. 8, No. 4: 140–53.

Larson, Arthur D. (1974) 'Military Professionalism and Civil Control: a Comparative Analysis of Two Interpretations'. *Journal of Political and Military Sociology*. Vol. 2, Spring: 57–72.

Linz, Juan J. (1978) 'Crisis, Breakdown, and Reequilibration', in Linz, Juan J. and Stepan, Alfred (eds.) (1978).

   (1990) 'Transitions to Democracy'. *Washington Quarterly*. Vol. 13, No. 3.

   (1992) 'La Transición a la Democracia en España en Perspectiva Comparada', in Cotarelo, Ramón (1992).

(2000) *Totalitarian and Authoritarian Regimes*. London: Lynne Rienner Publishers.

Linz, Juan J and Stepan, Alfred (eds.) (1978) *The Breakdown of Democratic Regimes*. Baltimore: The Johns Hopkins University Press.

(1995) 'Democratic Transition and Consolidation in Southern Europe, with Reflections on Latin America and Eastern Europe', in Gunther, Richard, Diamandouros, P. Nikiforos and Puhle, Hans-Jürgen (eds.) (1995).

(1996) *Problems of Democratic Transition and Consolidation: Southern Europe, South America, and Post-Communist Europe*. Baltimore: The Johns Hopkins University Press.

Lleixà, Joaquim (1986) *Cien Años de Militarismo en España*. Barcelona: Anagrama.

López Garrido, Diego (1983) 'La Posición Constitucional de las Fuerzas Armadas'. *Revista de Administración Pública*. No. 100–102: 949–71.

López Ramón, Fernando (1987) *La Caracterización Jurídica de las Fuerzas Armadas*. Madrid: Centro de Estudios Constitucionales.

Losada Malvárez, Juan Carlos (1990) *Ideología del Ejército Franquista (1939–1959)*. Madrid: Istmo.

Luttwak, Edward (1994) 'Washington's Biggest Scandal'. *Commentary*, 97, No. 5: 29–33.

Machiavelli, Niccolo (2003) [1520] *Art of War*. Chicago: University of Chicago Press.

Mainwaring, Scott, O'Donnell, Guillermo and Valenzuela, J. Samuel (eds.) (1992) *Issues in Democratic Consolidation: The New South American Democracies in Comparative Perspective*. Indiana: University of Notre Dame Press.

Maravall, José M. and Santamaría, Julián (1986) 'Political Change in Spain and the Prospects for Democracy', in O'Donnell, Guillermo, Schmitter, Philippe and Whitehead, Laurence (eds.) (1986a).

Martin, Michel Louis and McCrate, Ellen Stern (eds.) (1984) *The Military, Militarism and the Polity: Essays in Honor of Morris Janowitz*. London: Collier Macmillan.

Martín Pérez, Ángel (1995) 'La mujer y las Fuerzas Armadas', in Ramírez Jiménez, Manuel (coord.) (1995).

Martín Villa, Rodolfo (1984) *Al Servicio del Estado*. Barcelona: Planeta.

Marx, Karl (2005) [1852] *The Eighteenth Brumaire of Louis Bonaparte*. New York and Berlin: Mondial.

Mérida, María (1979) *Mis Conversaciones con los Generales. Veinte Entrevistas con Altos Mandos del Ejército y de la Armada*. Madrid: Plaza & Janés.

Ministerio de Defensa (1986) *Memoria de la Legislatura (1982–1986)*. Madrid.

(1989) *Memoria de la Legislatura (1986–1989)*. Madrid.

(1993) *Memoria de la Legislatura (1989–1993)*. Madrid.

Morlino, Leonardo (1998) *Democracy Between Consolidation and Crisis: Parties, Groups and Citizens in Southern Europe.* Oxford: Oxford University Press.

Moskos, Charles C. (1977) 'From Institution to Occupation: Trends in Military Organization'. *Armed Forces and Society.* Vol. 4, No. 1, November.

(1985) 'La nueva organización militar: ¿institucional, ocupacional o plural?', in Bañón, Rafael and Olmeda, José Antonio (eds.) (1985).

(1986) 'Institutional/Occupational Trends in Armed Forces: An Update'. *Armed Forces and Society.* Vol. 12, No. 3, Spring.

(2000) 'Toward a Postmodern Military: The United States as a Paradigm', in Moskos, Charles C., Williams, John Allen and Segal, David R. (eds.) (2000).

Moskos, Charles C, Williams, John Allen and Segal, David R. (eds.) (2000) *The Postmodern Military: Armed Forces after the Cold War.* New York: Oxford University Press.

Mozo, Antonio (1995) 'Las Fuerzas Armadas y su Ordenamiento Jurídico'. *Revista Española de Derecho Militar.* No. 65: 609–29.

Nunn, Frederik (1976) *The Military in Chilean History: Essays in Civil–Military Relations 1810–1973.* Albuquerque, New Mexico: University of New Mexico Press.

O'Donnell, Guillermo (1994) 'Delegative democracy'. *Journal of Democracy.* Vol. 5, No. 1 January: 55–69.

(1997a) *Contrapuntos. Ensayos recogidos sobre autoritarismo y democratización.* Buenos Aires: Editorial Paidós.

(1997b) 'Transiciones, continuidades y algunas paradojas', in O'Donnell, Guillermo (1997a).

(1997c) 'Otra institucionalización', in O'Donnell, Guillermo (1997a).

(2001) 'Reflections on Contemporary South American Democracies'. *Journal of Latin American Studies.* No. 33: 599–609.

O'Donnell, Guillermo, Schmitter, Philippe C. and Whitehead, Laurence (eds). (1986a) *Transitions from Authoritarian Rule: Southern Europe.* Baltimore and London: The Johns Hopkins University Press.

O'Donnell, Guillermo, Schmitter, Philippe and Whitehead, Laurence (eds.) (1986b) *Transitions from Authoritarian Rule: Comparative Perspectives.* Baltimore and London: The Johns Hopkins University Press.

Oliart, Alberto (2002) 'Las Fuerzas Armadas y los Gobiernos de UCD', in Aracil, Rafael and Segura, Antoni (eds.) (2002).

Olmeda Gómez, José Antonio (1988) 'The Armed Forces in the Francoist Political System', in Bañón, Rafael and Barker, Thomas M. (eds.) (1988).

Osorio, Alfonso (1980) *Trayectoria Política de un Ministro de la Corona.* Barcelona: Planeta.

Parada, Ramón (1997) 'Prólogo', in Domínguez-Berrueta de Juan, Miguel *et al.* (1997).

Payne, Stanley G. (1968) *Los Militares y la Política en la España Contemporánea*. Paris: Ruedo Ibérico.

Pérez-Díaz, Víctor M. (1993) *The Return of Civil Society: The Emergence of Democratic Spain*. Cambridge: Harvard University Press.

Perlmutter, Amos (1982) *Lo militar y lo político en los tiempos modernos*. Madrid: Ediciones Ejército.

Pion-Berlin, David S. (ed.) (2001) *Civil–Military Relations in Latin America: New Analytical Perspectives*. Chapel Hill: The University of North Carolina Press.

(2005) 'Political Management of the Military in Latin America'. *Military Review*. January–February: 19–31.

(2006) 'The Defence Wisdom Deficit in Latin America: A Reply to Thomas C. Bruneau'. *Revista Fuerzas Armadas y Sociedad*. Vol. 20, No. 1: 51–62.

Pion-Berlin, David S. and Arceneaux, Craig (2000) 'Decision-Makers or Decision-Takers? Military Missions and Civilian Control in Democratic South America'. *Armed Forces & Society*. Vol. 26, No. 3: 413–36.

Platón, Miguel (2001) *Hablan los Militares. Testimonios para la Historia (1939–1996)*. Barcelona: Planeta.

Powell, Charles (2001) *España en Democracia. 1975–2000*. Barcelona: Plaza & Janés.

Powell, Colin L. (1992) 'U.S. Forces: the Challenges Ahead'. *Foreign Affairs*. Winter 1992/93: 32–45.

Preston, Paul (1977) *España en Crisis. La Evolución y Decadencia del Régimen de Franco*. Madrid: Fondo de Cultura Económica.

Pridham, Geoffrey (1995) 'The International Context of Democratic Consolidation: Southern Europe in Comparative Perspective', in Gunther, Richard, Diamandouros, P. Nikiforos and Puhle, Hans-Jürgen (eds.) (1995).

Przeworski, Adam (1991) *Democracy and the Market: Political and Economic Reforms in Eastern Europe and Latin America*. Cambridge and New York: Cambridge University Press.

(1992) 'The games of transition', in Mainwaring, Scott; O'Donnell, Guillermo and Valenzuela, J. Samuel (eds.) (1992).

Puell de la Villa, Fernando (1997) *Gutiérrez Mellado. Un Militar del siglo XX (1912–1995)*. Madrid: Biblioteca Nueva.

Ramírez Jiménez, Manuel (coord.) (1995). *La Función Militar en el Actual Ordenamiento Constitucional Español*. Madrid: Trotta.

Rice, Condoleezza (2001) 'Campaign 2000: Promoting the National Interest'. *Foreign Affairs*. January/February.

Rodrigo, Fernando (1985) 'El Papel de las Fuerzas Armadas Españolas durante la Transición Política: Algunas Hipótesis Básicas'. *Revista Internacional de Sociología*. Vol. 42, Fasc. 2: 349–69.

(1989) *El Camino hacia la Democracia: Militares y Política en la Transición Española*. Doctoral Thesis. Universidad Complutense de Madrid.

Rodríguez Sahagún, Agustín (1986) 'La Reforma Militar de los Gobiernos de Suárez'. *Revista Española de Investigaciones Sociológicas*. No. 36: 189–94.

Rustow, Dankwart A. (1970) 'Transitions to Democracy: Toward a Dynamic Model'. *Comparative Politics*. Vol. 2, No. 3: 337–63.

Sarkesian, Sam C. (1984) 'Two Conceptions of Military Professionalism', in Martin, Michel Louis and McCrate, Ellen Stern (eds.) (1984).

Schiff, Rebecca L. (1995) 'Civil Military Relations Reconsidered: A Theory of Concordance'. *Armed Forces & Society*. Vol. 22, No. 1: 7–24.

Schmitter, Philippe C. (1995) 'Organized Interests and Democratic Consolidation in Southern Europe', in Gunther, Richard, Diamandouros, P. Nikiforos and Puhle, Hans-Jürgen, (eds.) (1995).

Schmitter, Philippe C. and Karl, Terry Lynn (1991) 'What Democracy is... and is not'. *Journal of Democracy*. Vol. 2, No. 3: 74–88.

Schumpeter, Joseph A. (1950) *Capitalism, Socialism and Democracy*. New York: Harper & Brothers Publishers.

Snider, Don M. and Carlton-Carew, Miranda A. (eds.) (1995) *U.S. Civil–Military Relations: In Crisis or Transition?* Washington DC: The Centre for Strategic and International Studies.

Stark, David (1992) 'The Great Transformation? Social Change in Europe'. *Contemporary Sociology*. Vol. 21, No. 3, May.

Stepan, Alfred (1988) *Rethinking Military Politics: Brazil and the Southern Cone*. Princeton University Press.

Suárez Pertierra, Gustavo (1994) *Legislación sobre Defensa Nacional*. Madrid: Tecnos.

(1988) 'Regulación jurídico-constitucional de las Fuerzas Armadas'. *Jornadas de Estudio sobre el Título Preliminar de la Constitución*. Madrid. Ministerio de Justicia. Vol. IV: 2359–414.

(2000) 'La Significación de las Reales Ordenanzas en el Contexto de la Reforma Militar'. *Revista de Derecho Político*. No. 48–49: 259–87.

(2004) 'Veinticinco años de Constitución y Fuerzas Armadas'. *Revista de Derecho Político*. No. 58–59, 95–116.

Valenzuela, J. Samuel (1992) 'Democratic Consolidation in Post-transitional Settings: Notion, Process, and Facilitating Conditions', in Mainwaring, Scott, O'Donnell, Guillermo and Valenzuela, J. Samuel (eds.) (1992).

Weber, Max (1968) *Economy and Society*. New York: Bedminster Press Incorporated (edited by Guenther Roth and Claus Wittich).

Weigley, Russell (1993) 'The American Military and the Principle of Civilian Control from McClellan to Powell'. *The Journal of Military History*. Vol. 57, No. 5: 27–59.

Wells, Richard S. (1996) 'The Theory of Concordance in Civil/Military Relations: A Commentary'. *Armed Forces & Society*. Vol. 22, Winter: 269–75.

Whitehead, Laurence (1986) 'International Aspects of Democratization', in O'Donnell, Guillermo, Schmitter, Philippe and Whitehead, Laurence (eds.) (1986b).

Index